WITHDRAWN

AF699193

Management of Transportation Carriers

Grant M. Davis
Martin T. Farris
Jack J. Holder, Jr.

The Praeger Special Studies program—utilizing the most modern and efficient book production techniques and a selective worldwide distribution network—makes available to the academic, government, and business communities significant, timely research in U.S. and international economic, social, and political development.

Management of Transportation Carriers

PRAEGER SPECIAL STUDIES IN U.S. ECONOMIC, SOCIAL, AND POLITICAL ISSUES

Praeger Publishers New York Washington London

Library of Congress Cataloging in Publication Data

Davis, Grant Miller
Management of transportation carriers.

(Praeger special studies in U. S. economic, social and political issues)
Includes biographical references and indexes.
1. Transportation—United States. 2. Transportation—United States—Laws and regulations.
3. Carriers—United States. I. Farris, Martin T., joint author. II. Holder, Jack J., joint author.
III. Title.
HE203.D38 380.5'0973 73-21465
ISBN 0-275-08680-1

PRAEGER PUBLISHERS
111 Fourth Avenue, New York, N.Y. 10003, U.S.A.

Published in the United States of America in 1975
by Praeger Publishers, Inc.

All rights reserved

© 1975 by Praeger Publishers, Inc.

Printed in the United States of America

PREFACE

There is considerable literature on transportation, and its study has a long history. As early as 1850, a special volume on transportation, Railway Economics: A Treatise on the Art of Transportation, by Dionysius Lardner, appeared in London, and in 1870, the first separate applied economics course in transportation in America was taught by President Hadley of Yale University.

Much of the general literature on transportation concerns its history, economic theory, geography, and regulation. Another portion emphasizes the user side and concerns industrial traffic management, physical distribution, and business logistics. Still another deals with the various modes of transportation and is made up of books on railway, highway, water, and air transportation. Surprisingly, there is little literature about transportation carriers in general, as compared to modal studies, and there is practically no literature specifically about the management of transportation carriers.

In higher education there has been a marked tendency to move away from the modal transportation courses. Emphasis has been placed on the shipper or user side of transportation, and a high degree of sophistication has developed in physical distribution and business logistics literature. The supply or carrier side is typically considered in a single course on carrier management, if it is covered at all, although most basic transportation texts give some emphasis to carriers in general. Yet very little formal literature exists specifically about carrier management.

The goal of this book is to offer a discussion of transportation solely from the viewpoint of carrier management. As such, it should prove useful to academic classes in carrier management as well as carrier managers and those involved in the day-to-day operation of carriers. It may also prove useful for policy makers and others who wish to learn another viewpoint on transportation.

The philosophy of this book is simple: We believe that transportation is different. While we agree that all firms face problems of management, and that many of these problems are similar in nature, irrespective of the type of firm and product or service involved, we see transportation as the major exception to the truism that "management is universal."

After a general discussion of the transportation system, Part I, "Regulatory Concepts: A Factor in Transportation Management," sets forth in detail the five constraints faced by carrier management that makes transportation different. Part II, "Managerial Responses and Techniques," discusses carrier management in the setting of these five constraints. Finally, Part III, "The Outlook for Carrier Management," contains our appraisal of the future. We hope in this manner to provide a complete picture of the management of transportation carriers.

This book is a joint effort, and each author had something to do with each chapter. However, Grant Davis took primary responsibility for Chapters 8, 9, 11, 12, and 15; Martin Farris for Chapters 1, 2, 3, 4, 5, and 16; and Jack Holder for Chapters 7, 10, 13, and 14. Chapter 6 was written jointly by Grant Davis and Martin Farris. We are, of course, collectively responsible for all errors of omission or commission.

CONTENTS

Chapter		Page
9	CARRIER MARKETING	148
	The Marketing Concept	148
	Carrier Product Strategy	155
	Market Strategy	158
	Price, Promotion, and Distribution	159
	Summary	162
	Notes	162
10	PUBLIC RELATIONS AND ADVERTISING	166
	Total Program Concept	167
	Measuring the Effectiveness of Advertising	168
	Objectives of Carrier Advertising	169
	Advertising Impact	171
	Types of Advertising by Carriers	172
	Public Relations	173
	Amount Devoted to Promotion	176
	Summary	178
	Notes	178
11	EQUIPMENT SELECTION	179
	Net Investment in Transportation Equipment and Facilities	180
	Types of Transportation Equipment	180
	Maintenance Programs and Safety Regulations	190
	Summary	194
	Notes	194
12	FINANCE AND CREDIT	197
	Capital Expenditure Programs	197
	Rate of Return and Investment Analysis	199
	Rate Levels	217
	Sources of Funds	219
	Lease-or-Buy Decisions	220
	Federal Financial Regulations	221
	Summary	222
	Notes	222

LIST OF TABLES

Table		Page

LIST OF FIGURES

LIST OF ABBREVIATIONS

AFL	American Federation of Labor
AST & T	American Society of Traffic and Transportation
BPI	Buying Power Index
CAB	Civil Aeronautics Board
DF	Damage Free
DOT	Department of Transportation
EEOC	Equal Employment Opportunity Commission
FAA	Federal Aviation Administration
FHA	Federal Highway Administration
FMC	Federal Maritime Commission
FRA	Federal Railroad Administration
FOB	Free On Board
GNP	Gross National Product
IATA	International Air Transport Association
IC Act	Interstate Commerce Act
ICAO	International Civil Aviation Organization
ICC	Interstate Commerce Commission
ISA	Index of Sales Activity
LASH	Lighter Aboard Ship
LTL	Less Than Truckload
MATE	Motors for Additional Tractive Effort
NLRB	National Labor Relations Board

NTSB	National Transportation Safety Board
PI	Profitability Index
PV	Present Value
QI	Quality Index
SEABEE	Seabarge
SMSA	Standard Metropolitan Statistical Area
STOL	Short Take-Off and Landing
TAA	Transportation Association of America
TEI	Trucking Employers, Inc.
TOFC	Trailer-On-Flat-Car

PART

I

REGULATORY CONCEPTS: A FACTOR IN TRANSPORTATION MANAGEMENT

In order to fully appreciate the problems of the management of transportation carriers, it is necessary to set forth clearly the character of the transportation system and the constraints it imposes on managerial decision making. The six chapters that follow attempt to delineate these factors.

CHAPTER

1

THE DOMESTIC TRANSPORTATION SYSTEM

Since the subject of this book is the management of transportation carriers, it is proper to set down the overall approach or philosophy of the discussion at the outset. In this manner, the reader will be able to see how the various parts and chapters fit together as a whole. Each chapter or subject can be considered as a separate entity and, indeed, each is analyzed here as a separate topic. However, when considered together, each topic becomes but a part of the entire discussion.

It is often said that management is universal. That is, irrespective of the type of firm, product or service rendered, or industry involved, the managerial principles used to solve the problems of the business entity are the same. This concept has been repeated so often that it has almost become conventional wisdom or a fundamental truth.

Like all conventional wisdom and fundamental truths, they allow exceptions. One such exception is transportation. Transportation is different. The various factors and constraints faced by the transportation firm are so diverse and unusual that the universal principles of management do not find complete application in the management of transportation carriers. And, because it is different, somewhat different principles and devices must be applied in managing the carrier or supply side of transportation.

THE REGULATORY ENVIRONMENT

One of the major differences about transportation is that it operates in a regulatory environment. All firms face various regulations or rules that society has deemed desirable. Antitrust rules, regulation of weights and measures, laws on fraud and misrepresentation, and control over the monetary system are examples of general business regulation. Regulation in this sense is almost universal. But the supply of transportation must be rendered within the constraints of a much more comprehensive regulatory structure than that facing other firms in the economy. Along with the local service monopolies (sometimes called public utilities), transportation is considered the regulated sector of our economy. By the very term "regulated," it is implied that additional constraints over and above those commonly applied to all firms are found in transportation.

This added and more comprehensive regulatory constraint vitally affects the management of transportation carriers. It seems that at every turn, carrier management is faced with rules, printed regulations, institutional restraints, and barriers to the free decision making so revered as management's prerogative in our society.

In order to understand the management of transportation carriers, one must understand this all-prevailing regulatory environment. While this is not a book on transportation regulation, regulatory development and its rationale and a basic understanding of what is meant by "regulation" is mandatory in order to manage a transportation carrier. Hence, our first task must be to sketch the overall regulatory system as a constraint on managerial action, which we will undertake in Chapter 2.

In addition to this constraint of the regulatory system, there are four further restraints within which transportation is supplied: a given route structure within which day-to-day operation must take place; a system of intermodal, carrier, and market-product competition, which affects almost all decision making; an ownership pattern that affects that operation; and a system of prices or rates that limits the adaptation of the firm. These plus regulation itself make up the five constraints on carrier management.

This is not to imply that these restraints or conditions cannot be changed. Indeed, much of our analysis will be involved with a discussion of the manner in which these conditions can be changed over time and the advisability of attempting to change, and the effects of changing, the route structure, the ownership pattern, the structure of intermodal and market competition, and the system of prices or rates. Even so, the compelling fact remains that these restraints impose limits on managerial action.

THE TRANSPORTATION SYSTEM

Before analyzing the five restraints imposed on the management of transportation carriers, it is appropriate to gain some knowledge of the transportation system itself. While changes in transportation occur constantly and transportation is a dynamic force in the U.S. economy, one must appreciate that it is a system made up of numerous interrelated and interacting parts. While it is possible to consider highway, rail, air, or any type of transportation in isolation (and it may be desirable to do so under certain circumstances), it is more important to understand the concept of transportation as a single, unified system.

Measurements of the Transportation System

One way to not only appreciate the immensity of the total transportation system, but also to get some idea of the relative parts and their importance to the whole, is to analyze some of the commonly available measurements of the importance of transportation.

National Transportation Bills

One widely used measure of the transportation system is the estimated total freight and passenger bill of the entire economy. The Transportation Association of America (TAA) makes available such estimates, and by close inspection of these figures the reader can gain some idea of the immensity of the transportation system in the United States.

Table 1.1 contains the estimate of the nation's freight bill for 1972, and Table 1.2 contains the estimate of the nation's passenger bill for 1972. For purposes of comparison, the gross national product (GNP) is noted, and each of the respective bills as a percentage of the GNP is given. Although these are published as estimates, they are frequently used and are the only data that attempt to measure the total system. Note the comparisons to GNP: 10.04 percent of the GNP is involved in the National Freight Transportation Bill, and 10.89 percent of the GNP is included in the National Passenger Transportation Bill. Collectively, over 20 percent of the GNP is involved in transportation. Hence, it is common to hear the statement that "one dollar out of every five expended in the economy goes for transportation." In 1972, this came to $248.8 billion.

Note that sizable amounts were expended for nonregulated highway transportation, a fact that will become significant when we consider carrier revenues. Note that a single mode, say air transportation, appears in several categories of passenger bill (in this case, both intercity and international). Note also that the passenger bill includes the cost of new and used cars, automobile services, and so forth. While these are certainly transportation costs, it is somewhat difficult to include them in the management of transportation carriers

TABLE 1.1

The Nation's Estimated Freight Bill, 1972

	Millions of Dollars	Percent
Highway		
Truck--intercity		
ICC-regulated	18,700	
Non-ICC-regulated	22,968	
Truck--local	50,498	
Bus	134	
Total	92,300	79.3
Rail		
Railroads	13,508	11.6
Water		
International	3,501	
Coastal, intercoastal	764	
Inland waterways	588	
Great Lakes	205	
Locks, channels, etc.	425	
Total	5,483	4.7
Oil Pipeline		
ICC-regulated	1,338	
Non-ICC-regulated	255	
Total	1,593	1.4
Air		
Domestic	880	
International	585	
Total	1,465	1.3
Other Carriers		
Forwarders and REA Express	358	0.3
Other Shipper Costs		
Loading and unloading freight cars	1,130	
Operation of traffic departments	424	
Total	1,554	1.3
Grand Total	116,261	
GNP	1,158,000	
Grand Total as Percent of GNP	10.04	

Source: Transportation Association of America, *Transportation: Facts and Trends*, 10th ed., July 1974, p. 4.

TABLE 1.2

The Nation's Estimated Passenger Bill, 1972

	Millions of Dollars	Percent
Private Transportation		
Auto		
New and used cars	46,389	
Tires, tubes, and accessories	8,320	
Gas and oil	30,027	
Tolls	720	
Insurance	5,366	
Interest on debt	6,485	
Auto registration fees	1,800	
Operator's permit fees	251	
Repair, greasing, washing, parking, and rental	12,278	
Total	111,636	84.1
Air		
Aircraft	743	
Operating costs	2,992	
Total	3,735	2.8
Total private	115,371	87.0
For-Hire Transportation		
Local		
Bus and transit	1,651	
Taxi	1,580	
Railroad commutation	177	
School bus	1,547	
Total	4,955	3.7
Intercity		
Air	8,227	
Bus	838	
Rail	330	
Water	14	
Total	9,409	7.1
International		
Air	2,592	
Water	268	
Total	2,860	2.2
Total for-hire	17,224	13.0
Grand Total	132,595	
GNP	1,158,000	
Grand Total as Percent of GNP	10.89	

Source: Transportation Association of America, *Transportation: Facts and Trends*, 10th ed., July 1974, p. 5.

unless the term "carrier" is extended to the personal automobile. Tables 1.1 and 1.2 do, however, give an overall picture of the total transportation system.

Our interest here is primarily in carrier or for-hire transportation. Therefore, we shall hereafter generally exclude consideration of the private automobile. Likewise, the whole area of for-hire passenger transportation is so specialized that it deserves separate treatment. Therefore, we shall limit ourselves to for-hire freight transportation. Finally, international transportation is in itself an area of special study and one that involves both foreign affairs and carriers under different regulations than domestic carriers. While we shall mention it when the occasion presents itself, by and large the discussion here will be limited to domestic for-hire freight transportation.

Our next task is to measure the transportation system, within these limitations. This measurement, and understanding of the domestic for-hire freight transportation system, can be found by considering four bases: the cost of the system, the inventory of the system, the performance of the system, and the resources used by the system.

Cost of the Transportation System

A measurement of the cost of the transportation system can be found by considering operating revenues of the carriers. The carriers that are regulated are required to report these matters in some detail. Thus, the best data available concern only regulated carriers. Table 1.3 includes the freight operating revenues of the regulated carriers in domestic transportation in 1972.

TABLE 1.3

Total Freight Revenues of Regulated Carriers in Domestic Operation, 1972

	Millions of Dollars	Percent
Railroad	13,508	37.5
Truck	18,700	51.8
Oil pipelines	1,338	3.7
Freight forwarders	728	2.0
Water carriers	525	1.5
Air carriers	880	2.4
Bus	134	0.04
REA Express	240	0.06
Total	36,053	

Source: Transportation Association of America, Transportation: Facts and Trends, 10th ed., July 1974, p. 6.

This more than $36 billion of total freight revenues is less than the total freight bill of the nation as indicated in Table 1.1 because significant portions of transportation are not regulated and therefore do not report statistics to regulatory authorities. In trucking, for example, Table 1.1 indicates $50.4 billion of expenditures for local freight and $22.9 billion of expenditures for nonregulated trucking that is not included in Table 1.3. Significant portions of water transportation are not regulated and do not report. Table 1.3 also excludes international operations. Table 1.3 does, however, give an idea of the importance of the various carriers or modes from the viewpoint of gross revenue.

Inventory of the Transportation System

A third measure of the transportation system is its inventory, as seen in the number of carrier firms, employees, miles of way, and vehicles.

Table 1.4 lists the number of carrier firms. Obviously, there is a relatively small number of firms in most modes. However, the large number of firms in motor transportation is deceptive. First, there are some very large, as well as some small, motor carriers included in the Class 1 grouping; that is, operating revenues over $1 million gross annually include both the few giants of the industry and many small firms. Second, the larger carriers tend to do the lion's share of the motor carrier business. Note again that some carriers--air, for example--serve primarily the passenger transportation market, and are included here only for purposes of comparison. In total, more than 15,000 carrier firms exist in the transportation system, the vast majority of them being motor carriers.

Table 1.5 indicates the number of employees in the various parts of the transportation system in 1970. Some of these employees --air, for example--are mainly involved in passenger service, and both international air and maritime employees are included in this data although we have restricted ourselves to domestic transportation. Even so, more than 3.6 million people are directly employed by the transportation system, and motor carrier employees make up two-thirds of the transportation labor force.

Table 1.6 notes the miles of way available for the transportation system. This is a common view of the domestic transportation system and emphasizes the physical size of the system available for shipping in the economy. Note that only mileage of airways under control of the Federal Aviation Administration (FAA) is included. Likewise, no mileage figure is listed for maritime transportation, but only inland water channels. Finally, the agencies controlling the highways and streets are noted as well as a breakdown between rural and municipal mileage. In effect, the motor carrier could operate over almost all of the miles of streets and roads in the United States, although regulated motor carriers are restricted as to route, as we shall see in Chapter 4. In any case, over 4.3 million miles are available in the total transportation system, over three-fourths of which are streets and highways.

TABLE 1.4

Number of Carrier Firms in Transportation, 1970

	Carrier Firms
Air	
Certificated, domestic and international	39
Supplemental, domestic and international	14
Total	53
Motor Carrier	
Class I	1,295
Class II	2,061
Class III	11,468
Total	14,824
Water	
Class A and B, inland and coastal	81
Maritime	19
Total	100
Railroads	
Class I only	71
Total	71
Oil Pipelines	
Regulated firms only	99
Total	99
Total Carrier Firms	15,147

Note: Class I Motor Carrier: annual gross revenues over $1 million. Class II Motor Carrier: annual gross revenues $300,000 to $1 million. Class III Motor Carrier: annual gross revenues less than $300,000. Class A Water Carrier: annual gross revenues over $500,000. Class B Water Carrier: annual gross revenues under $500,000. Class I Rail Carrier: annual gross revenues over $5 million.

Source: U.S. Department of Transportation, Summary of National Transportation Statistics (November 1972), pp. 15, 24, 29, 31, and 33; and Interstate Commerce Commission, 84th Annual Report (1970), p. 127 for Class II and Class III motor carriers of property.

TABLE 1.5

Number of Employees in the Transportation System, 1970

Breakdown of System	Employees
Air	
Domestic	246,687
International	53,188
Total	299,875
Motor Carriers	
Truck drivers and delivery men	1,678,000
Service, trucking, and warehouse	1,083,000
Total	2,761,000
Water	
Class A and B, inland and coastal	7,811
Maritime	14,845
Total	22,656
Railroads	
Total	566,282
Oil Pipelines	
Regulated companies	15,017
Total	15,017
Total	3,664,830

Source: U.S. Department of Transportation, Summary of National Transportation Statistics (November 1972), pp. 15, 24, 29, 31, and 33.

TABLE 1.6

Miles of Way in the Domestic Transportation System, 1970

	Miles
Air	
Low altitude	138,295
Jet routes	108,171
Total	146,466
Motor	
Rural mileage	3,169,412
State control	707,002
Local control	2,274,714
Federal control	187,696
Municipal mileage	560,670
State control	74,103
Local control	486,567
Total	3,730,082
Water	
Commercially navigable inland channels	25,543
Total	25,543
Rail	
Total	206,265
Oil Pipelines	
Regulated and unregulated crude oil only	218,604
Total	218,604
Total miles of way	4,326,960

Source: U.S. Department of Transportation, Summary of National Transportation Statistics (November 1972), pp. 19, 29, 31, and 33; and Federal Aviation Administration, Statistical Handbook of Aviation (1970), p. 11, for controlled airway mileage in contiguous 48 states.

The final measure of the inventory of the transportation system is the number of vehicles operated, as indicated in Table 1.7. These data include all commercial aircraft (even though the service rendered may be principally passenger), exclude maritime water transportation, and include all registered trucks. Obviously, many of the trucks are private and are not directly involved in for-hire carrier transportation. In that sense Table 1.7 is not an inventory of carrier vehicles so much as total vehicles operated in the system, both private and for-hire or carrier. Even so, Table 1.7 does indicate another dimension of the inventory of the domestic transportation system, which is that over 20 million vehicles are operated in domestic transportation, over 18 million of which are trucks.

TABLE 1.7

Total Vehicles Operated in the Domestic Transportation System, 1970

	Number of Vehicles
Air (domestic and international)	
Certificated	2,564
Supplemental	195
Total	2,759
Motor	
Private and commercial	17,789,980
Government-owned	968,441
Total	18,748,421
Water	
Barges	19,171
Towboats and tugs	4,248
Total	23,419
Rail	
Freight cars	1,423,573
Locomotives	27,086
Total	1,450,659
Grand Total	20,225,258

Source: U.S. Department of Transportation, Summary of National Transportation Statistics (November 1972), pp. 15, 24, 29, and 31.

In summary, the inventory of the transportation system is made up of over 15,000 carrier firms directly employing over 3.6 million people operating over 20 million vehicles over 4.3 million miles of way.

Performance of the Transportation System

How has the transportation system performed? An analysis of ton-miles carried, vehicle-miles produced, average haul, and average load will give us some idea.

One common measure of performance is ton-miles (one ton moved one mile), as presented in Table 1.8. Obviously, carriers that move very heavy loads many miles, such as railroads and waterways, will have a large number of ton-miles; carriers moving lighter loads on shorter journeys, such as trucks, will produce fewer ton-miles. The relative share of ton-miles produced in 1972 can be compared roughly with the relative share of revenues given in Table 1.3 to gain some ideas of rates. Hence, railroads carried 38 percent of the ton-miles and received 38 percent of the revenues, trucks carried 22 percent of the ton-miles but received 52 percent of the revenues, water carriers carried 16 percent of the ton-miles but received only 1.5 percent of the revenues and so forth. (Exact comparisons are difficult, however, because some of the revenues of freight forwarders and REA Express came from ton-miles moved by both railroads and motor carriers.)

TABLE 1.8

Ton-Miles Produced in Domestic Transportation, 1972

	Millions of Ton-Miles	Percent
Air carriers	3,800	0.2
Oil pipelines	457,000	22.2
Railroads	785,000	38.2
Motor carriers--intercity	470,000	22.9
Inland water carriers	339,000	16.5
Total Ton-Miles	2,054,800	

Source: Transportation Association of America, Transportation Facts and Trends, 10th ed., 1974, p. 8.

Since ton-miles give undue emphasis to weight and distance, a vehicle-mile measure is sometimes used. In 1970, air carriers reported over 2 million vehicle-miles, motor carriers 214 billion, and Class I rail carriers 427 million.[1] Unfortunately, neither pipelines nor inland water transportation reports on a vehicle-mile basis. Consequently, ton-miles and vehicle-miles are not completely comparable. Even so, a vehicle-mile measure does give emphasis to the many short journeys of the motor carrier.

The length of the average haul, as presented in Table 1.9, shows another dimension of the transportation system. Note that only intercity movement is reported. In the case of trucks, a large amount of transportation is produced in short journeys within metropolitan areas and is hence excluded from these data. Also note that average length of haul data for railroads are reported both by carrier and by the rail system as a whole. Since the equipment is interchangeable from one firm to another, it is common for a shipment to travel over the tracks of two or more railroads, and a system figure is quite realistic. Oil pipeline data are reported by type of pipeline, either crude or refined petroleum product, each type of pipeline transportation having its own system.

TABLE 1.9

Average Length of Freight Haul in Intercity Domestic Transportation, 1972

	Miles
Air	991
Oil pipeline (crude)	299
Oil pipeline (product)	347
Railroads (per carrier)	287
Railroads (system)	512
Motor carriers (Class I--common)	280
Water (rivers and channels)	350
Water (Great Lakes)	504
Water (coastal)	1,449

Source: Transportation Association of America, *Transportation: Facts and Trends*, 10th ed., July 1974, p. 14.

The average load carried gives a final measure of performance. Data on this topic are found in many places and obviously would not apply to carriers such as pipelines. However, it has been estimated that railroads carry an average load of about 57 tons per freight car, motor carriers about 12 tons per intercity truck, and water carriers about 1,800 tons per barge on inland waterways.[2] The average load for air carriers varies, depending on whether the shipment is air freight, air express, or airmail, and is expressed in terms of pounds, not tons.

Resources Used in Domestic Transportation

A final dimension of the domestic transportation system is the amount of resources used. Considerable investment in capital by both carriers and governments is necessary to produce the immense amounts of transportation noted earlier under performance. Three measures of this investment are net investment in equipment and facilities, expenditures for new plant and equipment, and governmental expenditures for transportation facilities.

While the data are now somewhat dated, Table 1.10 presents estimates of the net investment in transportation equipment and facilities in the nongovernment sector of the economy. Around $64 billion was invested in the transportation system, exclusive of governmental investment in 1968. A comparison of the relative share of net investment with the number of firms, as indicated in Table 1.4, will give some idea of the cost structure of the firms involved. For example, the railroads, with 71 firms and $31.7 billion net investment, obviously have high fixed costs; the motor carriers, with 14,824 firms and $17.6 billion net investment, do not have as great a problem with fixed costs.

TABLE 1.10

Net Investment in Nongovernment Transportation Equipment and Facilities, 1968

	Millions of Dollars
Air carriers	7,965
Trucks and trailers	17,568
Oil pipelines	3,842
Railroads	31,748
Water carriers	2,930
Total	64,053

Source: Transportation Association of America, *Transportation: Facts and Trends*, 10th ed., 1974, p. 26.

Another measure of investment is expenditures for new plant and equipment, as presented in Table 1.11. Great care must be used with these figures, however. First, in some years expenditures for new equipment may be very high due to re-equipment problems. For example, in 1970, air transportation spent an estimated $3.03 billion --almost twice the 1971 figure--much of it for the new generation of wide-bodied jets. Second, some transportation equipment--for example, rail--lasts for many years, whereas other equipment--such as truck--has a much shorter life. These problems will be discussed in greater detail in Chapter 9.

TABLE 1.11

Estimated Expenditures for New Plant and Equipment in the Transportation System, 1972

	Billions of Dollars
Air transportation	2.46
Rail transportation	1.80
Pipeline and water transportation	1.46
Motor transportation	1.83
Total	7.55

Source: Transportation Association of America, Transportation: Facts and Trends, 10th ed., 1974, p. 29.

Various levels of government also make considerable expenditures in fixed transportation investment, such as highways, waterways, and airways, as well as in the operation of the ways. Table 1.12 contains these data and illustrates the third measure of investment. Naturally, these amounts will vary from year to year since some programs, such as highways and airports, tend to be built in crash programs like the Interstate System, originally scheduled for construction between 1956 and 1972, and the Airport Improvement Program, scheduled for 1970 to 1980. Even so, considerable public money has been invested in transportation facilities and it is estimated that between 1947 and 1973, $425.9 billion ($113.4 billion federal, $312.5 billion state and local) was expended on domestic transportation, $320 billion of which was spent for streets and highways.[3]

But transportation is also responsible for considerable revenues into government in the form of income taxes, excise taxes such as those on gasoline and fuel, property taxes, licenses and permits, and so forth. In 1971, total federal taxes that were transportation related were estimated at $31.3 billion (16.3 percent of all federal taxes); total state taxes were $51.5 billion (29 percent of all state taxes).[4] Of course, these government sources include the private automobile (including corporate income taxes on transportation equipment manufacturers) and must therefore be used with care. However, anyone who has paid four cents a gallon federal tax and from five to ten cents a gallon state tax for gasoline has had experience with these transportation related taxes. The sources of tax revenue and the manner of collection vary but the fact remains that the function of transportation pays into government huge sums and governments pay out equally huge sums to provide transportation facilities.

TABLE 1.12

Federal and State Expenditures for Transportation Facilities, 1971

	Millions of Dollars
Airways	
All federal	1,398
Total	1,398
Airports	
Federal	215
State and local	1,061
Total	1,276
Rivers and Harbors	
Federal	385
State and local	504
Total	889
Highways	
Federal	5,646
State and local	15,560
Total	21,206
Grand Total	24,769

Source: Transportation Association of America, Transportation: Facts and Trends, 10th ed., 1974, p. 26.

A final measure of the total transportation system (including the private automobile) is found in the degree of resources consumed by transportation. In 1973 it was estimated that transportation used 75 percent of all rubber, 53 percent of all petroleum, 67 percent of all lead, 36 percent of all zinc, 24 percent of all steel, 27 percent of all cement, 21 percent of all aluminum, and 12 percent of all copper produced.[5]

In summary, the resources used in the transportation system are prodigious. Private investment in transportation was approximately $64 billion in 1968, new equipment and plant expenditures were around $7.5 billion in 1972, governmental expenditures for facilities were almost $24.8 billion in 1971 and $426 billion between 1947 and 1973, transportation related activity was responsible for 16 percent of all federal and 29 percent of all state taxes collected, and substantial amounts of physical resources were consumed by the transportation system.

SUMMARY

Overall statistics on total transportation are overwhelming. The total transportation bill--freight and passenger--of the nation is over 20 percent of the GNP. Huge amounts of both private and public expenditures, taxes, and resources are involved.

Since our concern here is primarily in terms of for-hire carriers, the transportation system can best be summarized in terms of the various modes of transportation, as illustrated in Table 1.13, which summarizes data for 1972.

Each mode has separate characteristics and an inherent advantage. The few air carrier firms (53) produced a relatively small amount of the total freight carried (0.2 percent of total ton-miles) over great distances (991-mile average haul) and over a large airway system (146,466 miles) at relatively high revenues (1.5 percent of total). Air transportation specializes in fast freight at high rates and is concerned mainly with passenger transportation.

Motor carriers produced 23 percent of the ton-miles with the many firms (14,824) operating over a very large and extensive way (over 3.7 million miles) with a huge number of vehicles available (over 18 million) with an average length of haul of 280 miles intercity, an average load of 12 tons, and received 51.8 percent of total transportation revenues. The motor carrier specializes in short-to-intermediate distance movement at intermediate-to-low rates.

Rail carriers produced 38 percent of all ton-miles--by far the greatest number of any mode, with an intermediate-to-small number of firms (71) operating over a relatively large way (206,265 miles) with a large number of vehicles (over 1.4 million freight cars) with

TABLE 1.13

Summary of Transportation System by Mode of Carrier, 1970

		Percent of Total
Air Carriers		
Freight revenues	$880 million	1.5
Number of carrier firms	53	
Employees (domestic and international)	299,875	
Miles of way	146,466	
Vehicles available	2,759	
Ton-miles produced	3,800	0.2
Vehicle-miles produced	over 2 billion	
Average length of haul	991 miles	
Motor Carriers		
Freight revenues	$18,700	51.8
Number of carrier firms	14,824	
Employees	2,761,000	
Miles of way	3,730,082	
Vehicles available	18,748,421	
Ton-miles produced	470,000 million	23.0
Vehicle-miles produced	214 billion	
Average length of haul (intercity)	280 miles	
Average load (intercity)	12 tons	
Rail Carriers		
Freight revenues	$13,508	37.5
Number of carrier firms (Class I)	71	
Employees	566,282	
Miles of way	206,265	
Vehicles operated (freight cars)	1,423,573	
Ton-miles produced	785 million	38.0
Vehicle-miles produced (Class I)	427 million	
Average length of haul (system)	512 miles	
Average load	57 tons	
Water Carriers		
Freight revenues	$525 million	2.0
Number of carrier firms (including maritime)	100	
Employees (including maritime)	22,656	
Miles of way (excluding maritime)	25,543	
Vehicles available (excluding maritime)	23,419	
Ton-miles produced (excluding maritime)	339,000 million	17.0
Average length of haul (excluding maritime)		
Rivers	350 miles	
Great Lakes	504 miles	
Coastal	1,449 miles	
Average load (barge)	1,800 tons	
Pipeline Carriers		
Freight revenues	$1,338 million	3.7
Number of carrier firms	99	
Employees	15,017	
Miles of way (crude only)	218,604	
Ton-miles produced	457 million	22.0
Average length of haul		
Crude	299 miles	
Product	347 miles	

Note: Freight revenues, ton- and vehicle-miles produced, and average length of haul are for 1972.

Source: See source notes for Tables 1.4-1.9, and fn. 1.

a long average haul (512 miles) of large average loads (57 tons) and received 37.5 percent of the total transportation revenues. By and large, rail carriers specialize in carload and heavy bulk commodity movement between major terminal points at low rates.

Water carriers produced 17 percent of the ton-miles with an intermediate number of firms (100) operating over a small way (25,543 miles) with a small number of vehicles (23,419) operating over considerable distances (350 to 1,449 miles) with large loads (1,800 tons per barge) and received 2 percent of total transportation revenues. Water carriers tend to specialize in bulk and heavy items that do not require speed and can be loaded and unloaded mechanically. They are, of course, limited to service in geographic areas where waterways exist.

Finally, pipelines specialize in liquid freight, produced 22 percent of the ton-miles with an intermediate number of firms (99) over a large way (218,604 miles of crude lines) with an intermediate-to-long average haul (299 to 347 miles) and received 3.7 percent of total transportation revenues.

NOTES

1. U.S. Department of Transportation, Summary of National Transportation Statistics, November 1972, p. 42.
2. Roy J. Sampson and Martin T. Farris, Domestic Transportation: Practice, Theory and Policy, 3rd ed. (Boston: Houghton Mifflin Co., 1975), pp. 55, 63, 73.
3. Association of American Railroads, Governmental Expenditures for Highways, Waterways and Air Facilities and Private Expenditures for Railroad Facilities, May 1973, Table 1.
4. Transportation Association of America, Transportation: Facts and Trends, 10th ed., 1973, p. 27.
5. Ibid., p. 1.

CHAPTER 2
THE REGULATORY SYSTEM

Now that the transportation system has been outlined and analyzed, our next task is to turn to the regulatory system. This is the major constraint or factor that makes the management of transportation carriers different from management in general.

VARIOUS MEANINGS AND TYPES OF REGULATION

There are several types of regulation and many uses and definitions of the term. Broadly speaking, there are three facets of the regulatory system: economic regulation, regulation of the physical aspects of transportation, and regulation by social policy. Economic regulation of transportation generally refers to the control or regulation of price (rates), entry of new firms and economic expansion or contraction of existing firms, and control of services from an economic viewpoint. The regulation of the physical aspects of transportation refers to control over the conditions of transportation. Regulation by social policy refers to the negative and positive results of aiding and supporting one means of transportation over another, or transportation as a function as compared to another economic function; the ownership patterns allowed; and environmental restraints. Each will be outlined in this chapter and analyzed in detail in subsequent chapters.

Regulation can also be classified as direct or indirect. Thus, the economic regulation of transportation is all direct--it is directly on the firms supplying the transportation service. Social regulation is all indirect--it affects the economic climate within which transportation operates and the financial conditions under which transportation takes place. The regulation of the physical aspects of transportation is a mixture of direct and indirect. Very often it is direct when such things as safety rules are imposed on carriers and private operators. Sometimes it is indirect when it involves rule-of-the-road and standard operating procedures.

Finally, it should be noted that there is a multiplicity of agencies involved in the regulatory system. Some are well known, others less so, but all are organized and operated differently and distinctively. In effect, these agencies are institutions that interact on one another and on transportation in a complex and sometimes inconsistent manner. Transportation regulation is filled with inconsistent and conflicting rules and regulations enforced by a large group of conflicting and competing regulatory institutions. Indeed, the struggle for consistency and the resolution of conflict is found in all aspects of transportation regulation.

GOALS OF REGULATION

Before analyzing the three facets of the regulatory system, we should attempt to examine the general goals of regulation, which are the protection of the public and the promotion of the best possible system of transportation.

While it is easy to state these general goals, their implementation is considerably more difficult, as they contain some inherent conflicts. To attain the best possible system of transportation, the carriers and manufacturers must be strong economically. An economically marginal carrier does not produce the best possible service nor does a manufacturer who is losing money necessarily produce the highest quality of equipment. On the other hand, the public must not be exploited in price or service. Conflict is apparent. So too with safety and environmental protection. The public demands that its interests be taken into consideration. But safety and environmental controls cost money and their provision may weaken the financial health of the carrier or the manufacturer. The inherent conflict of the two goals is evident.

The result is conflict and countervailing powers or forces that must somehow be accommodated. This accommodation is usually a compromise and the conflict of countervailing forces may be only partially resolved; as a result, the goals of regulation are probably never completely fulfilled. The public is not completely protected, nor is the best possible system of transportation attained. Indeed, given the inherent conflict in these goals, one could question whether it would ever be possible to fully attain them.

ECONOMIC REGULATION

The economic aspect of transportation regulation encompasses three devices of control: price or rate regulation, entry regulation, and regulation of transportation service.

Rate Regulation

Transportation has long been regulated in the public interest. Even in medieval times, the cabby and the drayman providing urban transportation were controlled by the sovereign or the city within which they operated. Historically, the number of suppliers of transportation has usually been restricted by way of some control over entry, and the charges have been limited in some way. While we will discuss entry controls in Chapter 3, "Transportation Competition," and Chapter 4, "Route Structure," it is well to point out that all three devices of economic control are part of a system that interacts and is interdependent. Historically, transportation has been organized as a monopoly or near monopoly, and has had its charges or prices controlled by society.

In modern times, in a situation with one or a few firms, the problem becomes one of how a commission or board acting as the sovereign can substitute for the forces of competition. Some administrative device is established to attempt to be a proxy for the marketplace. Society desires the benefits of restricted numbers of suppliers but wishes to protect itself from potential exploitation by the firms it has favored with this limitation. This is the age-old problem of regulation, and turns on rate control.

In general, rate regulation means the control of the prices that for-hire carriers charge. But more specifically, rate regulation encompasses both the level of rates and the rate structure. "Level of rates" refers to the earnings of the carrier, while "rate structure" refers to the specific prices or rates charged. This division of rate regulation has existed for a very long time and involves the two legal and economic concepts of reasonableness and discrimination.

Rate Level

The level of rates is related to the reasonableness of the carrier's earnings and charges. By controlling prices, the public controls the carrier's earnings. Prices can be set both too high and too low. If they are too high, the public will be exploited and pay unreasonably high prices, and the firm will enjoy unusual monopoly earnings. If they are too low, the carrier may be forced to provide service at a loss, and ultimately will have its property economically confiscated. The problem of the level of rates and reasonableness is a difficult one.

In the United States, rate regulation goes back to the post-Civil War period and the attempts by some states to regulate the railroad monopolies of that day. In the so-called Granger Movement, several Midwestern states established boards to set rail rates, or else legislatures set rail rates by statute.[1] While this movement was short-lived, it was determined to be a legal and constitutional exercise of state powers in the famous case of Munn v. Illinois (1877).[2] However, the problem of rate level remained and was not legally resolved until the equally famous case of Smyth v. Ames (1898).[3]

In this latter case, the United States Supreme Court stated that rates should be established for a regulated firm in such a way as to yield no more than a "fair return on a fair value" of the property committed to public use. In effect, this meant that a standard was established for the determination of the level of rates deemed reasonable in all regulated firms.

The long history of the problem of defining what is meant by a "fair value" and a "fair return" need not delay us here. Obviously, what is fair is a matter of judgment. More often than not, a court has finally had to arbitrate what was meant by a "fair return on a fair value" in a case-by-case method. "Fair value" can mean original cost, or cost of reproduction, or a combination of both. "Fair return" can mean earnings comparable to other regulated firms, earnings high enough to attract capital, earnings high enough to compensate for risk, and many other things. The long and interesting history of this problem can be found in most standard textbooks on public utility economics.[4]

Suffice it to say at this point that the legal doctrine of a fair return on a fair value is the reason we find the Interstate Commerce Commission's (ICC) ruling that the railroads may earn up to 6 percent on fair value, or the Civil Aeronautics Board's (CAB) determining that airlines may earn 10 to 12 percent and that rates that yield more or less than this are "unreasonable." In effect, these institutions are acting in the ancient role of sovereign and are determining what level of rates or earnings is fair and reasonable.

It should be noted that the determination of the rate level under the fair return and fair value criterions is theoretically a type of target rate level. Legally, if the firm earns more than the target, rates will be decreased; if the firm earns less than the target, rates will be increased. In recent times, rather than determining a specific target of, say, 6 percent, a "zone of reasonableness" approach has been adopted.[5] Hence, rate levels yielding between 10 and 12 percent are not legally unreasonable in the airlines. The target becomes a zone of reasonable earnings level.

It is not expected that each and every year the firms will earn the target return, or even the return found in the zone of reasonableness. Further, the legal doctrine is specifically not a guarantee of any sort--it merely means the regulated firm should have the opportunity to reach the target.[6] There is a tendency to apply rate level earnings control on the upside--that is, decrease rates if earnings exceed the target of reasonableness, and to disregard the target of reasonableness on the downside--that is, a hesitancy to raise rates when less than a reasonable rate of return is earned. This is not a bit surprising, given the fact that in transportation considerable competition and elasticity potential or substitution exists, as will be discussed in Chapter 3, "Transportation Competition." If regulatory authorities were to raise the level of rates to meet the "fair return on a fair value" target, it could well mean even lower earnings for a carrier, if customers were induced to use other modes. Also, note that the legal doctrine of rate level control is based on the historical fact of monopoly control. However, the conditions of monopoly are at best only partially relevant to transportation.

Finally, given the problem of determining what constitutes a fair value and a fair return, and given the degrees of competition involved in the industry, some commissions on some modes have used the operating-ratio approach to rate level control. The operating ratio is defined as the operating expenses over the operating revenues multiplied by one hundred--for example, an operating ratio of 85 would mean that 85 cents out of every dollar of revenue went for operating expenses. By determining a target operating ratio of, say, 92, the commission hopes to avoid the problems inherent in the fair-return-on-a-fair-value approach. This substitute has been widely used in motor transportation, where the carriers are great in number and determination of fair value becomes burdensome. It should be noted that the operating-ratio approach is a poor substitute for an already vague level of reasonableness, and has many pitfalls inherent in it as well.[7]

In summary, the regulation of the level of rates means determination of the reasonableness of prices. A legal concept has grown over the years in which the rate level must yield a fair return on a fair value. Much difficulty exists in defining these terms where a specific problem of rates exists. The rate-level approach may not act as a guarantee for the firm, but is rather an ideal or target to be sought. Since it is based on monopoly control and the industry has many degrees of competition, this approach is far from perfect. The conclusion is that there is considerable difference between the legal world of regulation and the real world of transportation.

Rate Structure

The structure of rates is concerned with the economic and legal concept of discrimination. The concept of avoidance of discrimination has a long legal and economic history like that of the concept of reasonableness. Both came out of the common carrier obligations found in the common law, which we will discuss directly.

Discrimination implies unequal treatment. It is possible that the schedule of transportation rates could cause unequal treatment for a given city, or a given class of freight, or a given geographical point such as a district, port, airport, or region. Given the historically monopolistic or near monopolistic type of organization of the transportation firms, this type of arbitrary action was to be avoided. Historically, the railroads in this country tended to lower rates to points where they competed with each other, and raise rates to points where they possessed monopolies. In effect, they were following the economic theory of differential pricing discussed in Chapter 6 under "Transportation Rate Theory." While it was perfectly good economics, it was not equitable to all users and caused great public concern over discrimination. Public outcry led to a congressional investigation,[8] and when the Supreme Court ruled that the existing state laws had no jurisdiction over discrimination in interstate commerce,[9] Congress acted in 1887 to regulate interstate commerce and prohibited discrimination in the rate structure.[10]

The term "discrimination" has many meanings. The legal definition is not always the economic definition which, in turn, is not always the social definition. The economist defines discrimination in terms of differences in price not reflecting differences in costs. Sometimes the legal definition of price discrimination is similar, and sometimes it is not. However, because of these multiple meanings, transportation regulation typically prohibits "undue" discrimination and allows a board or commission to determine what is "undue." Discrimination can work in two ways, of course, both for and against a point or class of freight. Hence, the statutes typically prohibit "unduly preferential or unduly prejudiced rates," and let a commission determine what is meant by "undue," "preferential," and "prejudiced," subject to judicial review.[11]

It should be clearly understood that rates or price schedules are set forth initially by the carriers. While it is commonly said that the CAB or the ICC "makes rates," this is really not the case.

The commission or board is given the power to approve or disapprove rate schedules--it does not set the prices. If the regulatory body finds rates to be unduly discriminatory (or unreasonable, when considering rate levels), it may specify what prices or rates it will approve as nondiscriminatory or reasonable. In this instance, and only in this instance, does the administrative commission actually set the rate.

While the distinction noted here may seem to be minor and somewhat burdened with legal niceties, it is, in fact, an important distinction. In spite of what the headlines say about the CAB's setting rates, and in spite of the often heard complaint by carrier personnel that the ICC sets rates too low (or too high), it is up to the carrier to set its rates as it sees fit, given the demand and cost as it perceives them. The regulatory authority then either approves or disapproves of the carrier's proposal. A great deal more innovation in pricing or rate making might be approved if the carrier would only try and propose it. The entire process of rate making will be discussed in detail in Chapter 6, "Pricing and Rate Making." But, as is also implied in Chapter 6, it is sometimes the path of least resistance on the carrier's part to compete on a basis other than price, and to shift the blame to the convenient regulatory board.

In actual practice, it is more often than not a competitive carrier that resists and offers a complaint to price or rate innovation. While cities and classes of shippers sometimes protest discrimination before regulatory groups, it is the carriers who are most alert to changes in the rate structure of their competitors. If the case alleging discrimination has merit, the commission or board must specify what it considers to be nondiscriminatory. It is for this reason that one finds the ICC concerned with the relationship of less-than-carload rates to carload rates and multiple-carload rates, or rates to inland points relative to rates to seaports for the same commodity, or rates to one distribution center as compared to another distribution center, and so forth. These are all examples of potential discrimination.

In summary, rate structure regulation concerns potential preferential or prejudicial treatment. Under the law, this must be "undue" discrimination, and a commission or other regulatory institution is given the authority to determine the meaning of this term, subject to judicial review. Actual prices are originally determined by the carrier and only approved or disapproved by the regulatory authorities. The most frequent parties protesting discrimination are not the shippers, but rather competitive carriers. Once undue preference or prejudice has been found, the regulatory authority can specify the exact rate that removes the alleged discrimination.

Entry Regulation

The second device of economic regulation is the control of entry of new carriers and the change in the operating route structure of existing carriers. This device is obviously interrelated with the other two devices of rate control and the regulation of service. Indeed, historically, it was the granting of monopoly or near monopoly status that led to the need for rate structure and rate level control.

Basically, the question is that of how many carriers will be allowed to compete on a given route or in a given area. Too much competition among carriers can be just as bad as too little. The financial health of the carrier and the needs of the public to be served are two sometimes conflicting criterions that must be weighed in these entry decisions.

Two regulatory devices have historically been used to control entry--the franchise and the certificate of public convenience and necessity. The franchise has been used to control entry on the city streets, alleys, and byways, and is typically issued by the city council to a bus, street-railway, or rapid-transit system. While most franchises are exclusive, that is, guaranteeing only one firm, they are not all so, and several firms sometimes have franchises to serve a given area or city. However, the number of possible firms is limited by the potential inconvenience to the public of having too many vehicles on a street, irrespective of potential bankruptcy due to excessive competition.

The certificate of public convenience and necessity is typically issued by a regulatory board or commission, such as the ICC or the CAB, where intercity transportation is involved. While there are potential space limitations, and facilities such as airports, train stations, ports, and the like can become overcrowded, it is more a matter of economic competition that is involved. Once more the problem is one of balancing the public's need for service with the need to maintain an economically sound carrier.

It is not an easy task to decide how many carriers should be allowed to serve between two geographic points or on a given route. But once the decision as to "how many" carriers has been made, the equally difficult decision as to "which" carriers is also involved. Because the public must be served, there is a distinct tendency to favor existing carriers over new carriers when this decision is reached.

Further, the tendency to favor existing carriers has been reinforced by the regulatory statutes. It must be remembered that, at one time, almost all areas of operation were unregulated as to entry. As each geographic area or economic area (such as motor carriers or air carriers) was brought under regulation, the problem of what to do about the existing carriers had to be faced. Typically, a "grandfather clause" was used to solve this problem.

Under the grandfather clause, the existing carriers were allowed to continue their operation in the same manner as they had been operating on or near the date of regulation, as "a matter of right." That is, the existing carriers were not required to show that their operations were necessary or that they served a public need. These carriers are sometimes called "grandfather carriers" and often refer to these privileges as "rights." The operating authority is, however, a privilege under the law, not a right like the right to vote or the right of peaceful assembly, and as such can be revoked for just cause. It is common in transportation, however, to speak of "operating rights."

While the matter will be analyzed again in Chapter 4, it is well to note that all new carriers and any changes in an existing carrier's operations had to show that public convenience would be served and that a necessity for the service existed. Hence the term "certificate of public convenience and necessity." Once the need was established, the entrant had to show that this need could be adequately served by proving it was "fit, willing, and able" to serve under the law. This applied to new carriers as well as to changes in the operating rights of existing carriers.[12] While the term "fit, willing, and able" is subject to interpretation and is difficult to define specifically, it generally refers to past operating experience that demonstrates ability, financial fitness and soundness (with emphasis on past financial history), and operating equipment and organization (once more based on past operations). In all cases, it is difficult for a new carrier to demonstrate that it is "fit, willing, and able," particularly since much of the interpretation of the term depends on experience or past operation. It is much easier for existing carriers to extend their operations into a new territory and develop as demand grows than for new carriers to enter a market under regulatory statutes.

The obvious result of the use of certificates of public convenience and necessity, plus the grandfather clause, plus the requirement of being "fit, willing, and able," plus regulatory policy, is that competition is controlled. There is a definite preference for existing firms and it is almost impossible for new firms to enter the transportation market. Empirical investigation shows that in most modes of transportation, the existing firms have continued since the time of regulation (grandfather carriers) and have expanded and changed as the market has expanded and changed. Very few new firms have begun under regulation.[13]

Additionally, as part of entry controls (as well as financial controls) of carriers, all mergers have to be approved. This concept was originally found in the Transportation Act of 1920, which dealt mainly with railroads, and was based on the idea that the carrier might endanger itself financially by undue expansion through mergers and consolidations, and hence impair the ability to serve. The idea was that regulation should promote economically strong carriers in order to assure good service. Control over mergers was incorporated in each act subsequent to the Act of 1920 as the newer modes of transportation were regulated.

In addition to the original rationale, it should be realized that if mergers were not controlled, the carrier could subvert the regulation of entry and routes by simply taking over existing firms. Merger controls and certificates of public convenience and necessity are mutually interdependent regulatory devices. However, the result of this logic is that even firmer control of entry and the pattern of competition exists than simply regulating new entrants.

Finally, there are many possible patterns of competition in transportation. Competition between substitute modes or means of transportation, such as truck versus rail, or air versus truck, is called "intermodal competition." Competition between substitute carriers of the same mode, such as two competing truck lines, two competing railroads, or two competing airlines, is generally called "intramodal competition" or "carrier competition." Finally, the shipper may also supply his own transportation, usually by privately owned truck or barge. This type of competition is also involved. These types of competition will be analyzed in depth in Chapter 3. Suffice it to say for now that the control of entry into the transportation market is not absolute, and that various patterns of existing and potential competition exist.

Service Regulation

The final device of economic regulation is the control over the level of service of the carriers. This aspect of regulation, although not as well known as price and entry control, is equally a part of, and is interrelated with, price and entry regulation as a system of economic regulation.

From a philosophical viewpoint, the goal of regulation in this area is to see that the public is offered good service. Economically, service regulation must accompany price and entry regulation, because when a monopoly or near monopoly is granted and prices are set there may be a natural tendency on the part of the firm to maximize by decreasing the quality and level of service. Once a carrier is granted the "right" to operate exclusively, the natural stimulus of competition is removed. The whole point of service regulation is to substitute administrative action for the stimulus of the impersonal marketplace, which causes firms to compete and try to serve best in order to gain more business and higher profit.

Service regulation is a very old concept, and the natural tendency to have deteriorating service levels once entry is controlled has existed almost as long as regulation itself. Historically, this problem was solved by imposing a series of rights and duties on the carrier or regulated firm by the sovereign. Hence, in exchange for the right to operate exclusively, the regulated firm assumed four duties: to serve, to deliver, to avoid discrimination, and to charge only reasonable prices. Later, these duties became part of the common law or the doctrine of common callings and were uniformly recognized as part of the fabric of regulation.[14]

The duty to serve means that the regulated firm must serve all comers. It may not limit its public except for due cause and unless physically limited in some way. Likewise, once given the right to serve a point, a carrier may not abandon its service without permission.

The duty to deliver concerns delivery to the consignee with dispatch, in the same physical condition as originally tendered to the carrier, and to the correct party. The annoying problem of freight claims that plagues carriers is due to the failure to adequately fulfill the duty to deliver.

The duty to avoid discrimination and the duty to charge reasonable prices have been formalized in rate control as noted above. Discrimination here refers to both price and service discrimination (both preferential and prejudicial) between points and between classes of freight. "Reasonableness" as used here refers to both the rate level and the rate structure as previously noted, and in general means that a carrier may not exploit its monopoly privilege. In both of these duties, an administrative commission has been granted the task of interpreting the meaning of the terms, subject to court review, and establishing regulatory rules and regulations to see that those duties are fulfilled.

These duties are open to considerable judgment and interpretation. For instance, once operating authority to serve a point has been granted, the carrier must continue to serve and must carry all freight tendered. In the words of the law, the carrier must "hold himself out to serve all comers." It should be pointed out, however, that the extent of service is usually not closely regulated. By "extent of service" we mean simply "how often?" Certainly a minimum of service exists, such as a train once a week, a plane once a day, or a truck once a day, in order to fulfill this duty, but beyond this there is little concern. Should the extent of service be too limited, the carrier risks having competitive service instituted in order to adequately fulfill the public-convenience-and-necessity feature of its rights, but typically a wide degree of latitude exists before competitive carriers are enticed into a market.

There has generally been little concern with maximum levels of service. The assumption has been that the carriers would follow the profit motive and would not serve more often than was necessary in their own self-interest. It should be noted, however, that this automatic regulator of maximum service may not work perfectly. That is, complaints of too much competition are sometimes heard among carriers, and generally refer to a situation in which there are several carriers heavily competing in a small market, and to decrease the extent of service would adversely affect the market share of the carrier taking such action. More analysis of these situations will appear in Chapter 3, "Transportation Competition."

Finally, there has been little concern with the condition of service. By the term "condition of service" we mean the adequacy of equipment, the treatment of the customer, and general environment within which the service is rendered. Once more the assumption was made that the carrier would render some mimimum standard of service in order to meet competition in the marketplace. If the condition of service were inferior, the shipper would simply shift to another carrier or another mode--that is, intermodal and intramodal competition and elasticity could be relied on to regulate the condition of service.

This position fails to recognize the interrrelated nature of the regulatory system. Poor conditions of service can exist, especially where monopoly privilege is found and it is not possible for all shippers to shift to other modes. Likewise, the conditions of service can become a vehicle of discrimination against points or classes of customers or freight, as well as a competitive tool to assure a large share of the market. Some have suggested that this has taken place relative to small shipments.

To make rate and entry regulation effective, conditions of service as well as extent of service may have to be controlled. Recognition of this necessity to control service in a comprehensive manner (both minimum and maximum) has come slowly and reluctantly to regulatory boards and commissions, if at all. Failure to recognize the fact that, once entry is controlled and price regulated the third aspect of service must also be regulated, is one of the problems of the regulatory system.

Consistency

It is fairly obvious that the three devices of economic regulation--price, entry, and service regulation--are a whole package or system of interrelated controls. It is sometimes difficult to regulate one without affecting the other. A cut in rates may mean a cut in frequency of service or the quality of service; a rise in rates to meet a desired revenue level may cause discrimination and preference. Too many carriers in one market can lead to economic chaos for all if wasteful service levels are not controlled or frequency of service becomes too great. All sorts of compromises and trade-offs are necessary, and the entire system of economic regulation must be considered as a whole, not as individual regulatory devices.

Unfortunately, economic regulation has not always been consistent. Rates have been raised or lowered without concern for regulation of services; entry has been allowed with little recognition of its effects on earnings or on service. Much of this inconsistency arises from the failure to realize that economic regulation is a system of three interrelated and complicated devices.

Inconsistency in the application of economic regulation of for-hire transportation is matched by inconsistency in the pattern of providing and controlling transportation. As we shall discuss shortly, all modes are not regulated equally and some modes, such as private transportation, are not economically regulated at all.

Direct Regulation

Finally, it is well to note that the system of economic regulation is imposed directly on the for-hire carriers by some board or commission such as the ICC, the CAB, or the Federal Maritime Commission (FMC). While regulation and control of the for-hire carrier system may be clothed in a legal framework, its effect is directly economic. The carriers must live in this regulatory environment and system for the public has come to expect it in its pursuit of the goals of protecting the public and promoting the best possible system of transportation. In short, it is an economic fact of life.

After discussing the regulation of the physical aspects of transportation and social regulation, we shall turn to the various agencies imposing these controls.

REGULATION OF THE PHYSICAL ASPECTS OF TRANSPORTATION

The second type of control in the regulatory system concerns the physical aspects of transportation. In general, these are regulations imposed on the conditions of transportation by society as a whole and the industry itself, in some instances.

The term "regulation" as used here is somewhat different from economic regulation. All systems must have ground rules or rules of the road. Some structure or operating procedures are necessary for an ordered and efficient society. Many of these ground rules or operating procedures are called "regulations," but irrespective of what they are called, they serve the same function--establishing order and relative operating efficiency in the daily life of society. But like specific economic regulation, these rules of the road restrict and impinge upon the freedom of the individual. In this sense they are regulations as surely as the actions of an administrative commission or board are regulations.

Objectives of Physical Regulation

Two specific interrelated objectives seem to be at the base of all the ground rules or regulation of the physical aspects of transportation--safety and reliability.

Perhaps the most important objective of physical regulation is the safety of the user and the co-user of the highway, airway, street, railway, and ocean shipping lane. Society acts to protect itself and its parts from physical danger. Interrelated with safety is the desire to have a reliable transportation system. Many rules are imposed with the idea that, not only will the public be served in a safe manner, but it will be served when it demands service, and with some assurance that a shipment, once started, will be completed. While the objective of reliability might be thought of as economic, and, indeed, is involved in two of the economic regulatory devices, control of entry and control of service, we are concerned here with physical reliability. The close connection between physical reliability and economic reliability illustrates once more that rules are interconnected and interrelated and that a system of regulation exists.

Finally, it should be noted that the objectives of safety and reliability fit nicely into the general goals of the regulatory system as noted above: the protection of the public and the promotion of the best possible system of transportation.

Devices of Physical Regulation

Most physical regulation of transportation is found in three groups or devices of control: regulation of the conditions of equipment, the qualifications of operators, and operating procedures.

Regulation of Condition of Equipment

Rules and regulations governing the physical condition of equipment are found in every phase and type of transportation. In private automobile transportation, it is becoming common for states to require periodic safety checks of brakes, lights, steering mechanisms, windshields, and so forth. Generally this is carried on under state jurisdiction, but federal action is involved in requiring that a portion of federal highway grants be withdrawn unless approved safety inspection programs are enacted by states.

Commercial highway vehicles were checked and standards prescribed by the ICC for many years. This work was shifted to the Department of Transportation (DOT) in 1966. State authorities check safety features of trucks and prescribe weight, height, width, and length regulations, with the safety of the co-user of the highway as at least part of the rationale. Protection of the highway itself from damage is generally also a rationale for these regulations.

In air transportation much of the work of the FAA, also part of the DOT, concerns the condition of equipment and the airworthiness of planes. Inspections are but a part of this task, and levels of maintenance are specified as well. Parts must be replaced or reconditioned after a specified number of hours of operation, and rigorous requirements to protect the safety of the user of air transportation are common. Navigational aids and devices are also controlled by the FAA and become part of the physical equipment necessary for air transportation. Even in international air transportation, rules and regulations relative to equipment are prescribed by the International Civil Aviation Organization (ICAO), closely associated with the International Air Transport Association (IATA).

In water transportation, the U.S. Coast Guard, now a part of the DOT, inspects the condition of equipment and is concerned with operating safety. In rail transportation, the Federal Railroad Administration (FRA), also a part of the DOT, sets standards for roadbed, alignment, gauge and surface structure, conditions of the rails, and so on. The effects of the regulation of the condition of equipment will be discussed further in Chapter 11, "Equipment Selection."

Regulation of Qualification of Operators

Rules and regulations governing the qualifications of personnel --particularly operating personnel--are common in transportation. In the private automobile transportation sector, the requirement that everyone have a current driver's license is a familiar example.

Driving tests are common to assure knowledge of safety laws, and regulation is almost uniformly found in all jurisdictions. In most states operator qualification requirements are more rigorous where commercial vehicles are involved.

In for-hire passenger transportation, operator qualifications may be regulated by several boards or groups at several levels. Not only is the highway operator expected to qualify for a commercial operator's license at the state level, but federal rules relative to hours of rest and hours of continuous service are involved for highway vehicles. In commercial air transportation, pilot training is supervised, operating personnel must submit to periodic physical examinations, and conditions of operation, such as hours of service, rest, and so forth, are rigorously specified. In water transportation, ships' pilots are licensed and must meet regulatory qualifications.

Some inconsistency may be involved in having different qualifications for private owners as compared to for-hire operators but, as noted above, transportation is filled with inconsistency. In general, operators' qualifications are highest in the for-hire intercity area of transportation and lowest in the private transportation area.

Regulation of Operating Procedures

There are a host of regulations and rules concerning operating procedures, some quite obvious, such as limits on speed, and others quite indirect and less obvious, such as driving on the right side of the road in some countries and on the left side in others. It would be impossible to list all the rules of the road in transportation, but everyone knows that highway vehicle speeds are regulated; stoplights and traffic signals restrict traffic flow; planes must fly at specified altitudes; ships pass one another in a specified fashion; cars traveling in the same direction use a certain side of the highway; the physical distance between planes and railroad trains is regulated; buses must stop before crossing railroad tracks; planes approach airports in a prescribed fashion, irrespective of where in the world the airport is located; and so forth. The point is that there a series of systems of operating procedures for each means of transportation prescribed by many authorities and levels of government and principally designed to accomplish the objectives of safety and reliability of transportation. It might be added that the regulation of operating procedures tends to be similar irrespective of ownership (with a few exceptions), whereas regulation over the qualification of operators and condition of equipment tends to be stricter for for-hire transportation firms than for the private passenger transportation sectors.

REGULATION BY SOCIAL POLICY

The third aspect of the regulatory system is regulation by social policy. It is common, of course, to refer to economic regulation--rates, entry, and service--as "social policy," since an agency of government typically imposes these controls. Likewise, it is common to refer to the regulation of the physical aspects of transportation as "social policy," since society imposes ground rules to protect itself with safety and reliability in mind. But even beyond this, there remain the broader social aspects of public support and repayment, the ownership patterns and structure of competition permitted, and the relatively new environmental restraints that have been imposed. We call this portion of the overall regulatory system "regulation by social policy."

Public Support and Repayment

Society has always imposed its general economic philosophy on individuals in the form of rules and regulations that set a framework within which economic activity takes place. Examples of this are the statutes prohibiting fraud and misrepresentation, the money and credit system, the weights and measures system, and the legal system protecting ownership. In the United States the system of antitrust and the reliance on the economic philosophy of competition is a further illustration. These all tend to be negative aspects of social policy, in the sense that each forces economic activity into a desired framework.

Positive aspects of social policy also exist, of course. By the use of public resources--both monetary and physical--the taxing power, or public economic power, such as tariffs and import quotas, various economic activity can be aided, promoted, and directed into various desired areas. Social policy is not all negative, and the positive aspects are of particular interest in the study of transportation.

Historically, transportation has been aided and promoted in the United States. Almost without exception, each mode of transportation has benefited from either direct or indirect aid by the whole of society as it developed. The railroads had their land grants; motor transportation benefited from programs to develop highways; air transportation has been aided technologically by public research and development, been directly subsidized, and continues to have the airway provided and operated for its benefit; water carriers have been subsidized; public transit receives federal developmental grants, and the private automobile uses public streets at least partially provided by property taxes. For an analysis of the means, goals, and methods of public aid, consult any basic transportation text.[15] All of transportation has been greatly aided by these methods of social policy.

There is also the broader question of promoting transportation as an economic function as compared to other economic functions. Public resources at any given moment are not infinite. Priorities must be established and choices made. Whether it is more in the social good to promote transportation and not, say, water resource development, the public school system, slum clearance, agricultural production, or any other socially worthwhile program, is a very real problem. We shall assume here that transportation is indeed aided and promoted by society, and concern ourselves with some of the ramifications of that fact.

Also a part of social policy is the provision for repayment of public aids. While some support has been in the form of outright grants, more often than not the firm or the user of the means of transportation has made some repayment through the tax system, or by way of services of some nature, or by some other means. The problems arise not from the existence of public support, but rather from the uneven application of the public support, the various methods or lack of methods of repayment, and the competitive ramifications of aiding one mode of transportation over another at a given period of time.

Social policy has many rationalizations and is a study in itself. In effect a type of social environment exists at any one period of time and this affects the operation of the carriers involved. Public aid and repayment plans are an integral part of this social policy. The point is, some transportation operations have been aided, promoted, and subsidized while in competition with other operators not equally aided, promoted, or subsidized at that point in time. This unevenness of public aid has caused considerable economic problems and shall concern us in Chapter 3.

Ownership Patterns and Structure of Competition

Obviously, various repayment devices plus subsidy of one mode at one time to the exclusion of a competitive mode causes a problem. Social policy has, in effect, structured competition in transportation. It makes considerable difference if one mode has an operating subsidy, and hence needs to charge a somewhat lower rate to survive in a world of competitive choice (air or maritime transportation versus rail or truck transportation). So too, repayment of an indirect subsidy by means of user charges, which are carrier operating costs, is quite different from repayment of capital invested, at interest, where the way is privately provided (the rail versus the truck). Thus, social policy directly or indirectly affects the structure of competition.

Finally, ownership patterns are also a reflection of social policy. By and large our system of transportation has been based on the pattern of private ownership of the means of transportation with public ownership of the transportation way. For example the truck is privately owned by a for-hire firm, the highway is publicly provided; the airline is a private profit-seeking firm, the airway is publicly owned and operated. Ownership patterns are mixed, with both private and public ownership existing together. Rail transportation provides the major exception to this pattern. Traditionally, both the means of carriage and the way were privately owned.

Further, regulatory policy has generally controlled the ownership of one means of transportation by another means. Hence, rail ownership of trucks has been restricted, ownership of airlines by any other transportation firm has been prohibited, and so forth. Some of these types of ownership patterns have lacked consistency and have been applied more with historical accident than logic. Additionally, the same ownership regulations have not been applied worldwide, and some of our neighbors have successfully experimented with different types of ownership of carriers patterns.

In summary, these ownership patterns and their exceptions are, in a very real sense, social policy. As a nation we have deliberately chosen to maintain private ownership of the means of transportation and public ownership of the transportation way, with the exception of rail. Many nations have chosen to have public ownership of both means and ways. We will return to these ownership patterns and their effect on the operation of carriers in Chapter 5.

Environmental Restraints

A final type of regulation by social policy is found in the recent concern over the quality of life and the effect of human action on the environment. Perhaps somewhat belatedly, society has moved to impose environmental restraints on transportation. Standards of permissible emissions of hydrocarbons, lead, nitrogen compounds, monoxides, and dioxides are being developed; noise pollution standards are of some concern; water pollutants emitted from ships and the ever present problem of petroleum spills in oceans are being controlled. Another environmental concern is with congestion, and some progress is being made in dealing with airway, highway, and street congestion. In each case it is society operating through public policy with a concern with the environment that is involved.

It should be noted that these restraints should be imposed irrespective of ownership. The privately owned automobile should be controlled just as strictly as the for-hire vehicle, and environmental restrictions on for-hire vehicles should be equal to those on private vehicles. Unfortunately, this is not always the case. The problem may turn, in the case of private automobiles, on the multiplicity of ownership and the natural hesitancy of the individual to forgo his freedom to act as he wishes. This is the reason, of course, why social control and the imposition of standards at the manufacturing level holds out the chance of some positive action, and is being pursued.

These environmental restraints are destined to become more important, not less, in the future. This type of social action is, of course, the basis of a whole series of problems. For the carriers, total solutions and their effect on the management of transportation carriers are not evident at this time. While the future is unclear, it is certain that social control in this area presents a real problem that will continue for some time.

In summary, regulation by social policy is concerned principally with methods of public aid and promotion and the accompanying structure of repayment systems; the patterns of ownership imposed by society and the resultant structure of competition developed or allowed; and, finally, the host of new environmental restraints, which are still developing but which are destined to become more important as a future type of social regulation.

AGENCIES OF CONTROL

The whole regulatory system made up of economic regulation, regulation of the physical aspects of transportation, and regulation by social policy, is imposed and administered by a host of agencies, boards, commissions, and groups. We designate these as the agencies of control. While we do not intend to analyze in depth each group, some elementary discussion of the major agencies of control is necessary to understand the conflicting and interrelated aspects of the regulatory system.

It is possible to classify these agencies of control in two groups: agencies of primary control, and agencies of ancillary control. This classification is based mainly on the function of the agency and does not imply that the action taken by it is not direct or important. Rather, some agencies have a primary function of controlling transportation, whereas others have the control of transportation as one of many functions or, in some cases, have a primary function in an area other than transportation, with transportation control being secondary. Finally, it should be noted that our discussion does not include every agency that affects transportation, an approach that would be beyond the scope of this book. Many other agencies not discussed here exist and exert influence on carrier transportation.

Agencies of Primary Control

Ten agencies, five of which are part of the DOT, are primarily concerned with administering economic regulation and controlling the physical aspects of transportation.

Interstate Commerce Commission

The oldest of the federal agencies directly concerned with transportation is the ICC. Established in 1887, this agency has led the way in the development of the economic regulation of transportation. Its role is now basically to control rates and earnings, issue certificates of public convenience and necessity, and control the service aspects of surface for-hire transportation in interstate commerce. Many of the regulations of the physical aspects of transportation developed initially in the ICC were transferred to the DOT in 1966. The ICC is an independent regulatory commission with its 11 commissioners appointed by the president with the consent of the Senate for staggered seven-year terms with no more than six commissioners from one political party. The president designates the chairman of the commission.

The ICC is divided into three divisions that illustrate its regulatory role. These are the Operating Rights Division; the Rates, Tariffs and Valuation Division; and the Finance and Service Division. Besides control of rates and certificates of public convenience and necessity, the ICC controls mergers and acquisitions, prescribes accounts, controls the issuance of securities, and has numerous controls over freight transportation. The ICC is the most important of the agencies discussed in this section.

Civil Aeronautics Board

Established in 1938 to undertake the conflicting tasks of promoting air transportation while regulating the economic aspect of the air transportation industry, the CAB is concerned mainly with economic control. The board has five members, no more than three of which are from one political party, appointed by the president with consent of the Senate, for staggered terms of six years each. The president designates the chairman and the vice chairman of the board.

The board grants authorizations to carriers to engage in interstate and foreign air transportation. Domestic carriers must secure certificates of public convenience and necessity, while foreign carriers are issued permits to engage in air transportation between the United States and foreign countries. The CAB has jurisdiction over tariffs, rates, and fares, and authorizes and pays subsidies to certain air carriers for service to communities where the traffic does not pay the cost of service. Additionally, the CAB passes on mergers, agreements, acquisitions of control, and interlocking relationships between carriers. It also has jurisdiction over unfair competitive practices of air carriers and ticket agents. Finally, the CAB regulates air carrier accounting and requires each carrier to file regular financial and operating reports.

Federal Maritime Commission

Established in 1920, the FMC's jurisdiction and functions were revised and clarified by Reorganization Plan No. 7 in 1961. The commission is composed of five members, no more than three of which are from one political party, appointed by the president with the consent of the Senate, for staggered terms of five years each. The president designates the chairman of the FMC.

While the FMC is primarily concerned with international maritime transportation, the movement of goods over the seaways often becomes an integral part of domestic for-hire transportation. Basically, the FMC approves or disapproves agreements filed by common carriers and conference agreements, regulates shipping practices, controls tariffs or charges of carriers, issues or denies certificates of financial responsibility, and administers the passenger indemnity laws. The FMC was also given control in 1970 of issuing certificates of financial responsibility where oil spills were involved.

National Transportation Safety Board

The National Transportation Safety Board (NTSB) was created in 1966 simultaneously with the DOT, although it is independent of it. The board is composed of five members, no more than three of which are from one political party, appointed by the president with the consent of the Senate, for staggered five-year terms. The president designates the chairman and vice chairman.

The purpose of the board is to investigate, determine probable cause, and issue reports on all civil aviation and surface transportation accidents; make recommendations for the prevention of accidents and promotion of safety in transportation; and conduct safety studies, examine safety standards, and determine compliance with safety standards.

Federal Aviation Administration

The FAA, formerly called the Federal Aviation Agency, was an independent federal regulatory commission from 1958 until it became one of the major operating agencies of the DOT in 1967. As a part of the DOT, it is now a part of the executive branch of the federal government.

The FAA is charged with regulating air commerce to promote its safety and development; achieving the efficient use of the navigable air space of the United States; promoting, encouraging, and developing civil aviation; developing and operating a common system of air traffic control and air navigation; and promoting the development of a national system of airports. To accomplish this mission, the FAA physically operates a network of airport traffic control towers, air route and traffic control centers, and flight service stations. It also issues and enforces rules, regulations, and minimum standards of safety for manufacture, operation, and maintenance of aircraft, as well as rating and certification (including medical) of airmen and certification of airports. Further, the FAA installs and maintains air navigation facilities and operates visual and electronic aids to air navigation. It registers aircraft, including foreign aircraft, and participates in the ICAO. The FAA research and development program involved in developing and testing improved aircraft, engines, propellers, and appliances plus new systems of air navigation and traffic control is large and well known. Finally, the FAA administers a comprehensive airport planning and development program, including substantial grants of funds to assist other public agencies in airport development and improvement.

Federal Highway Administration

The Federal Highway Administration (FHA) is also a part of the DOT and has a three-part function that directly affects transportation: The administration of the federal aid program for highway planning and construction, highway safety, and motor carrier safety. Its major work is the administration of the highway trust fund and the federal aid aspects of highway construction through various revenue matching plans. The best-known highway program in the last few years has been the National System of Interstate and Defense Highways, commonly called the Interstate System, which has been a special program of improving and upgrading a small portion (42,500 miles, or about 1.5 percent of over four million miles of streets and highways) of intensively used streets and highways. Construction and safety standards involved in the Interstate System, as well as the federal, Primary, Secondary, and Urban Highway-Aid systems, come under the FHA. Standards are established as well as funds administered and highways coordinated. This program also includes beautification of the highways. Much of the work of this agency prior to 1966 was done under the Bureau of Public Roads in the Department of Commerce.

The final aspect of the FHA's work concerns the safety program for commercial motor carriers engaged in interstate commerce. Safety investigation and inspection, driver qualifications, hours of service on the road, truck accident investigation, and vehicle inspection are the main elements of this program, which was formerly in the Bureau of Carrier Safety under the ICC.

Federal Railroad Administration

The FRA, also an agency of the DOT, consolidated the administration of the Bureau of Railroad Safety and Services (formerly part of the ICC), the Office of High Speed Ground Transportation (formerly in the Department of Commerce), and the administration of the Alaska Railroad (formerly in the Department of the Interior). The work of this agency affects transportation in its concern with rules and regulation designed to promote railroad safety, the demonstration projects of the Office of High Speed Ground Transportation in the Northeast Corridor of the United States (the Turbo-train and Metroliner projects), and in the operations of the Alaska Railroad (service between Anchorage and Whittier, and Anchorage and Fairbanks).

National Highway Transportation Safety Administration

The fourth agency of the DOT involved in primary control of transportation is the National Highway Traffic Safety Administration. Various programs are involved, the best known of which is probably the Federal Motor Vehicle Safety Standards program of establishing and administering prescribed safety features in the private automobile, such as seat belts, shoulder harnesses, air bags, and vehicle design. The agency also carries on important research and development on vehicle design and the crashworthiness of vehicles. Further, it provides matching federal funds for state and local motor vehicle and driver safety programs. This agency was part of the Department of Commerce prior to 1966.

United States Coast Guard

The fifth and final agency of the DOT involved in transportation regulation is the U.S. Coast Guard, formerly part of the Department of the Treasury, and a branch of the Armed Forces of the United States. The Coast Guard maintains vessels and stations to pursue its programs of search and rescue; enforcement of federal laws on the high seas and navigable waters of the United States (including boat inspection); ocean stations (four in the North Atlantic and two in the Pacific) which provide meteorological information to ships and aircraft, search and rescue services, oceanographic data, and navigation information for ships and aircraft; merchant marine safety (including licensing personnel); inspection of vessels for safety of personnel and passengers; and aids to navigation (lightships, buoys, electronic aids, and so on). Other Coast Guard programs are boating safety, port security, icebreaking services, Great Lakes pilotage staff, and military preparedness.

State Commissions

At the other end of the spectrum of agencies of primary control are the regulatory commissions and boards of the various states. Almost every state has one or more agencies charged with the economic (and sometimes the physical) regulation of transportation. Jurisdiction over firms will vary by state, of course, but in all cases the authority of these boards is limited to intrastate transportation. Intrastate rail, airline, and truck rates are regulated, certificates or permits for intrastate operation are often issued, and occasionally the carriers' service is regulated. These state regulatory commissions are of particular importance in the regulation of motor carriers and, depending on the type of for-hire operation, may be the major regulatory agency for some carriers.

In concluding this section, it should be pointed out that some agencies are more concerned with economic regulation (the ICC, the CAB, or state commissions, for example), some are more concerned with regulation of the physical aspects of transportation (the FAA, the FRA, the National Highway Transportation Safety Administration, and the Coast Guard, for example), and some are more concerned with regulation by social policy (the FHA, for example). It should also be pointed out that a firm or an individual will often be subject to the regulatory action of more than one of these agencies, and that the problem of consistency remains a difficult and annoying one.

Agencies of Ancillary Control

Many agencies are involved in the control of transportation, of course. Some have a primary function that is other than the regulation of transportation, others affect transportation only indirectly. We have arbitrarily designated these as agencies of ancillary control and note only three broad groups of the many agencies involved herein.

State and Local Law Enforcement

Regulation of the physical aspects of transportation may often rest partially with state and local peace officers. Traffic control, speed limit enforcement, and operator qualifications are familiar aspects of this type of regulation. These agencies, such as state highway patrols, sheriff's forces, and local police, have functions other than transportation regulation and often have a primary function that is much more comprehensive than traffic control. Accordingly, they are a good example of agencies of ancillary control.

Municipal, County, and State Governments

A portion of the function of government is to regulate transportation through rules of operation. Local speed limits, weight and length limits, and restrictions on street use illustrate this regulation. Control also comes from capital decisions of these agencies, in allocating funds to street and road construction and improvement, airport construction and improvement, harbor and port development, and the like. The primary function of these governmental agencies is not to regulate transportation, but their rule-setting actions and capital decisions do a great deal to control transportation.

Federal Agencies

A whole group of federal agencies with primary functions in matters other than transportation regulates and affects transportation. Some familiar examples are the operation and rules of the Customs and Immigration Service, research grants and programs of the Department of Housing and Urban Development, the policies and operations of the U.S. Postal Service, the Environmental Protection Agency, and the operating procedures of the various branches of the Armed Forces. Since it is the largest single customer of transportation, the rulings and operations of the Department of Defense are of particular importance. Many of these actions regulate transportation in an indirect manner.

SUMMARY

The regulatory system in transportation has many interrelated parts and facets. The three main aspects of the system are economic regulation (rate, entry, and service regulation); regulation of the physical aspects of transportation (regulation of the condition of equipment, qualifications of operators, and operating procedures); and regulation by social policy (public support and repayment, ownership patterns and the structures of competition, and environmental restraints). These aspects of the regulatory system are imposed and administered by a multitude of governmental and private agencies, some of which are primarily concerned with transportation control and some of which are primarily concerned with other than transportation control. In view of the complexity of the regulatory system, it is not surprising that regulations are often inconsistent and overlapping, and that a person or firm is subject to many regulations by many agencies at many levels. This is part of what we mean by a regulatory system. Even so, the regulatory system does, in general, seem to succeed in attaining its goals of protecting the public and promoting the best possible system of transportation. Finally, in pursuit of these goals, and given the complexity of the regulatory system, it is not surprising that many problems arise. We shall concern ourselves next with some specific areas of regulation and their operation as a constraint on the management of transportation carriers.

NOTES

1. The most comprehensive study of this agrarian revolt is found in S. J. Buck, _The Granger Movement_ (Cambridge: Harvard University Press, 1913).
2. 94 U.S. 113 (1877).
3. 169 U.S. 466 (1898).
4. See Martin T. Farris and Roy J. Sampson, _Public Utilities: Regulation, Management, and Ownership_ (Boston: Houghton Mifflin Co., 1973), pp. 79-93, 118-36.
5. _Federal Power Commission_ v. _Natural Gas Pipeline Co._, 315 U.S. 575 (1942).
6. _Public Service Commission of Montana_ v. _Great Northern Utilities Co._, 289 U.S. 130 (1935).
7. D. Philip Locklin, _Economics of Transportation_, 7th ed. (Homewood, Ill.: Richard R. Irwin, 1972), pp. 709-12, contains a good review of the argument.

8. U.S., Congress, Senate, Select Committee on Interstate Commerce, 49th Cong., 1st Sess., 1886, S. Rep. 46, better known as the Cullom Committee Report.

9. Wabash, St. Louis & Pacific Railway Co. v. Illinois, 118 U.S. 557 (1886).

10. Act to Regulate Commerce, 1887, later known as the Interstate Commerce Act (IC Act).

11. These terms were originally used in Sec. 3 of the Act to Regulate Commerce, and have been used again in every statute regulating the other modes of transportation.

12. In the case of the domestic airlines, the CAB decided early not to allow additional firms to enter the industry. Specifically, it stated in the Delta Air Corporation case (2 CAB 447, 480 [1941]): "The number of air carriers now operating appears sufficient to insure against monopoly in respect to the average new route case . . . in the absence of particular circumstances presenting an affirmative reason for a new carrier there appears to be no inherent desirability of numerically enlarging the industry."

13. An interesting study on creating competition by expanding the routes of existing carriers is found in Samuel B. Richmond, Regulation and Competition in Air Transportation (New York: Columbia University Press, 1961), pp. 62-97, 98-100.

14. Roy J. Sampson and Martin T. Farris, Domestic Transportation: Practice, Theory and Policy, 3rd ed. (Boston: Houghton Mifflin Co., 1975), pp. 109-22.

15. Ibid., pp. 437-54.

CHAPTER

3

TRANSPORTATION COMPETITION

In addition to regulation, each carrier faces a constraint from the marketplace. This constraint turns on the type and degree of competition it faces. Therefore, another pivotal factor in the management of transportation carriers is transportation competition.

Essentially, carrier management must be aware of, and map strategy in terms of, three general types of competition: intermodal, carrier, and market-product competition. By "intermodal competition" we mean competition between transportation modes such as truck versus rail, rail versus water, truck versus air, and water versus pipeline. "Carrier competition" is sometimes called intramodal and refers to competition of firms within a given mode. Examples of carrier competition are one railroad competing with another railroad, or one truck line competing with another trucker. Finally, "market-product competition" refers both to the competition between geographic locations as markets and as producing areas, and the competitive characteristics of the goods themselves in their own particular markets.

The degree and type of competition for a given transportation carrier is a direct response to the regulatory constraint noted earlier, including national transportation policy, and is manifested in route structure and ownership patterns, which will be discussed shortly. It should be stressed that competition is but one facet of a system of interacting and interdependent constraints faced by carrier management. No one facet (regulation, competition, route, ownership, price system) stands alone; rather, all five interact and are part of a system of constraints.

INTERMODAL COMPETITION

Competition between modes of transportation is well known. Some people tend to assume that regulation means a lack of competition, while just the opposite may be the case--regulation often promotes competition. This is particularly true in intermodal competition, where regulation often increases the number of firms in one mode with little concern for the number of firms in another mode already in a market.

While it is true that regulation was necessary in the nineteenth century because of the abuse of monopoly power in the hands of the railroads, even then some intramodal competition existed. But, beginning in the late 1920s in America, competition between modes began to appear. This intermodal competition arose, at least partially, as competitive transportation modes were fostered and encouraged by public transportation policy. For example, with the advent of federally aided highway improvements in 1916, the means for expansion of the motor carrier industry were at hand. Trucks were not technologically enough developed prior to that date to be an effective competitor to railroads in freight transportation. But by the late 1920s, the motor truck had advanced technologically, and just at the time when highways had been improved to the point where motor carrier competition with railroads was possible. So too with air transportation as a competitor with railroads, buses, and the private automobile, in intercity travel. By the mid-1950s, aircraft had advanced to the point where the cost of air travel was competitive with rail travel, if the traveler's time was given any value, and public policy had fostered air transportation by providing the airway free to all. The era of intermodal competition thus began in America around 1930.[1]

From a carrier management viewpoint, each firm must recognize that, in each market, freight and passengers can and will shift from mode to mode in response to factors such as price, service claims, and advertising. Chapter 9, "Carrier Marketing," will analyze in detail some of the factors that cause these shifts. Suffice it to say at this point that a potential shifting is always present. We call this potential "modal substitutability."

But modal substitutability is not unlimited. A wise carrier management will realize that some of its customers are more responsive to changes in one of the many factors involved in modal choice--say, price--than other customers. Some customers will shift in response to service factors. Other factors may also cause traffic shifts. Recognition of modal substitutability as a fact of transportation life, and recognizing that a carrier can specialize somewhat in the areas where modal substitutability is smallest, can be a very important point for management.

In many ways, this recognition is similar to the principle of comparative advantage that operates in international economics. Nations tend to specialize in the products in which they have a comparative advantage. Of course, where one nation has an absolute advantage--say, the production of coffee beans in Brazil--specialization of production is obvious. But even a nation with a high cost of coffee bean production may specialize in this commodity if its comparative advantage is greater in that commodity than in any of the other commodities it can produce.

So too with transportation firms. Given a route structure, an ownership system, and a regulatory environment, each carrier should strive to specialize in the service that it does best. The problem is identifying this service, identifying the customers for this service, analyzing why its service is superior, and mapping strategy to develop this comparative advantage.

The concept of comparative advantage in transportation is called "inherent advantage." National transportation policy since the Transportation Act of 1940 has recognized that each mode has an inherent advantage that should be preserved and developed. This concept is contained in the preamble to that act which states, in part: "It is hereby declared to be the national transportation policy of the Congress to provide for fair and impartial regulation of all modes of transportation subject to the provision of the Act, so administered as to recognize and preserve the inherent advantage of each. . . ."[2] Therefore, the concept of inherent advantage is firmly established in national transportation policy.

The problem for both carrier management and national transportation policy is not the concept or principle of inherent advantage. Even those in carrier management who have not studied national transportation policy recognize intuitively the concept that each mode has some job that it performs better than a competitive mode. The problem lies in the implementation of the policy of inherent advantage. The managerial strategy should be to identify markets and services where the particular inherent advantage lies, and to take steps to develop this potential. The target of each carrier should be its inherent advantage.

For example, motor carriers may have a special advantage over railroads in movements for distances of less than 500 miles. This is because the economics of rail transportation call for large volume shipments in order to spread heavy fixed costs over many units of freight.[3] Railroads must provide their own railway as well as marshalling yards, collector systems, and so forth. With such high fixed costs, railroads are prone to accumulate shipments until enough volume is available to make it profitable to send a freight train composed of many railway cars.

Motor carriers, on the other hand, tend to have a very small ratio of fixed or constant expenses and the vast majority of its costs are variable in nature.[4] This is partially due to the fact that the motor carrier pays for his use of the public highway and streets as he uses them--on a variable basis. If shipments do not move, no highway costs are incurred. In rail transportation, the railroad must pay for the railway, since it owns it, whether it uses it or not. Many other motor carrier costs are also connected to use. Further, the unit load in motor carriers is smaller than in rail transportation, so service can be more frequent and delay is not necessary.[5] The result of these economic characteristics is that motor carriers can provide faster service at a cheaper price on short-distance freight and on less-than-carload or smaller loads.[6] In this instance, the inherent advantage of motor carriage lies with speed and the smaller unit movement, and the inherent advantage of rail carriage lies with unit or volume loads over considerable distances. Both modes should strive to develop their particular inherent advantage.

Another example involves air transportation. Air transportation is very fast but very expensive. The size of the shipment is limited by the size of the vehicle and its ability to lift weights, and much of the high cost is a result of the labor-intensive nature of loading, unloading, ticketing, maintenance, and so forth. On the surface, there seem to be few inherent advantages to air transportation in a modal substitutability situation.

However, time can be an important factor for both passengers and freight. All other modes are slow compared to air. The airlines have tended to stress the advantage of speed. Time is especially valuable to busy people, so air transportation has for years stressed the movement of passengers--the business traveler being the base of the air travel demand. The labor-intensive nature of air transportation has been turned from a disadvantage into an advantage by stressing the number of personal services available, such as stewardesses, meals, and the absence of tipping. The cost per pound of air transportation is high, so the airline firms have stressed passenger service, where the rate per pound they can charge is similarly high.

Distance tends to magnify the effect of speed. Time savings in air transportation between continents as compared to the modal substitutability of water travel or maritime freight is particularly striking. A movement from North America to Europe takes hours by air, and days by water. Given these technological facts, air transportation tends to stress the savings in inventory and carrying costs when freight moves by air as compared to maritime movement. With the high costs of inventory and the need to utilize expensive working capital most efficiently, this is an excellent strategy. Many firms will be willing to pay premium transportation charges in order to offset or lower other costs, such as inventory or carrying charges.[7] Airline companies have tended to stress and develop their inherent advantage. This is a good example of a strategy of exploiting that which the carrier does best.

Modal substitutability is, however, not limitless. All modes do not compete with all other modes in all freight. The physical characteristics of the goods moved imposes some limitation to modal substitutability. Obviously, pipelines do not compete with rail and water in the movement of steel, nor do airlines compete with rail and water in the movement of crude oil. Economic characteristics, particularly value, also limit modal substitutability. That is to say, some items, such as sand and gravel, are of such low value that they cannot afford to pay the freight rates of air transportation, or even motor transportation, over much distance. Movement of these commodities over distance is restricted to rail or water, due to their low value.

Shipping characteristics also tend to limit modal substitutability. Some items are very sensitive to rough handling and must be handled with great care. Examples of these goods are sophisticated electronic gear such as computers or delicate scientific instruments. Their value is very high, and rates are not a factor in choice of mode, but potential damage is an important one. Such freight will tend to go to motor or air, where specialized personal service is available and the chance of damage is smaller.

Thus, each mode has certain inherent advantages in each market and with each class of freight or passengers. Carrier management must understand this and implement it by carefully analyzing the various options open to it. Once again, the target is inherent advantage.

Finally, it should be pointed out that exploiting inherent advantage will be modified by other constraints, such as routes. If a carrier is not authorized to serve on a given route, it cannot exploit an inherent advantage, no matter how great. Ownership and social policy may also be constraints. Price or rates (as connected to value) have also been mentioned. Unless a competitive price or rate is possible at a given service level, modal substitutability can not be expected. Regulation may also serve as a constraint. The obligation of the common carrier concept may mean a firm must serve points, routes, freight, or passengers that are not within its inherent advantage. Common carriers must, within their capability, serve all comers at reasonable rates and without discrimination, and must deliver the goods or passengers on time to the proper destination and in the same physical condition as tendered. This common carrier obligation may restrain transportation management from completely utilizing the concept of inherent advantage. Yet, within the constraints or limitations imposed, carrier management can exploit modal substitutability by keeping the idea of inherent advantage firmly in mind.

CARRIER COMPETITION

A second type of competition deals with a particular modal market. This is sometimes called intramodal competition or carrier competition, since it is based on competition between firms of the same mode. Carrier competition concerns a particular market and can be compared to the market-share concept in unregulated industry.

This type of competition extends beyond the concept of inherent advantage. Once a modal inherent advantage has been identified, the next question concerns how a particular firm can operate so as to take special advantage of that specialization. Or, in market-share terms, how can the share of a particular market where inherent advantage exists be increased by a given firm or carrier?

Every firm faces these problems and must map strategy to attack these market share problems. Chapter 9, "Carrier Marketing," will detail some of the various strategies that can be used to approach this problem. Obviously, the degree of the problem will depend on the other constraints already noted. Thus, route structure becomes pivotal. If a particular carrier firm is the only air carrier serving a city, the problem is one of intermodal competition. If there are two air carriers operating between two markets, the problem is one of both intermodal and carrier competition.

It is likely that some carrier firms have less market share competition than others, due to their economic structure. As noted in Chapter 1, some modes have fewer carrier firms than others, such as railroads, airlines, and pipelines. The reason for this smaller number of competitors is a combination of economic, historical, and regulatory developments. Hence, most points in the United States are served by only one railroad (if they have rail service), or, at best, two railroads. Only a very few points have rail service from more than two railroads. The costs of building a rail line are so high that the city must be a very large shipping point in order to economically support more than one or two railroads. In addition, railroads came early in U.S. transportation history. Once a point was served it was questionable that a competing line would be a profitable venture. Other unexploited territory existed and there was a tendency to extend the rail network extensively before developing it intensively.

Further, intensive expansion of the rail network had to await economic growth to the extent that competition could survive. The best grades, passes, and locations were typically taken by the first rail carrier built. Competitive rail carriers were not only expensive to build but were generally high-cost to operate. History is full of examples of competitive rail lines built late in the rail movement that were financial failures. After 1920, rail expansion was also controlled by regulation.[8]

Air transportation provides an example of the effect of regulatory policy on carrier competition. While air transportation is expensive, particularly as concerns the cost of the vehicles, the airway was free until recently, and the capital costs of terminals, offices, and ground facilities were either low or a rental/lease situation prevailed. But as the youngest and sometimes the favorite mode, air transportation has been both highly regulated and highly promoted by government policy.[9] For example, in the Civil Aeronautics Act of 1938, Congress directed that U.S. policy should be "the encouragement and development of an air transportation system properly adapted to the present and future needs of the foreign and domestic commerce of the United States, of the Postal Service, and of national defense."[10] Regulatory or remedial provisions were also involved, but the important point for carrier competition was the clear charge to promote and develop air transportation.[11]

The CAB faced a decision very early in its existence as to the number of firms necessary for intramodal competition. It decided, in the Delta Air Corporation case of 1941, not to allow additional firms, and stated the following:

> The number of air carriers now operating appears sufficient to insure against monopoly in respect to the average new route case. . . . In the absence of particular circumstances presenting an affirmative reason for a new carrier there appears to be no inherent desirability of increasing the present number of carriers merely for the purpose of numerically enlarging the industry.[12]

Thereafter the CAB increased intramodal or carrier competition by awarding new routes to existing carriers and by not allowing more airline firms. Consequently, intramodal competition in air transportation has taken the form of service competition, such as scheduling, types of aircraft, classes of service, meals and drinks, attractive stewardesses, leg room, and lounges.[13]

In pipelines, the degree of carrier or intramodal competition is governed by economic, historical, and technical factors. Huge fixed investment is necessary to build a pipeline and risks are very high because of the limited life of oil fields. Crude oil pipelines, which came first, were typically built on an undivided-interest basis. That is, several petroleum companies pooled resources and each took a portion of the risk of the investment of a pipeline from an oil field to a refining center. This placed the shipper--the oil company --in a position of being the owner of the carrier--one of the few places where a public or common carrier is owned by its customers --and brought on subsequent regulatory problems when pipelines were declared common carriers in 1906. Additionally, a pipeline's thru-put can be increased somewhat by factors such as a greater number of pumps before it has to be "looped" (a parallel line built). But even when a line is looped, the clear advantage is to the existing pipeline firm, since land easements are already available, pumping sites developed, storage tanks available, and so forth. Consequently, it is often much easier to expand an existing pipeline than to build a competitive one. The result is that carrier competition in crude oil pipelines has been limited.

The same situation does not prevail completely in product pipelines from the refinery to the market. Here the ownership pattern, the risk factor, and the ease of expansion carry over from crude oil pipelines, but not the limited life of the resources factor. Even so, intramodal competition is limited in this part of pipeline transportation, too--probably because of the traditional way of pipelining. In any case, it is possible to say that the degree of carrier competition is small in pipeline transportation, just as it is in rail and air transportation. One can also say that historical, regulatory, technical, and economic factors have caused limited carrier competition in those modes.

The opposite is true for motor carriers and water carriers. In these modes, the number of carriers is large and it is quite likely that a high degree of carrier competition exists in a given market.

Of prime importance are the characteristics of the way. The highway and the waterway have been traditionally furnished by the public as part of the social overhead capital of the nation, as noted in Chapter 2. In the case of highways, payment for the facility has been on the basis of use. Water carriers pay little or no user charges for use of the waterway. This is in contrast to railways and pipelines, where the carriers own the way and must pay for it, irrespective of use. Consequently, motor carriers and water carriers have a high degree of variable costs and a low ratio of fixed costs, as noted above. Entry of new firms is economically fairly easy where fixed costs are low and a small investment is all that is necessary to start up a carrier.[14]

Under such circumstances, regulatory policy has been the factor limiting and controlling carrier competition. In the case of motor carriers, the low cost of entry plus the newly improved highways led to a proliferation of trucklines in the late 1920s and early 1930s. This movement was accelerated by the Great Depression and the ease of buying trucks on a time-payment-pay-as-you-use plan. State authorities had attempted to regulate entry in the 1920s, but their jurisdiction had been limited by the Supreme Court cases in 1925.[15] After a long struggle, the federal government regulated motor carriers in 1935.[16]

Some idea of the results of relatively easy entry and economic conditions that favored the start of trucklines can be gained from this regulatory experience. Hugh S. Norton states that over 89,000 applications for "grandfather rights" were filed with the ICC after the 1935 regulatory act.[17] Given the inherent advantage of motor carriers, there was undoubtedly an excessive number of carriers, and carrier competition was chaotic. The task of regulation was to limit the number of firms and control the degree of carrier competition. This was accomplished by rigorous control of entry, route, and types of service. Additionally, relatively liberal allowances on motor carrier mergers coupled with restrictive entry requirements has drastically reduced the number of regulated motor carrier firms. However, there were over 15,000 regulated motor carriers in 1970, so the degree of carrier competition continues to be substantial.

While 81 regulated inland water carriers does not seem to be an excessive number, the extent of the inland waterways is limited. Carrier competition cannot be measured exclusively by the number of carriers, and each market will vary in the degree of competition. Using the data for number of carrier firms (Table 1.4) and miles of way (Table 1.6) for 1970, we can come up with a figure for the number of carriers per mile of way that will allow us to compare the various modes. Thus, the number of carrier firms per mile of way operated in domestic transportation in 1970 is as follows:

rail	.00034
air	.00036
pipeline	.00045
inland water	.00317
motor	.00397

Note that in both motor carriage and inland water transportation, the ratio of carriers per mile of way is in the magnitude of 10 times as great as in rail, air, and pipeline transportation.

As we will discuss in Chapter 4, "Route Structure," each market is a separate study, and the degree of carrier competition is individually determined by such factors as the route system and the ease of interconnection or interlining. But the fact remains that motor carriers and water carriers typically face a high degree of both carrier competition and intermodal competition whereas rail, air and pipeline carriers typically have a problem of intermodal competition with a smaller degree of carrier competition.[18]

The degree of competition discussed above is primarily between regulated carriers, but an important additional competitive factor from private and exempt carriers exists in motor and water transportation. Once again the way is public and relatively easily available. Regulatory acts have traditionally excluded private carriage from all but safety regulation. Hence, any shipper can buy its own trucks and use the highway, or buy its own barges and use the rivers. Any firm could build its own railroad, too, but only a few find the heavy investment worthwhile.[19] Any firm could buy its own airplane, but, once again, a considerable volume of freight would have to be available to make it profitable. However, where the unit load is small, particularly in motor carriage, a firm often decides to own its own private truckline.

Furthermore, some of the regulatory acts exempt the movement of certain products or commodities from regulation. In motor carriage, agricultural commodities are exempt, and in water carriage, loads of three or fewer commodities in bulk are exempt. This has not only led to the development of a considerable amount of carrier competition between the regulated carriers and the exempt carriers, but to the difficult problem of the definition of what constitutes an exempt commodity or service.[20]

Carrier management must develop strategy to meet carrier competition as well as intermodal competition, and in some instances unregulated and private competition. Some carriers, such as motor and water carriers, face all types of competition, and in a particularly intense degree; other firms face principally intermodal competition and carrier competition, and in a lesser degree. However, all firms face competition and must learn to cope with this fact of transportation life. Competition is a challenge to carrier management and, in spite of regulation, exists in various degrees in various markets.

MARKET-PRODUCT COMPETITION

The final type of transportation competition comes from the derived nature of transportation demand; that is, the demand for a carrier's services is derived from the demand for the goods themselves, and carrier demand takes on the characteristics of the demand for the goods themselves. Hence the term "derived demand."

Derived demand explains how large changes can take place in the demand for a carrier's service when no significant changes have taken place in price, service, or any of the factors usually associated with changes in demand. If the demand for the goods shipped increases because of some factor unrelated to the transportation of the goods, it will affect transportation demand. Derived demand also exists in passenger transportation. There may be wide changes in the demand for business travel that are unrelated to the transportation function. For example, if business is poor, business travel may be cut as a cost-saving device, even though the service and price of passenger transportation remain unchanged.

Extending the concept of derived demand into the area of competition, a carrier will find that the market characteristic of the goods hauled, on the one hand, and the characteristics of the geomarkets, on the other hand, provide a type of derived competition, and therefore a constraint to managerial actions of each carrier.

Consider first the market characteristic of the goods. Every market has a different competitive characteristic. Some goods are sold in highly competitive markets where a small change in price will cause a major change in quantity sold. Economists call the demand for these goods "elastic." Other goods are sold in markets with less competitive characteristics. Perhaps the seller is a regional monopolist or oligopolist, or the goods are so essential that few substitutes exist. Under such conditions, a small change in price may not cause a major change in the quantity sold. Economists call the demand for these goods "inelastic."

With goods possessing an inelastic demand in the ultimate market, or goods sold under conditions of oligopoly or regional monopoly, carrier management has more choice of action than if hauling highly elastic and competitive goods. If the demand is highly elastic, carrier management must realize that by raising rates it may cause a shift in the ultimate demand for the goods, and hence price itself out of that market. Goods that are inelastic can often absorb changes in freight rates without a major effect on ultimate demand. It is a wise carrier management that studies and understands something about the market characteristics of the freight it hauls.

Consider next the characteristics of the geomarkets. Every geographic location can be viewed for transportation purposes as both a point of production and a market for goods produced elsewhere. That is, both production center competition and consuming center competition exist. From a producing-center competition viewpoint, the interrelationship of geography and transportation is well known. Transportation costs affect the location of manufacturing or processing. The degree of this effect will vary with the dependency of the process on factors such as raw materials, labor costs, and tax costs, but the fact remains that transportation is one of the factors in the location of almost all industry. Realizing this, a carrier may choose to help establish manufacturing or processing in its service area by its rate or service policy. It may be able, in some instances, to create more business for itself by helping to attract industry.

Each location problem is a separate study in itself, and a well-developed theory of the location of industry does exist. A discussion of this theory will be found in Chapter 15, "The Location of Transportation Operations," although our application has to do with the location of transportation facilities, not industry.[21] Carrier management actions can be a factor in the location of many industries, and a wise management is alert to the possibility of assisting its service territory to grow economically.

Consuming-center competition, sometimes called "directional competition" or "market competition," refers to the effect of transportation costs on the location of markets for goods produced. Transportation is one of the largest costs of distribution and is a major factor in the ultimate price of all goods. The price of the goods is one of the major factors affecting competition. Hence, by lowering freight rates (and therefore price) from city X to city Y, the carrier may be widening the market for city X, to the detriment of city Y. Carrier action can sometimes broaden or extend a market for a city and affect the competition between cities or distribution points as well as production points. These ideas will be developed further in Chapter 6, "Pricing and Rate Making," and Chapter 9, "Carrier Marketing." The point is, a derived competition exists for all carriers of both a consumer-center and producing-center type, as well as a type of competition arising from the demand for the goods themselves. These types of derived competition must be recognized, and strategy mapped, by carrier management to utilize this knowledge.

SUMMARY

Carrier management faces many types of competition. Intermodal competition (modal substitutability) is faced by all carriers, and is the most important type of transportation competition for some carriers. Both carrier competition (intramodal competition) and intermodal competition are faced by other carriers. Additionally, competition from private and exempt carriage also exists. Motor and water transportation seem to have more competition of all types than other modes. Furthermore, each location or geomarket faces competition as a producing center and as a consuming center, as well as competition for the goods in their ultimate markets. This derived competition can also be important to carrier management. A wise carrier management is cognizant of the degrees and types of competition it faces and takes these factors into careful consideration in its decision-making process.

NOTES

1. For a detailed discussion of the rise of intermodal transportation competition, see Roy J. Sampson and Martin T. Farris, Domestic Transportation: Practice, Theory and Policy, 3rd ed. (Boston: Houghton Mifflin Co., 1975), pp. 337-42.

2. 54 Stat. 899 (1940).

3. D. Philip Locklin states that early writers on transportation used the ratio of two-thirds of railroad costs as fixed expenses. The degree of fixed costs will turn on a number of difficult definitional points, but they are certainly considerable in size. See Economics of Transportation, 7th ed. (Homewood, Ill.: Richard D. Irwin, 1972), pp. 143-46.

4. Some experts quote as low a figure as 10 percent of fixed costs. Ibid., pp. 651-52.

5. Charles A. Taff calls this "inherent flexibility," and cites it as one of the five advantages of truck transportation. See Commercial Motor Transportation, 4th ed. (Homewood, Ill.: Richard D. Irwin, 1969), p. 9.

6. See also references to "terminal cost effect" in Sampson and Farris, op. cit., p. 167.

7. This is the basis of the so-called total cost concept in physical distribution. See Sampson and Farris, op. cit., pp. 259-60; Grant M. Davis, "Managerial Techniques for Controlling Premium Transportation Charges," Journal of Purchasing, vol. 7, no. 4 (November 1971); and Grant M. Davis and Stephen W. Brown, Logistics Management (Lexington, Mass.: D. C. Heath & Co., 1974).

8. Perhaps the best discussion of railroad development is found in Locklin, op. cit., pp. 109-41, 404-20.

9. See Sampson and Farris, op. cit., pp. 352-67.

10. 52 Stat. 973 (1938).

11. Actually, competition in air transportation had been controlled at an earlier date through the use of airmail contracts. Because of the need for a stable revenue source, early airlines could not exist without the help of the Post Office. The Post Office Department exerted positive entry control by exercising its power to certificate airmail routes from 1930 to 1938.

12. 2 CAB 447, 480 (1941).

13. See Samuel B. Richmond, Regulation and Competition in Air Transportation (New York: Columbia University Press, 1961), pp. 62-97, 98-100; and William A. Jordan, Airline Regulation in America: Effects and Imperfections (Baltimore: The Johns Hopkins Press, 1970), pp. 14-56.

14. Even today, the average capital invested in operating property of Class I and II motor carriers is small--in 1971 it was $978,781. Compare this to an investment of well over $1 million

per mile for railway. Of course, averages are deceptive, and many of the larger carriers have millions of dollars invested in operating property.

15. See Michigan Public Utilities Commission v. Duke, 266 U.S. 570 (1925) and Buck v. Kykendall, 267 U.S. 307 (1925).

16. Taff, op. cit., pp. 377-80.

17. Hugh S. Norton, Modern Transportation Economics, 2nd ed. (Columbus, Ohio: Charles E. Merrill Publishing Co.. 1971), p. 239.

18. While it is generally true that airlines face a higher degree of intermodal than intramodal competition, it must be pointed out that CAB policy has sponsored competition between many key points by authorizing expansion of the routes of existing air carriers. Therefore, carrier competition does exist and is particularly intense between major traffic points as a matter of public regulatory policy. This only serves to emphasize the importance of route structure, of course.

19. Private railroads do exist, principally in the resources area, where the large volumes of movement make the heavy investment profitable. Examples can be found in lumbering, coal, copper, and iron ore.

20. Sampson and Farris, op. cit., pp. 349-50, 474-91; Locklin, op. cit., pp. 685-720, 745-69.

21. For a more detailed discussion, see Sampson and Farris, op. cit., pp. 217-33, 234-50.

CHAPTER

4

ROUTE STRUCTURE

In addition to the constraints of regulation and competition, each carrier, irrespective of mode, faces a third constraint of a given route structure.

ROUTE ENVIRONMENT

Route structure as a constraint on management can be considered from three vantage points: the importance of routes, the types of routes, and the characteristics of routes. Each will vary for a particular carrier in a specific situation. We will discuss them here in a general way, and try to lay a framework for the specific analysis that each carrier management team must make for itself.

Importance of Routes

It is axiomatic that each carrier can serve only where it is authorized to do so. The device of entry regulation was discussed in a general manner in Chapter 2, where it became clear that the regulatory philosophy of our nation is firmly based on limiting the number of carriers in a given market. While scholars argue about the desirability of such a policy and its effects over time, entry into transportation remains controlled.[1]

Controlling entry means, in effect, controlling competition. As discussed in Chapter 3, there are several types of transportation competition. Entry control will affect intramodal or carrier competition more directly and more completely than intermodal competition, as we have already noted. But entry control goes further than just limiting the number of firms and controlling intramodal competition. Entry control affects the competition on routes and establishes for each carrier a separate and very important facet of the problem of management. Entry control actually establishes a route structure, which is like a microcompetition or specific competition in each segment of a carrier's operation.

Consider the following illustration. The Snowball Express Trucking Company may serve points A, B, C, D, and E as part of its authorized routes. It is conceivable that Snowball Express could be the only carrier from A to B; compete with five other motor carriers from B to C; compete with a railroad and three other motor carriers between C and D; and compete with three other motor carriers, a contract carrier, two railroads, and an airline between D and E. In short, even though entry is controlled, each segment of an authorized route structure can have different degrees of intramodal and intermodal competition. Each segment is, in effect, a study of microcompetition.

It is apparent that the management of our hypothetical Snowball Express must be cognizant of, and plan strategy in terms of, each of these degrees of microcompetition. From management's viewpoint, the route structure is the ultimate constraint on its actions.

This is not to say that a given route structure cannot be changed. However, route changes occur very slowly and, since they involve not only regulatory processes but usually capital investment, they are also expensive. Hence, as far as the immediate and ongoing task of management is concerned, the route structure is a given factor and is one of the most important givens that management must face.

Types of Routes

There are many types of routes and many route classifications are possible. One way of considering routes is to think of them as line-haul, feeder, collector, and bridge routes.

Line-haul routes are those between major points of origination and destination or through major gateways. In rail transportation these may be called "mainline," in air transportation, "trunkline," and be known by other names under other circumstances, but they are usually the most intensively used routes, make up the major part of the route structure, and connect the major points or places in the route structure.

Feeder routes are those that feed in or bring together freight and passengers at the major origination and destination points. In rail transportation, the local freight train collecting and delivering railroad cars at smaller cities between division points would be feeder routes. Branch lines, which are of some importance in some parts of the country, would also be rail feeder routes. In air transportation, the so-called local service or regional airline serves this function. Many smaller trucklines feed the larger transcontinental carriers.

Collector routes are those routes used to distribute freight and passengers in a city or region, such as pickup and delivery routes of a motor carrier, marshalling yards and switching companies in railroads, and third-level airlines, such as air taxis, helicopter service, and air commuter operations.

Bridge routes would be those routes or portions of a route structure that connect other carriers or other modes. Many smaller but well-located railroads are bridge routes and generate little of their own freight, but connect rail carriers that originate and deliver large volumes of freight. Some trucklines specialize in bridge-route business by interlining with numerous other trucklines.

Bridge traffic is not necessarily for short distances. For example, the so-called Land Bridge and Mini-Bridge rail traffic involves moving international freight all the way across North America. In Land Bridge, it is between maritime connections on each coast, and in Mini-Bridge, between inland shipping points of origination or destination and foreign points via maritime connections. Likewise, in air transportation, due to restrictive regulations, some airlines served as the bridge across the United States for international flights between Europe and Asia. For example, American Airlines often formed the bridge connecting Pan American Airway international flights. Indeed, bridge routes can be both long and short.

In classifying routes, keep in mind that a given carrier can appear in several of these classes. For instance, a regional or local service airline can perform a mainline route function for some of its passengers while performing a feeder function for other passengers and a bridge function for still others. A good example of this is Allegheny Airlines, which mainlines between many smaller northeastern cities, feeds into Chicago, Pittsburgh, and New York, and is a bridge line with Pan American and Trans World Airlines on overseas travel. Many smaller trucklines perform similar multiroute functions as well.

Characteristics of Routes

Since each particular route has its own peculiar characteristics, generalizations can be dangerous. Yet routes do have characteristics that can be thought of as characteristics of physical geography, economic geography and commodity characteristics, and operational characteristics. Some routes combine all three; others reflect predominantly one of these aspects.

Physical Geography

The existence or lack of landforms gives a particular characteristic to a transportation route. Mountain passes, valleys, swamps, bodies of water, and canyons are some of the common landforms that affect the location and operation of transportation. Most routes seem to follow the path of least physical resistance, and it has been suggested that the basic transportation routes were actually surveyed by migrating animals milleniums ago as they moved about seeking food and water.[2] Given the lack of capital to tunnel, bridge, or blast and cut, transportation routes followed paths worn into the landscape, first by animals, then by Indians, explorers, and migrants on foot. Settlements or towns arose where transportation routes crossed or where transfer was made from one mode of transportation to another (for example, from water to land), and these settlements created the need for even more transportation following the same route. Landforms could have been overcome, but at an economic cost. Indeed, much of recent transportation investment has been involved with straightening, relocating, and correcting the location of older routes, which were built with the smallest possible capital outlay in an earlier period of capital shortage. Of course, rivers, bays, streams, and estuaries give rise to water transportation while providing obstacles to land transportation. Landforms and physical geography thus give the first characteristic to almost every route.

When one examines maps of the routes of highways, railways, and airways, it becomes apparent that there are corridors of principal routes that all these modes seem to follow. These routes tend to connect the various regions of the nation, and it is over these principal routes or corridors that the majority of U.S. transportation takes place.

Beginning in the East, one principal corridor extends along the seacoast from New England to Florida and lies between the Appalachian Mountains and the Atlantic Ocean. A second connects the Southeast region to the Great Lakes and lies west of the Appalachian Mountains. A third route connects the Great Lakes and the North Atlantic region, while a fourth follows the Mississippi from the Gulf of Mexico to the Great Lakes. These four major corridors compose the basic transportation route pattern of the eastern half of the nation.

In the portion of the nation lying west of the Mississippi River, seven route corridors are found that form almost a box with a shelf in the middle. First, a major route extends from the Gulf of Mexico to the central Great Plains. Another route extends from the northern Great Plains to the Great Lakes. Three basic east-west routes extend from the Mississippi-Great Lakes axis to the Pacific Coast. These are sometimes called the North Transcontinental, Central Transcontinental, and Southern Transcontinental. A fourth transcontinental route connects the south Pacific Coast region to the Great Lakes. Finally, the eleventh major route traverses the Pacific Coast itself.

Most major railroads, highways, and airways will follow one or more of these principal transportation corridors or routes. Physical geography has been part of the reason for these routes, but economic geography has also played a role.

Economic Geography and Commodity Characteristics

Every carrier manager should learn something about the physical and economic geography of the route structure of both his and his competitors' carriers. We shall confine ourselves here to four aspects of economic geography: raw materials location, manufacturing location, market location, and the attraction of traffic centers to each other. All of these give distinctive characteristics to a given route.

Raw materials location might be considered as physical geography, since raw materials are the work of nature. However, the existence of raw materials alone is not enough. Technology or process, plus transportation, plus a market or profitable end use is necessary in order for a raw material to become a resource. Many beds of minerals exist that are not economically utilized because they are too distant from potential users, or because technology is not highly developed enough to make their purification or processing worthwhile. One is reminded of the axiom of the famous economic geographer, Eric V. Zimmermann: "Resources are not, they become."[3]

But, given the existence of technology and transportation, raw materials become resources and give a route a distinctive characteristic. In past years, before the modern merger movement reduced the number of railroads, it was common to speak of "granger routes." These were railroads that served the massive Midwest and depended on agricultural products for a majority of their traffic (such as the Rock Island, Chicago Northwestern, and Chicago Great Western). Other railroads depended on coal (for example, the old Chesapeake & Ohio and the Norfolk & Western); others served large phosphate deposits (the old Seaboard Airline); others, iron ore (old Great Northern); still others depended on lumber (old Northern Pacific); and some were even known as "potato" roads (Bangor and Aroostock). Some railroads had a high percentage of merchandise traffic (the old New

York Central and the old Baltimore & Ohio are examples), where they served the industrialized Northeast. All these illustrate how economic geography can lend a type of characteristic to a route.

In the location of manufacturing or processing, the existence of transportation routes and the existence of manufacturing are interrelated. That is, manufacturing locates at a given point because of the existence of the means of transportation. Two types of transportation interaction are involved, as we noted in Chapter 3--the interaction of raw materials and resources used in the productive process and the interaction of markets for the end product of manufacturing. But it is also correct to say that the existence of manufacturing causes transportation. If adequate transportation services are not available, the location of a manufacturing plant will generate more service and additional carriers.

This is not to say that all manufacturing is located according to transportation services. Other factors, such as labor, power sources, taxes, subsidiaries, business climate, capital, and even personal preference of executives, have considerable influence in the location of some firms, and even some industries. It should also be pointed out that the locational effect of transportation for both resources and markets can be offset by rates or prices and service considerations. Carrier management should be especially alert to these possibilities and should acquaint itself with the rudiments of transportation location effects.[4]

Location theory goes back to the nineteenth century and the work of the German J. H. Von Thunen. Modern industrial location theory stems from the work of another German, Alfred Weber, who, in 1909, devised his classification of raw materials as either ubiquitous or localized and either pure (those that do not lose weight in manufacture) or gross (those that do lose weight in manufacture). Both August Losch and Frank Fetter did early work on the effect of transportation on market location, and modern-day location theory owes much to the works of Melvin Greenhut, Edgar Hoover, and Walter Isard.[5]

Finally, market location and the attraction of traffic centers are examples of the use of location theory in specific applications. Starting from a simple assumption of one seller and transportation costs equal to mileage and introducing more selling points, the boundaries of each market may be ascertained and a market defined. In attraction of traffic centers, gravitational models have been developed that give some quantitative dimensions to the pull or drag of one community on another. While such modeling may seem unduly complex, gravitational models have proved helpful in practical applications, such as route certification cases in air transportation where city pairs data is available.[6] Indeed, before another carrier can be authorized to serve, it should be clear that the markets to be served have the potential of sufficient traffic to make the service economically viable. More will be noted on this point directly in our discussion of certificates of public convenience and necessity.

Operational Characteristics

The final aspect of route characteristics can be called "operational characteristics." Obviously, physical geography causes some routes to be uphill or upgrade in motor transportation, some routes to be water-level in rail transportation (such as the old New York Central from New York City to Chicago), and some routes to be upstream in inland water transportation (routes from New Orleans to Cincinnati, for example). In effect, these cause the route to assume operational characteristics, such as the need for extra motive power, slowness, or speed. Likewise, pipeline routes can assume the character of the freight, depending on the oil field served. Hence, some routes are low-gravity crude routes or high-viscosity routes. These characteristics also cause operational problems.

In motor transportation, the regulatory system recognizes three sets of operational characteristics: type of carrier, type of service, and type of commodity.[7] There are five types of carriers: common, contract, private, brokers, and exempt, and each has its legal definition.

The operational characteristic of the type of service is an even better example. Here, the regulatory system also recognizes five types of service: (1) regular route, scheduled service; (2) regular route, nonscheduled service; (3) irregular route, radial service; (4) irregular route, nonradial service; and (5) local cartage service. Each type of service is carefully defined and described. Hence, regular route, scheduled service has a fixed schedule and a fixed terminus and irregular route, radial service has a fixed base but no limitations as to routes, and so forth. Obviously, the type of service specified in the certificate of public convenience and necessity sets an operational characteristic to motor transportation.

Finally, the regulatory system specifies the type of commodity the motor carrier is authorized to haul. There are 17 commodity classifications involved: general freight, household goods, heavy machinery, liquid petroleum products, refrigerated liquid products, refrigerated solid products, dump trucking, agricultural commodities, motor vehicles, armored car service, building materials, film and associated commodities, forest products, mine ore, retail store delivery, explosives or dangerous articles, and specific commodities not subgrouped. Each commodity group is carefully defined, usually by case decisions, and the ICC can furnish a detailed description of what each classification includes.

It should also be noted that the three sets of operational characteristics in motor freight are usually interconnected to form a complete description. Hence, a given firm might be authorized as a "common carrier of property, in irregular route-nonradial service, hauling household goods." Obviously, a rather detailed operational characteristic is provided in each case.

In summary, each route has definite characteristics. These are based on physical geography, such as the existence of landforms and principal transportation routes of the nation; economic geography, based on the location of raw materials, the location of industry and physical production, the location of markets, and the attraction of traffic centers; and each route has operational characteristics based on physical operating circumstances or regulatory route restraints.

CERTIFICATES OF PUBLIC CONVENIENCE AND NECESSITY

No factor is more important to route structures than the certificate of public convenience and necessity. These certificates are the devices through which the route structure is established. They are also the devices through which route structure is amended or changed.

Development of the Concept

Certificates of public convenience and necessity first appear in transportation law with the Transportation Act of 1920. Prior to that time, each state had the power to permit railroad extensions and construction, but the authority was neither uniform nor equally applied.[8] As part of the attempt to insure a system of transportation adequate for the needs of the nation, and to give the railroads an opportunity to earn enough revenue to provide an adequate system, Congress granted to the ICC authority over construction of new lines and the extension or abandonment of existing lines.[9] This entry-control device was granted to control competition and protect the carriers from destroying one another economically. Justice Brandeis, speaking of the congressional purpose for this control, noted the following:

> It recognized that the preservation of the earning capacity, and conservation of the financial resources, of individual carriers is a matter of national concern; that the property employed must be permitted to earn a reasonable return;

> that the building of unnecessary lines involves a waste of resources and that the burden of this waste may fall upon the public; that competition between carriers may result in harm to the public as well as in benefit; and that when a railroad inflicts injury upon its rivals, it may be the public which ultimately bears the loss.[10]

The device of entry controls by means of certificates was included as part of the Motor Carrier Act of 1935, in the Civil Aeronautics Act of 1938, in the Transportation Act of 1940 controlling water carriers, and in 1942 concerning freight forwarders.[11] Thus, certificates of public convenience and necessity are almost universally required in transportation.[12]

While exact route control is not specifically defined in the rail and motor carrier regulatory sections on certificates, by 1940 the certificates provision of the water carrier act stated that "such certificate shall specify the route or routes over which, or the parts to and from which, such carrier is authorized to operate."[13]

Definitions of Terms

The definition of the term "public convenience and necessity" was left up to the ICC. A whole series of decisions was involved in this process and, among other things, it was decided that "convenience" and "necessity" are used conjunctively and are not synonymous, but have separate and distinct meanings.[14] In general, public convenience and necessity can be defined as "a strong and urgent public need," with "public" being defined as "more than a few shippers."[15]

In determining whether public convenience and necessity will be served by the proposed service, three questions must be asked: (1) Will the new operation serve a useful public purpose responsive to a public demand or need? (2) Will this public purpose be served as well by existing lines or carriers? (3) Can the public purpose be served by the applicant without endangering the operations of existing carriers?[16] Since an applicant for a certificate of public convenience and necessity must bear the burden of the proof, the law clearly protects existing carriers.

A further protection of existing carriers is contained in the provision that the applicant for new authority must show that he is "fit, willing, and able."[17] While each case is determined on its merits, six major criterions are considered in motor carrier cases: length of time in operation, financial fitness, experience and skill of personnel, ability to buy new equipment, reputation with respect to dependability of service, and adequate insurance coverage.[18] Since past experience is given considerable weight in determining fitness, it is difficult for a new carrier to qualify. Existing carriers wishing to extend their routes are obviously in a much better position to show that they are fit, willing, and able.

"Grandfather Clause"

One further regulatory provision affecting route structure is the so-called "grandfather clause" contained in the statutes regulating motor, air, water, and freight forwarders.[19] As noted in Chapter 2, this refers to carriers in existence at the time federal regulation was begun. These carriers were granted certificates of public convenience and necessity to continue their operations if they could show that they had bona fide operations prior to regulation. These certificates, sometimes called "grandfather rights," were issued as a matter of right and without having to prove public convenience and necessity. Only when routes were to be extended or changed was it necessary to prove that public convenience and necessity existed, and that the carrier was fit, willing, and able. In effect, the regulatory system for all railroads began with route structure authority operated just prior to regulation, and included strict controls for new entrants and changes in operations by existing carriers.

Procedures in Certificate Cases

Proving that public convenience and necessity exists is not always easy. The matter is judgmental and turns on both legal and economic factors. Too often in the past, it has been a matter of legal or procedural maneuvering that has led to the granting or denial of extensions of service or new entrants into transportation. Actually, the economic factors should outweigh the legal or procedural factors. Wise carrier management not only employs a lawyer who is experienced in the area of public convenience and necessity, but also an economic or transportation consultant to generate retail sales and market data, changes in freight tonnage or passenger travel, personal income changes, employment data, business indices of various types, and other data designed to show that additional service is necessary. Economic data on the effect on existing carriers is difficult to generate, but, given the regulatory structure, must be considered. Each case is a separate study in itself and generalizations are difficult, but full consideration of all legal and economic aspects should be undertaken.

It was stated earlier that the route structure of a carrier could be changed, but that it was a time-consuming and expensive process. In some modes, particularly motor carriers, where many grandfather rights have been issued, it is far easier to purchase existing route authority. Indeed, most major motor carriers have chosen the buying of existing trucklines as the preferred method of adjusting their route structure. While the regulatory system does control the merging of carriers, these controls are considerably less strict than those over new or expanded route authority.

Finally, it should be mentioned once more that the term "rights" or "operating rights" has a special meaning in transportation. In fact, a certificate of public convenience and necessity is a privilege, not a right like an individual's constitutional rights. As a privilege, it can be revoked and amended by the governmental agency that issued it (either the ICC or the CAB). The law makes it clear that operating rights are revokable.[20]

Certificates of public convenience and necessity, then, are the devices that establish the route structure of a given carrier and the characteristics of the particular service on a particular route.

SUMMARY

Carrier management faces a constraint in the form of the route structure of the carrier. Unless authorized, a carrier cannot serve. Existing routes reflect geography, economics, history, and regulatory acts of the past. Routes can be changed only slowly, and then only at considerable expense, since changes involve certificates of public convenience and necessity. Therefore, it behooves management to be alert to all aspects of the existing route structure and consider the given factor of transportation life not as a hindrance but as a challenge.

NOTES

1. The literature on the entry issue is immense. For more detail consult Alfred E. Kahn, _The Economics of Regulation: Principles and Institutions_, vol. 2, "Institutional Issues" (New York: John Wiley and Sons, 1971); Dudley F. Pegrum, "Restructuring the Transportation System" in _The Future of American Transportation_, Ernest W. Williams, Jr., ed. (Englewood Cliffs, N.J.: Prentice-Hall, 1971), pp. 59-82; Ann F. Friedlaender, _The Dilemma of Freight Transport Regulation_ (Washington, D.C.: The Brookings Institution, 1969), p. 216; Charles F. Phillips, Jr., _The Economics of Regulation_, rev. ed. (Homewood, Ill.: Richard D. Irwin, 1969),

pp. 483-536; Martin T. Farris and Roy J. Sampson, Public Utilities: Regulation, Management and Ownership (Boston: Houghton Mifflin Co., 1973), pp. 155-74; Dudley F. Pegrum, "Regulatory Requirement for Motor Transport" in Modern Transportation: Selected Readings, 2nd ed., Martin T. Farris and Paul T. McElhiney, eds. (Boston: Houghton Mifflin Co., 1973), pp. 98-102; Martin T. Farris, "Rationale: The Regulation of Motor Carriers" in ibid., pp. 93-98; Richard N. Farmer, "The Case for Unregulated Truck Transportation" in ibid., pp. 102-13; Thomas Gale Moore, Freight Transportation Regulation, Surface Freight and the Interstate Commerce Commission (Washington, D.C.: American Enterprise Institute for Public Policy Research, 1972), pp. 98.

2. Roy J. Sampson and Martin T. Farris, Domestic Transportation: Practice, Theory and Policy, 3rd ed. (Boston: Houghton Mifflin Co., 1975), pp. 89-90.

3. Eric V. Zimmermann, World Resources and Industries, rev. ed. (New York: Harper and Brothers, 1951), pp. 3-20.

4. For a good general survey, see Farris and Sampson, op. cit., pp. 217-32.

5. Some elementary location theory is reviewed in ibid., pp. 234-50.

6. Some examples of gravitational analysis and use of city pairs data are contained in Stanley C. Hollander, ed., Passenger Transportation: Readings Selected From a Marketing Viewpoint (East Lansing, Mich.: Michigan State University, Graduate School of Business, 1968), Systems Analysis and Research Corp., "Demand for Intercity Passenger Travel in the Washington-Boston Corridor," pp. 62-72; John B. Lansing, Liu Jung-chao, and Daniel B. Suits, "An Analysis of Interurban Air Travel," pp. 104-13; B. J. Elle, "The Economics of Convenient Airline Service," pp. 123-38; and Edward J. Taaffe, "A Map Analysis of United States Airline Competition," pp. 521-38.

7. See Charles A. Taff, Commercial Motor Transportation, 4th ed. (Homewood, Ill.: Richard D. Irwin, 1969), pp. 109-31, or William S. Hudson and James A. Constantin, Motor Transportation: Principles and Practices (New York: Ronald Press Co., 1958), pp. 175-202, for a detailed analysis of these classifications.

8. ICC v. Oregon-Washington Railroad and Navigation Company, 288 U.S. 14, 32-3 (1920).

9. Sampson and Farris, op. cit., p. 331.

10. Texas and Pacific Ry Company v. Gulf, Colorado and Santa Fe Ry Company, 270 U.S. 266, 277-8 (1926).

11. 49 USC 306 (b); 49 USC 1371 (a); 49 USC 909 (c); 49 USC 1010 (c).

12. Contract carriers by motor must secure "permits" [49 USC 303 (a) (15)]; contract carriers by water must also secure "permits" [49 USC 909 (f)]; and air freight forwarders must secure "operating authorizations" from the CAB [14 CFR 296, 297].

13. 49 USC 909 (d) (1940).

14. For a definitive discussion see John Guandolo, Transportation Law, 2nd ed. (Dubuque, Iowa: Wm. C. Brown Co., 1973), pp. 1-42, 57-148, 158-71.

15. Ibid., pp. 59, 71-78.

16. Ibid., p. 60; Taff, op. cit., p. 407; Hudson and Constantin, op. cit., pp. 497-99.

17. 49 USC 307.

18. Hudson and Constantin, op. cit., pp. 502-3; Guandolo, op. cit., pp. 101-7; and Taff, op. cit., pp. 407-8.

19. 49 USC 306 (a); 49 USC 909 (d); 49 USC 1371 (d).

20. Taff, op. cit., pp. 416-18; Hudson and Constantin, op. cit., pp. 505-7; and Guandolo, op. cit., pp. 265-71.

CHAPTER

5

OWNERSHIP PATTERNS

The fourth constraint faced by carrier management is that of ownership patterns. This is the least apparent or visible constraint, but is of importance in some carrier management situations. Ownership patterns are also of concern to the public in certain situations. There are two approaches to ownership patterns in transportation--the broad social approach, which concerns public policy and modal development, and the firm organizational approach, which concerns the operational pattern of the individual carrier. Regulatory policy as a reflection of public concern is involved in both approaches.

PUBLIC POLICY AND MODAL DEVELOPMENT

We have already discussed many of the ramifications of public policy on modal development in Chapter 2 under "Regulation by Social Policy." What is involved is the manner in which the way is owned, supported, and developed, and the various repayment processes. As noted previously, some modes, such as railroads and pipelines, develop, own, maintain, and pay taxes on their own ways as private property. Other modes, such as motor, air, and water, use the publicly supported, maintained, and owned ways. Of these, motor and air carriers and other co-users of the highways and airways pay user taxes, which are designed to recoup a portion of the investment costs of those ways. Typically, operating and maintenance costs and, in some instances, part of the investment costs, are not recovered. In such a manner, the public policy on the ownership of the transportation way may pick up a portion of the costs of transportation which other modes must pay themselves. In water transportation, no user charges at all are assessed. Accordingly, the existence or lack of publicly provided way and user charges not only causes the operating costs of the railroads and pipelines to be heavily weighted with fixed charges (and the motor carriers, air carriers, and water carriers to be heavily weighted with variable expenses), but may promote the development of one mode at the expense of another. The area of public aids and promotions is both complicated and controversial, but carrier managers should have a basic understanding of it. This aspect of ownership, which involves public policy and modal development, operates as a given factor within which the management of transportation carriers must operate.[1]

OPERATIONAL PATTERN OF THE INDIVIDUAL CARRIER

Each carrier possesses a distinctive ownership pattern that can sometimes be important in operational decisions. At other times, ownership patterns are unimportant for operational purposes. Since the situation varies by carrier, we will only broadly outline some of the ownership aspects of each mode.

Development of Ownership Patterns

To a considerable degree, the ownership patterns in each mode are a reflection of the economic, regulatory, and historical factors involved in the growth of that particular mode. For example, all railroads are corporations, and many are very large corporations. This reflects the need for massive amounts of capital during the period of railroad construction and development (approximately 1830 to 1910). The economics of the way noted above are further reflected in the ownership pattern of railroads, whereby a large amount of corporate debt to fund the expensive railway is the predominant financial aspect of ownership. This debt is widely held by financial institutions and individuals, so a separate financial public exists alongside the shipping public or traveling public. Additionally, this large debt needs to be continually refinanced, so an added management burden is found in railroads.

Further, since some railroads were granted land as a device to help them build, many railroads today have large real estate holdings in many cities, or large land holdings scattered across the countryside. In some instances, these land holdings have been developed to the point where some railroads are considered by investors as resource companies rather than transportation companies. Rail holdings of coal, oil, and timber are particularly valuable today.

Many other railroads have large land holdings in the cities and towns they serve. Because of these land ownership patterns, the management of some rail carriers faces problems that are broader than transportation. Indeed, as we will note in Chapter 7, "Control and Organization," some railroads have separate real estate divisions and resources subsidiaries, such as oil and lumber companies.

In air transportation, the ownership pattern is again corporate and firms are quite large. Originally, the airline firms were either small or were subsidiaries of the aircraft manufacturers. However, after the airmail scandals of 1934, Congress forced the aircraft manufacturers to divest themselves of the ownership of airlines.[2] This is an example of how regulation affected ownership.

The capital cost of airplanes is very high, and maintenance and operating expenses are great. Hence, large amounts of capital are involved in a few pieces of equipment. Further, flying has been popular. Capitalizing on this popularity, the necessary capital for air transportation has come from common stock or equity ownership rather than from bonds, to a considerable degree. Most loans for equipment have been financed by banks and insurance companies on a relatively short-term basis, and long-term debt is the exception rather than the rule in air transportation.

Pipelines have very heavily fixed costs, and large amounts of capital invested in ventures with a potentially limited life. As noted in Chapter 4, this led to the undivided-interest ownership pattern of a syndicate of large petroleum companies, each sharing the risk of a pipeline by contributing a portion of the necessary capital. Here, the ownership pattern differs once again from that of rail or air, which have very little public ownership. Indeed, until only recently there was only one pipeline (out of 99) that was owned by investors or by the public. All others were owned by oil companies or by other pipelines. Thus, one finds neither publicly owned corporate bonds nor stock of pipelines, as a rule.

Motor and water carriers both started out as small-sized firms, sometimes as individual proprietorships or partnerships. While most of the carriers in these modes are corporations today, many are still small and closely held by the families of the originators of the carriers plus a few other original investors. In motor transportation, a few firms have gone public and have a large number of shareholders and shares that are regularly traded. However, these are but a very few of the many motor carriers, and the predominant ownership pattern remains a small, closely held corporation. Little or no corporate debt in the form of publicly held bonds is found in motor transportation. Some water carriers have become subsidiaries of other firms, but water carrier ownership resembles motor carrier ownership--small, closely held corporations. These ownership patterns reflect the economic structure of both of these modes--small fixed cost and small investment necessary for original entry.

In summary, ownership patterns developed reflecting economic, historical, and regulatory patterns. Additionally, one can expect different ownership patterns for each different mode. These may affect carrier management in that additional investing public may be involved. Also, pressure to cover the fixed charges on bonds or maintain dividends may affect some managerial decisions, whereas carriers not widely held by the public do not have these pressures.

Types of Ownership Changes

While ownership patterns reflect economic, historical, and regulatory aspects of transportation, they are subject to change. Two important types of ownership changes are carrier mergers and intermodal ownership. Both have become quite controversial at times and involve public policy.

Carrier Mergers

Most carriers grew by way of mergers. Historically, the railroads were built in disconnected parts or lines with a rail system ultimately emerging from a series of corporate mergers. Many early tycoons made their fortunes by manipulation of railroad securities, not by being good railroad managers or operators. Each merger changed the physical railroad, but it also changed the ownership and financial pattern of the railroad. Sometimes too much debt was created and, in a period before the close regulation of security markets, manipulation, deception, and fraud took place. Where debt was heavy, there was great pressure to earn the resultant heavy fixed charges, and financial pressure to take advantage of the naturally monopolistic structure of early railroads.

The result of all this financial manipulation plus monopolistic markets plus abuse of monopoly was that transportation mergers were considered antisocial and detrimental to the public interest. When regulation of railroads came, it prohibited the consolidation and merging of separate railroads. But prior to regulation, the rail merger was the method of growth for railroads.

U.S. railroads have witnessed three distinct periods of merger activity. The first was prior to regulation (up to 1887), as noted above; the second was following the Transportation Act of 1920, when rail merger provisions were relaxed (and extending into the Great Depression, when some changes in ownership pattern came about in an attempt to keep some railroads financially afloat); the third was a recent merger movement that started in the late 1950s and lasted until 1970.[3]

Air carriers have gone through a shorter period of mergers, since they were regulated in 1938, relatively early in their development. Additionally, as was noted in Chapter 3, CAB policy has been to sponsor growth of existing firms by additional route award rather than by certificating new carriers. Motor carriers have actually been in a merger movement since 1935, although truckline mergers are less noticed, since there are already so many firms in the industry, and since they typically involve a smaller geographic area than rail or air mergers. All of these mergers change the ownership pattern and present both management problems and opportunities.

Basically, there are two patterns of carrier mergers, the side-by-side and the end-to-end. In both types, the carrier can often increase its profit, but by different avenues. In the side-by-side merger, two carriers competing with each other can sometimes profitably merge. Where duplication of facilities exists or excess capacity is present in one or both of the merging carriers, economies can be effected and costs reduced. In the case of a high degree of fixed investment, such as in railroads, these economies can be considerable. Where the degree of fixed investment is small, such as in motor or water transportation, economies from side-by-side mergers are usually correspondingly smaller. The major advantage of side-by-side mergers in these cases is the reduction of the number of competitors.

End-to-end mergers are profitable mainly in terms of better or extended service. While some duplication can be eliminated at the point of juncture between the merging carriers, the major advantage comes in offering a superior service covering a larger territory. Even though interchange and interlining can be highly developed, some shippers prefer to deal with a single carrier that serves both point of origination and point of destination. By the merging of two interlining motor carriers, for example, some shippers might be persuaded to use the merger carrier, when they had avoided the small line with a smaller service territory. Other economies are also possible when the end-to-end merger allows the organization to be large enough to take advantage of mass purchasing, easier access to capital markets because of size, more specialization of labor (particularly staff functions), and the like. The end-to-end merger typically results in a larger carrier, whereas the side-by-side pattern is based on reduction in size or elimination of duplication.[4]

It should be added that most mergers are not clearly either side-by-side or end-to-end, but contain elements of both.

Intermodal Ownership

Another type of ownership change concerns intermodal ownership, where one mode buys and operates a carrier of another mode. This is sometimes referred to as "integration," that is, integrating several modes, as distinct from unification or consolidation, or merging several carriers of the same mode.

Once again, historical development is important. The railroads were the first form of transcontinental land transportation and were typically very large organizations. As such, they were in a position to buy up firms in other modes of transportation and integrate them into a transportation system. However, as the early major means of transportation, railroads were also the first to be regulated, and by 1912 they were forbidden to own any other form of transportation. Motor, air, and inland water transportation developed later and so were regulated by society later. Some integration of these modes took place prior to regulation (for example, railroads owned trucklines), but to a considerable degree, transportation integration in the United States has never fully developed. This was due partially to social regulation and partially to the slowness of railroad management in realizing that other modes had a role to play in the transportation system.

This is not the case in Canada, where fully integrated transportation companies exist. Hence, the Canadian Pacific Company owns one of the two major transcontinental railroads, an airline, truckline operations, steamships, and hotels, resorts, and other allied businesses, as well as resource companies. Somewhat in the British tradition of trading companies, the one firm was allowed to control many economic ventures as a matter of public policy. The Canadian National, while government owned, is also integrated.

The transportation-company concept of a fully integrated firm has long interested scholars.[5] The intriguing idea here is that one firm with operating divisions in each mode would, theoretically, allocate freight and passengers to the mode that could most profitably handle that particular business. Without doubt, there is a good deal of duplication in U.S. transportation, and intermodal competition can be wasteful. In this country, we have followed the policy of forcing the modes to compete and paying the price of duplication and wasteful transportation. As we will see, this has been a conscious social policy on our part. Yet the alternative of allowing the profit motive to allocate freight and passengers does exist. While it does not always work perfectly, the experiences of intermodal ownership in Canada present an interesting alternative to the limited integration allowed in the United States.[6]

Public Policy on Mergers

The public policy on transportation mergers has generally been one of strict control. This policy is firmly grounded in the philosophy of antitrust and fear of the business unit becoming too large and exploiting its size. As previously noted, an integral part of the first regulation of transportation was the prohibition of rail mergers.

Regulation by state law during the Granger Movement had typically contained an absolute prohibition of pooling of all types (both traffic and revenue), and was based on the concept of enforced competition.[7] This feature of regulation was repeated in Section 5 of the Act to Regulate Commerce in 1887, when federal control of railroads was begun.[8] In addition to these regulations prohibiting pooling and consolidation, the antitrust laws were applied to railroad efforts to act in concert, or to merge, or for one railroad company to control another.[9]

Public policy toward rail mergers was drastically changed by the Transportation Act of 1920, which attempted to assure that the carriers earned a fair return on a fair value and provided an adequate transportation system for the nation. Mergers were permitted if they conformed to a plan designed to reduce the number of carriers and assure an adequate system. William Z. Ripley of Harvard University was engaged to draw up the plan and some mergers did take place, as noted above.[10] But the important point is that mergers were permissible under certain conditions and thus were no longer absolutely prohibited. While subsequent legislation (the Transportation Act of 1940) abandoned the idea of a plan, public policy had evolved by 1920 to the point where mergers were permissible with regulatory controls. This policy position was generally the one adopted when motor, air, and water transportation were regulated in 1935, 1938, and 1940, respectively.

Public policy on transportation mergers today remains one of control by the regulatory institutions having jurisdiction--the ICC for rail, motor, and inland water transportation and the CAB for air transportation. The approach is strictly on a case-by-case basis, although some guidelines have evolved, at least for rail mergers, in Congress. Other merger guidelines have evolved out of administrative practice.[11] For example, in rail merger cases the ICC is required by Congress to consider the effect of the merger on the adequacy of service, the effect on competing rail carriers, total fixed charges resulting, and the effect on employees.[12] In motor carrier mergers, legislative guidelines exempt mergers of a smaller type from any commission control. This was contained in the earlier "20-vehicle rule," which was subsequently changed to the "$300,000 gross revenue" rule, in which a merger had to involve motor carriers reaching a certain size before the ICC had jurisdiction.[13]

During the early part of the most recent rail merger movement (approximately 1958 to 1970), there was considerable concern over the lack of a more definitive public policy on mergers. Many suggestions were made and a great deal of analysis took place as rail mergers accelerated.[14] However, public policy was not changed by Congress, and the case-by-case approach of individual hearings before a regulatory commission remains.

Public Policy on Intermodal Ownership

In addition to controlling mergers between carriers within the same mode (intramodal mergers), public policy controls mergers between carriers of different modes (intermodal mergers). As noted above, U.S. transportation policy has never allowed integration of the modes under a common ownership, such as in Canada, and, at most, only partially integrated transportation firms are allowed in the United States.[15] For example, many railroads own truck subsidiaries, and a few own pipelines and occasionally a water carrier. Some motor carriers own freight forwarders, but rarely any other means of transportation.

Regulations affecting intermodal ownership apply principally to railroads. The reasons for this are both historical and regulatory. The Panama Canal Act of 1912 effectively forced the railroads to divest themselves of steamship companies by denying use of the canal to water carriers owned by "any other carrier."[16] Railroad ownership of trucklines was restricted in Part II of the Motor Carrier Act of 1935 by Section 213 as well as by Section 5 (2) of the original act concerning mergers. The Civil Aeronautics Acts of 1938 restricted ownership of airlines by "other than air carriers." Ownership of inland water carriers by others must be approved by the ICC, and some intermodal ownership by rail has been allowed. Other carriers may own freight forwarders under public policy, but freight forwarders may not own other carriers.

The reason for the fear of rail ownership of competing modes is based partially on history and economics. Railroads came early in our regulatory history and were the first big business, as noted above. The fear that railroads would dominate and suppress the newer modes as they began to develop was real. Economically, railroads often possessed the financial resources to buy up firms in competing modes as well. Also, there was fear that, given the large degree of fixed costs and common or unallocatable costs, the natural response of rail ownership of other modes would be to suppress intermodal competition. While these reasons may have been valid in the past, some argue that this situation is no longer true.[17]

Where railroad ownership existed at the time of regulation, such as rail-owned motor carriers in 1935, highly restrictive provisions were enacted to assure that the motor operation would be ancillary and auxiliary to the rail service. This was accomplished by prohibiting rail-owned motor carriers from operating between "key points" or by requiring all shipments to go by rail "prior or subsequent to" the movement by motor.[18]

In general, it is possible to say that intermodal ownership has been as closely controlled as mergers, and that full integration has been denied as a matter of public policy.

Diversification and Conglomeration

The final types of ownership patterns found in recent times are carrier diversifications and the purchase of carriers by large corporate conglomerates. These are somewhat similar types of ownership changes in that both involve nontransportation enterprises.

Diversification

Diversification, the well-known business principle of investing in other business, has been practiced in transportation for many years. As noted previously, railroads own substantial amounts of resources, such as real estate, timber, oil, coal. Many transportation firms own real estate, some of it for nontransportation purposes. Some carriers have ownership in manufacturing companies of various types as well.

Historically, railroad ownership of coal mines caused the "Commodities Clause" to be enacted in the Hepburn Act of 1906.[19] This clause grew out of a Supreme Court case in which railroads were found to be discriminating in favor of traffic in which they possessed ownership positions.[20] Therefore, rail carriers were prohibited from transporting any commodity (except lumber) that is "manufactured, mined or produced by it." The effect was to separate railroad ownership from its nontransportation undertakings, and the usual pattern was to establish a holding company that owned the railroad, on the one hand, and the resource firm, on the other hand. However, the matter of actual rail management and control was given close attention by the courts and the commission with a considerable degree of restriction.[21]

In recent times, some railroads, having borrowing power due to their capital intensive nature, and faced with a rather low return on capital invested in transportation operations, have attempted to diversify further into nontransportation activities. This has taken the form of the so-called industries approach, in which the parent company becomes purely a holding company and changes its name to "X Y Z Industries." A number of railroads have set up this type of organization in recent times and have diversified into all sorts of undertakings (not just the traditional resource or land-based activities of the past). Some "industries" so set up have even subsequently sold the railroad that was the original base (Northwest Industries sold the Chicago & Northwestern Railway to its employees, and Bangor Punta Industries sold the Bangor & Aroostook Railway).

The goals sought were a better return on capital assets, utilization of borrowing power (and sometimes tax-loss-carry-forward balances), and a lessening of risk by having income from nontransportation sources. Additionally, the industries approach effectively bypassed the commodities abuse.

The ICC has been much concerned with actual and potential abuses under this holding-company-as-industries approach as well as under conglomerate control.[22] It is contended that transportation capital is often transferred to nontransportation activites, and other abuses are possible.[23] Of course, advantages are foreseen as well as disadvantages.[24]

Conglomeration

In conglomeration, it is usually a nontransportation firm that buys up control of a transportation firm. As noted above with the industries approach, the distinction between diversification and conglomeration can become blurred. Even so, there have been several instances of large nontransportation conglomerate firms buying up trucklines and bargelines as they diversify. The motives for these ownership changes are much the same--diversifying risks and not putting all your eggs in one basket. Further, some modes, such as motor carriers, have attained the status of growth industries in some investment circles, and have been prime targets for large conglomerates. Hence, in the late 1960s, conglomerates began to acquire trucklines, freight forwarders, bargelines, and airlines. A few transportation companies themselves became conglomerates in their efforts to diversify, with railroad holding companies owning a number of nontransportation firms, and at least one large bus company diversifying into meat packing, foods, and soaps and toiletries.

As usual, there have been conflicting ideas on the effect of this movement.[25] The charge of diverting transportation assets to nontransportation purposes is found here as well. The ICC has asked for power to control these ownership changes, because, at the present time, there is very little it can do about nontransportation firms gaining control over carriers.[26] The commission has undertaken several studies of the problem and seems able to detail detrimental effects of the movement.[27] There also seems to be some evidence that the bankruptcy of the Penn Central was due, at least partially, to some of the abuses of conglomeration.[28]

Congress has taken no action to change the regulatory structure, in spite of the disclosure of problems with diversification and conglomeration. While the sensational exposes in the press relative to the bankruptcy of the Penn Central highlighted this problem, it remains true that much of the activities of diversification and conglomeration are outside the jurisdiction of regulation.

Effects on Carrier Management

The effects of ownership patterns on carrier management will vary with the particular situation. We have already mentioned the effect of high fixed costs on operational decisions. Where a carrier is a subsidiary of a competing mode, specific effects on managerial decision making are possible. Where a carrier is part of a conglomerate, other effects are possible. To a considerable degree, the effects of ownership will depend on the amount of autonomy granted to carrier managers, the general management philosophy of the ownership, and the regulatory restrictions imposed. For example, a railroad owned truckline certainly operates differently and has a different management philosophy from an independent truckline. Likewise, a motor carrier that is part of a large conglomerate has a different image of itself than a truckline that is independently owned. The effects on the management of a carrier can be potentially great or minimal, depending on the situation and the circumstances.

SUMMARY

Ownership patterns can be a constraint on carrier management. Public policy and ownership of the way present a given for most carriers, but do affect decision making. Changes in carrier ownership through mergers, intermodal ownership, diversification, and conglomeration reflect historical, economic, and regulatory events. The effect of each of these ownership changes is generally controversial and subject to considerable debate. Public policy regulates some of these changes but is silent on others. The area of ownership as a study is changing and evolving as transportation changes and evolves, and it behooves carrier management to be cognizant of the issues involved and alert to the effects of ownership on its particular operation.

NOTES

1. For a more detailed discussion of the issues involved in public aids and promotions, see Roy S. Sampson and Martin T. Farris, Domestic Transportation: Practice, Theory and Policy, 3rd ed. (Boston: Houghton Mifflin Co., 1975), Chapter 7.

2. John H. Frederick, Commercial Air Transportation, 5th ed. (Homewood, Ill.: Richard D. Irwin, 1961), p. 75.

3. Perhaps the best treatment of rail merger developments during the second period of merger activity is found in W. N. Leonard, Railroad Consolidation Under the Transportation Act of 1920 (New York: Columbia University Press, 1946).

4. A more detailed discussion of these types of mergers is found in Sampson and Farris, op. cit., pp. 405-23.

5. Considerable literature exists on the problems of intermodalism. See W. Graham Clayton, Jr., "A Single Intermodal Transportation Company," Transportation Journal, Spring 1972, pp. 31-38; Orrin H. Fraley, ibid., pp. 53-58; Robert C. Lieb, "A Revised Intermodal Ownership Policy," Transportation Journal, Summer 1971, pp. 45-54; Peter S. Douglas, "The Economic Irrelevance of 'Common Ownership,'" I.C.C. Practitioners' Journal, July-August 1969, pp. 1794-1800; Robert C. Lieb, "Intermodal Ownership: Experience and Evaluation," I.C.C. Practitioners' Journal, July-August 1971, pp. 746-59; and James E. Suelflow and Stanley J. Hille, "The Transportation Company: An Economic Argument for Intermodal Ownership," Land Economics, August 1970, pp. 275-86.

6. Trevor D. Heaver, "Multi-Modal Ownership--The Canadian Experience," Transportation Journal, Fall 1971, pp. 14-29.

7. D. Phillip Locklin, Economics of Transportation, 7th ed. (Homewood, Ill.: Richard D. Irwin, 1972), p. 216.

8. Ibid., pp. 226, 315-18.

9. United States v. Trans-Missouri Freight Association, 116 U.S. 290 (1897); Northern Securities Co. v. United States, 193 U.S. 197 (1904); United States v. Union Pacific R.R., 226 U.S. 61 (1912) and 226 U.S. 470 (1913); and United States v. Southern Pacific Co., 259 U.S. 214 (1922).

10. Sampson and Farris, op. cit., p. 417.

11. For an excellent treatment of the subject, see John Guandolo, Transportation Law, 2nd ed. (Dubuque, Iowa: Wm. C. Brown Co., 1973), pp. 729-826, 845-54.

12. 49 USC 5(2) (c).

13. 49 USC 312 (b).

14. There is considerable literature on mergers. See Michael Conant, Railroad Mergers and Abandonments (Berkeley: University

of California Press, 1968); Kent T. Healy, The Effect of Scale in the Railroad Industry (New Haven: Committee on Transportation, Yale University, 1961); Roy J. Sampson, Obstacles to Railroad Unification (Eugene, Ore.: Bureau of Business Research, University of Oregon, 1960); John W. Barriger, "The Effects of Mergers on Competition," Transportation Journal, Spring 1968, pp. 5-17; Martin T. Farris, "Rail Mergers: New Interest in an Old Approach," Transportation Journal, Summer 1962, pp. 30-37; Robert W. Harbeson, "New Patterns in Railway Consolidation," The Quarterly Review of Economics and Business, February 1962, pp. 7-10; Kent T. Healy, "The Merger Movement in Transportation," American Economic Review, May 1962, pp. 436-44; W. N. Leonard, "Issues in Competition and Monopoly in Railroad Mergers," Transportation Journal, Summer 1964, pp. 5-15; Newton Morton, "Carrier Consolidation," I.C.C. Practitioners' Journal, January-February 1963, pp. 425-48. There were also congressional investigations on mergers. See U.S., Congress, House, Committee on the Judiciary, The Railroad Merger Problem, Committee Print, 88th Cong., 1st sess., 1963, and U.S., Congress, Senate, Committee on Interstate and Foreign Commerce, National Transportation Policy, Senate Report No. 445, 87th Cong., 1st sess., 1961.

15. An example of partial integration would be the Southern Pacific Company, parent of the Southern Pacific Railway, which owns trucklines and pipelines.

16. The whole subject of intermodal ownership regulation is well treated in Byron Nupp, "Regulatory Standards in Common Ownership in Transportation," I.C.C. Practitioners' Journal, November-December 1966, pp. 776-90.

17. See note 5, particularly the two articles by Lieb, and the Suelflow and Hille analysis.

18. Nupp, op. cit.; Guandolo, op. cit.; Charles A. Taff, Commercial Motor Transportation, 4th ed. (Homewood, Ill.: Richard D. Irwin, 1969), pp. 418-20; and William J. Hudson and James A. Constantin, Motor Transportation (New York: Ronald Press Co., 1958), pp. 509-17.

19. 49 USC 1 (18).

20. New Haven Railroad v. Interstate Commerce Commission, 200 U.S. 361, and later testing the clause United States v. Delaware and Hudson Co., 213 U.S. 366.

21. Guandolo, op. cit., pp. 614-28.

22. The ICC asked for power for broader control over both diversification and conglomeration in its 83rd Annual Report (1969), after several staff investigations.

23. A detailed discussion is found in Harrison F. Houghton, "The Interstate Commerce Commission Views Toward Conglomerate

Expansion and Holding Company Control of Railroads in the Light of General Public Policy Toward Conglomerates," I.C.C. Practitioners' Journal, May-June 1973, pp. 437-53; Colin Barrett, "Diversification of Scatteration," I.C.C. Practitioners' Journal, January-February 1970, pp. 198-208; and Perry M. Shoemaker, "Should Railroads Diversify for Growth and Profit?" Transportation Journal, Fall 1969, pp. 5-17.

24. Frederick G. Pfrommer, "Panel Discussion: The Effects of Diversification Into Other Modes of Transportation," I.C.C. Practitioners' Journal, September-October 1969, pp. 1989-2011 (panelists Allan Furth, Charles D. Matthews, William K. Smith, and George Peterkin).

25. L. L. Waters, "Panel Discussion: Pros and Cons of Conglomerates as They Affect Transportation," I.C.C. Practitioners' Journal, September-October 1970, pp. 963-86 (panelists J. W. Hershey, Roland W. Donnem, Robert J. Bernard, and Robert S. Hamilton).

26. Harrison Houghton, op. cit., and William J. DeWitt, "The Railroad Conglomerate: Its Relationship to the Interstate Commerce Commission and National Transportation Policy," Transportation Journal, Winter 1972, pp. 5-14.

27. One such study is contained in U.S., Congress, Senate, Subcommittee on Surface Transportation of the Committee on Commerce, Railroad Industry Overview, 92nd Cong., 1st sess., pp. 529-613.

28. U.S., Congress, Senate, Committee on Commerce, Failing Railroads, 91st Cong., 2nd sess., 1970, pp. 795-982.

CHAPTER

6

PRICING AND RATE MAKING

The fifth and final constraint on management of transportation carriers is the pricing and rate-making system. Price is important to transportation carriers, because price multiplied by weight or dimensions equals revenues for the carriers. Prices are called "rates" in transportation and are generally expressed in terms of the price required to move 100 pounds between two designated points. Rates are controlled by federal and state agencies in the regulated segment of the transportation industry, and must be just, reasonable, and not unduly preferential or discriminatory, as explained in Chapter 2.[1] Rates are published by rate conferences and individual carriers, and, unless an emergency exists, cannot be changed without a 30-day notice period.[2]

Transportation pricing is enormously complex, due to the institutional manner in which it is published and the sheer number of freight rates, of which there are trillions.[3] From this plethora of rates, only one legal, applicable rate can be assessed on a given shipment. Rates are also complex because, in part, they influence the size and extent of a business firm's geomarket and channels of distribution. We will examine three facets of carrier rate making (pricing): transportation rate theory, the conference method of rate making, and rate conferences and market strategy.

TRANSPORTATION RATE THEORY

Pricing in the transportation industry is basically very much like pricing in any other industry--prices are determined by supply and demand. However, both supply and demand in transportation are complex and reflect the economic characteristics of the suppliers (carriers), the complicated nature of the service offered, and the multitude of economic factors affecting the demand for service by demanders (shippers). An elementary discussion of these complicated supply and demand factors will provide a general framework within which some understanding of how transportation prices are established can be gained.

Transportation Costs

Transportation supply must reflect the cost of providing the service. Carriers have no source of revenue other than rates. Therefore, rates must reflect costs. A few elementary cost concepts will be helpful in determining which costs must be covered by rates.

Constant and Variable Costs

One way to look at transportation costs is to divide them into constant and variable costs. The distinction here is in terms of cost behavior in response to changed activity (more or less tonnage, more or fewer passengers). This division into constant and variable costs is a simple and much used cost distinction. While the term "fixed costs" is often used, we prefer the concept of constant costs. That is, few costs are actually fixed and cannot be changed--particularly if the time frame used is a long one. Likewise, when large additions are made to capacity, a whole new set of fixed costs is established. Accordingly, we prefer the term "constant costs" as a more realistic and descriptive approach.

By "constant costs" we mean those costs that remain essentially fixed within the relevant range of output (capacity) available in the time period under consideration in the decision at hand. Examples of constant expenses would be interest on debt; property taxes; many, but not all, administrative expenses; property insurance; minimum amounts of maintenance; cost of a minimum amount of working capital; licenses and fees; depreciation on the basis of time (not use); in short, any costs that do not increase or decrease as output (freight or passengers carried) changes. Once again, these are often called "fixed costs," but, in truth, most of them are avoidable should the business cease, or most will increase should the capacity of the firm change greatly.

By variable costs we mean those costs that vary with, or change as, output changes. Examples would be the cost of supplies and fuel; labor costs (some labor costs actually become constant by union contracts that force the carrier to keep on certain employees in the face of decreased tonnages); most advertising and promotion costs; depreciation caused by use; most marketing costs; some administrative costs; leasing costs; user charges (for motor and air transportation); in short, any costs that increase or decrease as output (freight or passengers carried) changes. It should be noted that the degree of change in cost in response to change in output is not the determining factor--some costs will increase proportionally to changed output; others will not change proportionally. The determining factor is whether costs change as output changes. Those costs that change are variable, those that do not change are constant.

Common and Traceable Costs

Another way of considering carrier costs is to divide them into common and traceable costs. The distinction here is one of assigning cost responsibility or assessing costs against a given department, function, division, or class of freight or passengers. If costs are to be used to determine price (or profit-center analysis), they must be assigned to specific functions or freight.

Traceable costs are those that can be readily assigned to a given function. In pickup and delivery, for example, it is fairly easy to assign costs to each shipment. Some handling costs, especially where special equipment is involved, can be assigned. Crew costs for operators can usually be assigned, billing and collection costs can be assigned, a few promotional costs (where a specific item or class of freight is involved) can be assigned, fuel costs can be assigned, user taxes can be assigned, and so forth.

However, there is a large number of costs that are incurred for the output as a whole; that is, they are common to all units of output and they can be assigned or traced only with the greatest difficulty. These are sometimes called "overhead," although the term has multiple meanings and we prefer the concept of common costs. Examples of common costs are most administrative costs, most sales or marketing costs, most investment or property costs, institutional or general advertising and promotion costs, most personnel costs, most utility costs; in short, any cost incurred for the whole operation and common to all functions or units of freight and passengers. Assignment of these costs can be done for pricing (and for profit-center analysis), but only arbitrarily, for they are difficult to trace to a specific function or unit of output.

It will be readily seen that the constant costs noted above are usually also common--that is, difficult to trace or assign. Who can say what portion of the president's salary should be assigned to the cost of moving a case of canned corn? But it is well to note that there are variable costs that are also common. The cost of traffic solicitors can be increased or decreased readily, but it is difficult to assign a portion of the salesman's salary to the rate on a given case of canned corn. Utility bills can be cut by changing shifts on a dock (which are variable), but it is impossible to attribute to a given item being moved anything but an arbitrary share of the power bill. Almost all constant costs are also common, but many common costs are not constant.

Functional Costs

A third way to consider carrier costs is by the function performed. The usual division here is into line-haul costs, terminal costs, and administrative costs. The distinction is purely by function, and the idea is to make comparisons for profit-center analysis or for comparison of mileage rates or blocks. All carrier costs are separated into one of the three categories, and a rate is found by aggregating or adding up the costs of each function associated with the particular movement. Because some modes of transportation have very large terminal costs (for example, railroads), the short-distance rates will have to be higher than modes having lower terminal costs (for example, trucks). Terminal costs similarly set minimum rates where they are used (such as motor carrier minimums). Where shipments move over very long distances, the proportion of terminal costs that must be recouped for each mile decreases as distance increases. This helps to explain why rates can be tapered--that is, increasing less than proportionally to distance. There are many other ways in which the distinction among line-haul, terminal, and administrative costs can be useful.

Transportation Demand

Turning to the other side of pricing, consideration must be given to the demand for the service. Domestic transportation is essentially producing a service when it moves goods and passengers from one geographical point to another. As such, the value of that service establishes the maximum rate level. For example, if a given product sells for $1.00 in city A and $1.50 in city B, the transportation rate between A and B cannot exceed $0.50 or the freight will not move. Transportation will be demanded only if the rate is less than the value of the service (in abstract terms). Conversely, we know that differences in price between geographic areas on a given product will also reflect transportation rates or the cost of transportation to the shipper. Hence, the reason why the price of the product is $1.50 in city B may be because transportation from city A costs $0.50. In fact, value of service does set a maximum on transportation rates, and transportation rates do establish differences in price. Demand for transportation is a combination of many factors, some of which are mutually determining.

Responses to changes in price or rates are also an important part of demand considerations. This is called "elasticity," and two types can be identified: elasticity of the demand for transportation, and elasticity of the demand for the commodity itself. Both of these factors have already been noted in Chapter 3, so we will only review them here.

As noted earlier, both potential modal substitutability and potential carrier substitutability (intramodal competition) exist. These potential shifts of traffic among modes and among carriers are the essential feature of elasticity of demand for transportation. With some commodities, a very small change in rates will cause a shift to or from a competitive transportation mode, or even an absolute decrease or increase in transportation demand as rates exceed or drop below the value of the service. This situation is one of elastic demand for transportation and it is illustrated in Panel B of Figure 6.1. Under these circumstances, a small decrease in rates (Q_1 to Q_2) causes a more-than-proportional increase in volume of transportation demanded, or, conversely, a small increase in rates in the same situation would cause a more-than-proportional decrease in volume of transportation demanded. The opposite case is inelastic demand illustrated in Panel A of Figure 6.2. Here, an increase in rates (P_1 to P_2) causes a small or less-than-proportional change in volume of transportation demanded (Q_1 to Q_2). Note that we are concerned here with demand for transportation from a given carrier or mode, and not demand for the commodity.

The second type of elasticity involves the effect of a rate change on the demand for the commodity itself. Many commodities have close substitutes, and a small change in price will affect the quantity of the product demanded more than proportionally. This is illustrated in Panel B of Figure 6.2 where a small increase in price (A to P_2) causes a more than proportional change in quantities demanded in the ultimate market (Q_1 to Q_2). Other commodities have fewer substitutes, and a small change in price will cause a less-than-proportional change in the quantity demanded. These are commodities with inelastic demands as shown in Panel A of Figure 6.2 where a change in price (P_1 to P_2) causes a less than proportional change in the quantity demanded (Q_1 to Q_2). Since an increase in freight rates is the same as an increase in price (and a decrease in freight rates is the same as a price decrease) for the commodity in its ultimate market, these demand characteristics must be considered in transportation pricing. The carrier should be particularly careful about

FIGURE 6.1

Elasticities of Demand for Transportation and Demand Pricing in Transportation

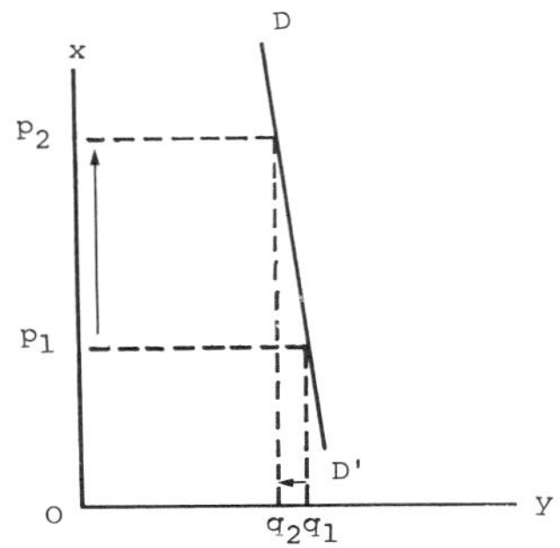

(A)
Inelastic Demand for Transportation

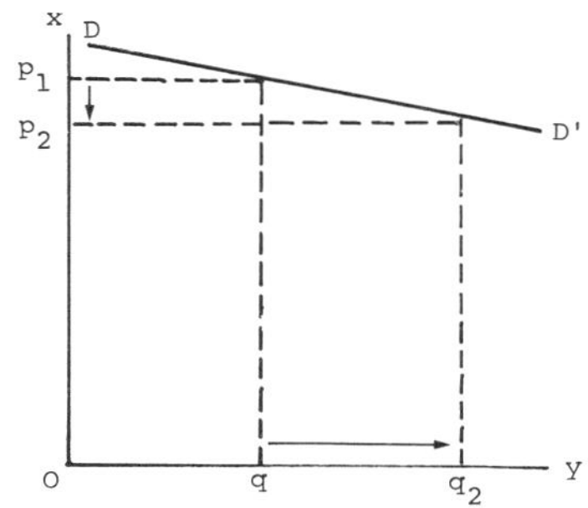

(B)
Elastic Demand for Transportation

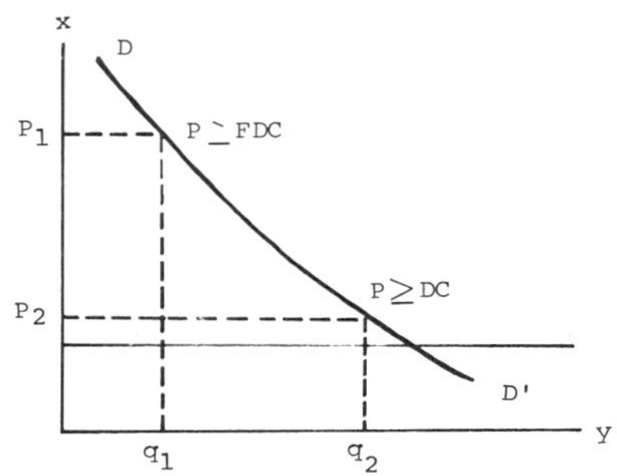

(C)
Demand Pricing in Transportation

FIGURE 6.2

Elasticities of Demand for Commodities in Ultimate Market

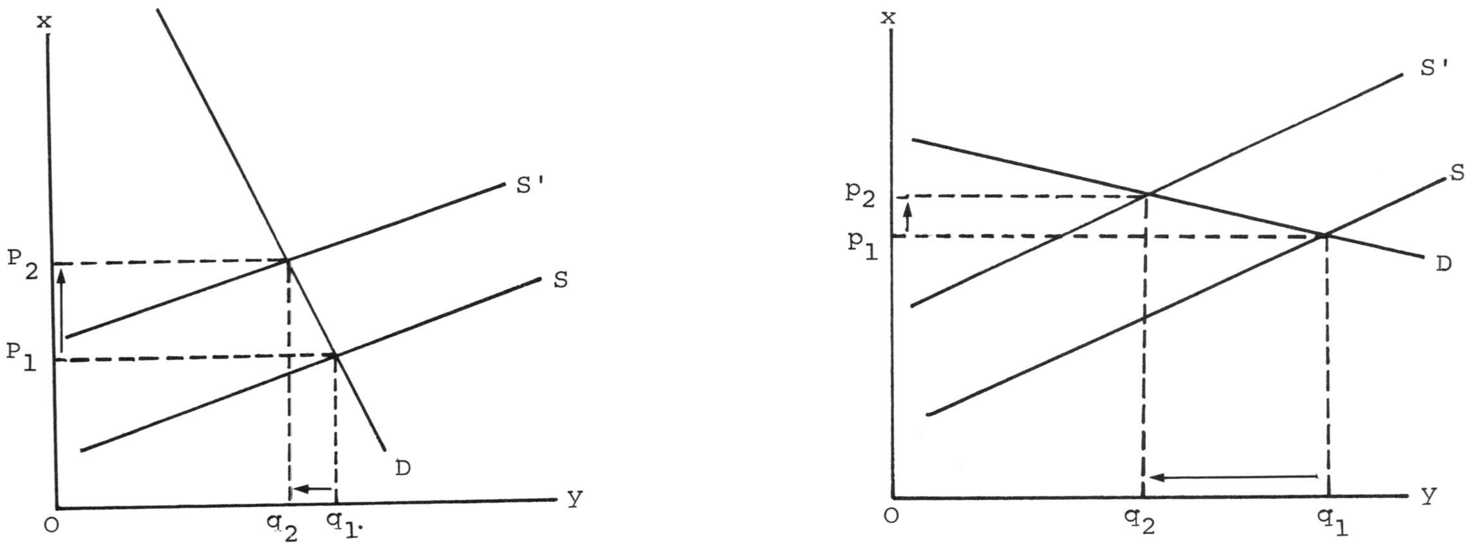

Inelastic Demand
(A)

Elastic Demand
(B)

raising freight rates on elastic commodities, for the result could well be that the freight rate increase would adversely affect the ultimate demand for the commodity. On commodities with enelastic demands in their ultimate market, the carrier has more flexibility to change freight rates.

Contribution Theory

When the basic supply (cost) factors and demand factors noted above are considered together, we have the well-known contribution theory. In the short run, and within the constraints of existing capacity to produce, the carrier must realize that the constant costs will continue, irrespective of freight volume. These constant costs are also common costs and thereby difficult to assign or allocate. Hence, the carrier should look to the variable and traceable costs as the key to short-run pricing. These costs must be covered, and they provide the minimum or floor below which rates cannot go.

Anything in excess of variable and traceable costs make a contribution to constant and common costs. Obviously, this contribution should be maximized in each freight rate, and in total, must cover the constant and common costs, if profit is to be realized. The degree of the contribution made by each rate will turn on the two elasticities already noted. That is, items with an inelastic demand for transportation and an inelastic demand for the commodity itself in its ultimate market should be assessed a freight rate that makes a large contribution to constant and common costs plus a markup for profit. Items with an elastic demand for transportation (potential substitutability by mode or carrier) plus an elastic demand for the commodity itself in its ultimate market (potential loss of ultimate market to small price change) should be assessed a freight rate that makes little or no contribution to constant and common costs. Between these two extremes, all sorts of combinations of elasticities can be found and should be given consideration in setting freight rates.

The theory of transportation rates can be concisely stated. "The freight rate on each commodity should cover variable and traceable costs and make the greatest total contribution to constant and common costs giving due consideration to demand conditions."[4]

Differential Pricing

In order to maximize the contribution and consider demand characteristics, the carrier must practice what is known as "differential pricing." That is, a different price is established for each and every commodity according to the cost characteristics, demand characteristics, and need for contribution and profit. Of course, this is exactly what happens in the use of freight rate classification and class rates--a different rate is established for each classification and reflects the transportation characteristics of the commodity in question. The same is true for commodity rates--different prices are established that are designed to promote large movement and maximize the potential contribution of that commodity group. Both are illustrations of the concept of differential pricing.

In the long run and in the aggregate, all costs must be recouped plus some fair return or profit earned or the carrier will go out of business. But in the short run and on an individual class or commodity basis, freight rates may be either above or below the arbitrarily allocated full costs.

Application of Differential Pricing

A strong argument can be advanced that carriers should not charge different prices for different goods because the service rendered is essentially the same--moving a commodity from one point to another.[5] Conversely, carrier managers correctly insist that cost differentials do exist between various classes of traffic and that price differentials are needed in order for plant facilities to be properly used.

It is clear from the above that elasticities of demand for both transportation and the commodity itself are of major importance.[6] Commodities with a relatively low value tend to move by the modes with the lowest rates, and these commodities generally have a high degree of elasticity of demand for transportation.

Conversely, commodities that normally have relatively inelastic transport demands often possess a high retail value, and transportation costs often represent only a small percentage of the free on board (FOB) destination invoice value.[7] High-valued goods, such as television and radio receiver sets, are normally charged rates that greatly exceed the fully distributed cost of providing the service by the carrier.[8] This is illuminated in Table 6.1 where the percentage of fully distributed cost ranges from a low of 58 on gravel and sand to a high of 250 percent on alcoholic liquors. If the transportation demand shown in Panel A of Figure 6.1 (inelastic) v.as for a truckload of whiskey, rates could be doubled and total revenue after the increase would be greater than before. Transportation rates in this instance usually represent less than one-tenth of 1 percent of the value of the item, and are insignificant to the buyer.

TABLE 6.1

Comparison of Carload Freight Revenues from Selected Commodities and Fully Distributed Cost, 1971

Commodity	Percent of Fully Distributed Cost
Butter	109
Flour, wheat	78
Cottonseed oil	105
Lettuce	73
Antracite coal	96
Iron ore	78
Gravel and sand	58
Pig iron	153
Drugs and toilet preparations	156
Agricultural implements	166
Machinery and machines	220
Airplanes and parts	218
Liquors, alcoholic	250

Source: Compiled from Interstate Commerce Commission, Bureau of Accounts, Distribution of Rail Revenue Contributed by Commodity Groups, State. No. 3-71 (Washington, D.C.: 1971).

On the other hand, articles that have relatively elastic transportation demands, normally inexpensive goods such as sand and gravel, are charged rates that barely exceed the direct cost of providing transportation service.[9] While prices for inexpensive goods are usually elastic, freight charges may constitute a substantial part of FOB destination invoice value.[10] Freight cost for sand, for instance, can be as high as 40 percent of the invoice cost. As illustrated in Panel B of Figure 6.1, by reducing rates slightly, a carrier's total revenue is greater after the price reduction than before; hence, a larger volume of traffic over which fixed costs can be allocated is encompassed.

In the transportation industry, a significant amount of cost cannot be allocated to a specific movement or commodity. A rail carrier, for example, may have as much as 15 to 20 percent of common or joint costs that are allocated arbitrarily. When a motor carrier goes from one point to another, return capacity is created and common cost must be allocated.[11] Although attacked by some critics, value-of-service pricing represents one method of rate making that, when properly functioning, allocates costs and facilitates efficient utilization of a carrier's plant.[12]

In transport pricing on the basis of demand (or value), is best reflected in Panel C of Figure 6.1. Cost is treated as constant, high-valued goods are charged a price that substantially exceeds fully distributed cost, and inexpensive commodities are charged a price that barely exceeds the cost of service. This form of pricing is analogous to the progressive income tax in that the more expensive commodities can stand the higher rates.[13] Although this type of pricing has been criticized by advocates of cost-oriented rates, a strong argument can be made that the expensive freight would be required to bear an even higher rate if the inexpensive commodities were not transported.[14] Needless to say, substantial diversions of traffic from one mode to another have seriously diminished the ability of carriers to employ this kind of rate making in all cases.

The conditions necessary to engage in value-of-service pricing are fourfold. First, the carrier must have some degree of monopoly power. This condition is easily satisfied by requiring certification for most common carriers by rail, air, truck, pipeline, and water. Second, transportation demand elasticity for a given product must be identified. Third, submarkets must be segregated--a condition satisfied by freight classification. And fourth, products cannot be resold. Since transportation is a service, this condition is easily met.

Establishing freight rates is an art, not a science, but, generally speaking, the principal determinates are cost and value of service.[15] While many experts contend that transportation costs are difficult to measure, distinct differences do exist in both the cost of providing a transport service and the demand for a given service. These are the following:

Cost of Service Factors[16]

1. loading characteristics of a commodity
2. susceptibility of a product to loss and damage
3. amount of carrier liability
4. volume of movement
5. regularity of movement
6. type of equipment
7. special services required

Transportation Demand Factors

1. commodity value
2. finished or raw material
3. commodity competition
4. financial condition of the industry

Even in private transportation, the general forces of supply and demand establish price over a period of time.[17]

CONFERENCE METHOD OF RATE MAKING

The management of transportation companies must, by necessity, frequently be performed within the constraints of many state, local, and federal laws concerning such subjects as discounts, unfair competitive practices, predatory pricing, service controls, and market entry. When selling transportation services, care must be exercised, because services and prices should ideally be structured toward classes of customers, and these must, in turn, be published in tariffs. The institutional mechanism through which freight rates are published, together with classifications and tariffs, are important to a carrier's marketing strategy and, hence, its financial success.[18]

Freight rates are contained in freight tariffs, which in turn are published through the medium of rate conferences. From the standpoint of developing carrier strategy, freight rates influence or determine physical market boundaries, the location of manufacturing and retail firms, packaging costs, and, ultimately, profits.[19] Rate bureaus are nonprofit corporations developed primarily to provide an avenue through which freight rates, rules, and services are formulated, discussed, and published in tariffs. Bureaus, or rate conferences, are financed by their carrier members, and membership fees are based on aggregate revenues. Carrier members file powers of attorney with their respective rate bureaus, which enables the organization to commit the carriers to various rates and rules.[20]

For an extended period of time, a major conflict existed between bureaus, the ICC, and the Justice Department. The original Act to Regulate Commerce required railroads to publish through routes and joint rates, a requirement that necessitated corporate cooperation regarding establishing rates and routes. On the other hand, the Justice Department's Antitrust Division contended that conference rate making essentially violated the Sherman Antitrust Act, which regulated collusive price agreements and prohibited the creation of monopolies.[21] This controversy was terminated in 1948, when Congress amended Title 49 of the United States Code by passing the Reed-Bulwinkle Act over President Truman's veto.[22]

Carrier rate conferences are now legal, insofar as they conform to rules and regulations promulgated by the ICC, in addition to permitting each member carrier the legal right to exercise independent action.[23] In essence, the Reed-Bulwinkle Act amended the Interstate Commerce Act by requiring accounts and records to be maintained by the conferences.

> Each conference, bureau, or committee, or other organization established or continued pursuant to

> any agreement approved by the Commission under the provisions of this section shall maintain such accounts, records, files, and memoranda and shall submit to the Commission such report. . . .[24]

The right to exercise independent action in effect represented an essential condition precedence for commission approval for any rail or motor carrier rate conference.

> The Commission shall not approve, under this section, any agreement which establishes a procedure for the determination of any matter through joint consideration unless it finds that in the agreement there is accorded to each party the free and unrestrained right to take independent action either before or after any determination arrived at through such procedures.[25]

Rate Bureau Functions

Each rate bureau performs four basic functions.[26] First, it disseminates pertinent information to carrier members. For example, weighing and inspection offices provide carrier members with specific data regarding weight violations and incorrectly described shipments. Second, a conference or bureau functions essentially as a catalyst for its carrier membership. That is, carriers can use the conference as a common point of interest for solving mutual problems. By discussing matters of mutual interest regarding, for instance, demurrage of detention, consensus can be attained in many instances. Third, a multitude of freight tariffs are published by conferences for both carriers and shippers to use. Although each carrier has the legal right to publish single-line tariffs, most carriers find that it is considerably less expensive to use conference tariffs than to publish their own. Fourth, conferences function as an institutional mechanism through which rates are published or definite procedures established, and various employee committees are used to consider any new rate or modification in existing rates or services.[27]

Rate conferences, moreover, are geographically aligned and rail carriers cannot be members of motor carrier bureaus or vice versa. Ten railroad rate territories exist and each territory maintains a separate rate bureau. There are 11 motor carrier bureaus. Interterritorial rates are published between each rate territory.[28]

Water Conferences

Rates and charges for exempt water transportation, like those for exempt transportation by truck, are negotiated between the carrier and shipper. Domestic inland water carriers that are regulated usually belong to waterway rate bureaus. Those regulated by the ICC, however, participate in freight tariffs published by both rail and water conferences. But, for the most part, regulated inland water carriers publish their own single-line tariffs.

With respect to international water transportation, most active trade routes have steamship conferences associated with them.[29] Unless an open rating situation exists, shippers may receive a lower rate if they agree to ship a specified amount by a conference carrier. Charter rates, on the other hand, are negotiated between carriers and shippers. Steamship conference rate agreements must be approved by the U.S. Maritime Commission.[30]

Other Carrier Conferences

While airlines, pipelines, buses, freight brokers, and forwarders do not belong to rate conferences, in most instances they publish single-line tariffs. In the areas of both passenger and cargo, regulated air carriers use the Air Traffic Conference of America to publish tariffs. This agency publishes a general rate tariff, pickup and delivery tariff, specific commodity tariff, and others.[31]

CARRIER MARKETING STRATEGY AND CONFERENCES

Publishing freight rates is the primary function of rate bureaus, although most people think this is a function performed daily by the ICC. Carrier managers should ideally use bureaus as a part of their overall marketing strategy. For example, suppose that the sales manager for the Ace Truck Line examines a computer run depicting profits associated with specific customer accounts. One such account is Rod Products, a firm manufacturing BB guns located at Rogers, Arkansas, that normally ships 2,000 pounds LTL (less than truckload) shipments. From a computer print-out, he notices that 10 volume shipments weighing 20,000 pounds each with a $2.00 per cwt. rate are moving each week from Rogers to Paris, Texas. After consulting with Ace's operating and traffic personnel, the sales manager explains to Rod's traffic manager that, due to the increased volume, Ace will attempt to have a commodity rate of $1.50 per cwt., volume minimum weight 20,000 pounds, published from Rogers to Paris. Ace's operations will be profitable at $1.50 per cwt. because of the volume of traffic involved and improved scheduling. The following procedure is followed to reduce the existing rate from $2.00 to $1.50 per cwt.:

1. Ace Truck Line files a proposal to publish a rate of $1.50 per cwt., volume minimum weight 20,000 pounds, published from Rogers, Arkansas to Paris, Texas, with the Southwestern Motor Freight Bureau, located in Dallas.
2. The Southwestern Motor Freight Bureau assigns an identifying docket number to the proposal and subsequently publishes a brief description of the proposed action in its weekly docket bulletin, a publication subscribed to by carriers and shippers. A hearing date is announced in the docket bulletin.
3. The Standing Rate Committee, an employee board, hears arguments concerning the proposals, and costs are emphasized.
4. Disposition of the proposal is announced in the next Southwestern Motor Freight Bureau weekly docket bulletin--the rate is published (in which case a tariff supplement number is designated), modified, or rejected.

In the event that the Standing Rate Committee denies the proposed reduction (usually on the grounds that the reduced rate would be detrimental to the industry), Ace's traffic representative can appeal to a general rate committee. Should this appellate action be denied, Ace could instruct Southwestern to independently publish the proposed rate of $1.50.

Figure 6.3 is a schematic diagram showing rate publishing procedures through three entirely different sets of circumstances—emergency, regular, and independent action for a hypothetical motor carrier bureau. While the ICC can initiate an investigation regarding the reasonableness of any given rate or service, the agency usually becomes involved in specific rate controversies when a carrier or rate conference petitions for a suspension of a given rate. Once the commission becomes involved in a rate matter, it can suspend the rate for 180 days to ascertain its reasonableness, deny the rate, or permit the rate to be published.

During recent years, rate conferences have received severe criticism from many sources. One transport study sponsored by Ralph Nader contended that rate bureaus were merely cartels and hence reduced competition.[32] The DOT is at present sponsoring legislation designed to eliminate various rate bureau activities.[33] Most criticism directed against rate bureaus arises from a widespread conference practice of petitioning the ICC to suspend rates

FIGURE 6.3

Rate Procedure Used by a Hypothetical Motor Carrier Bureau

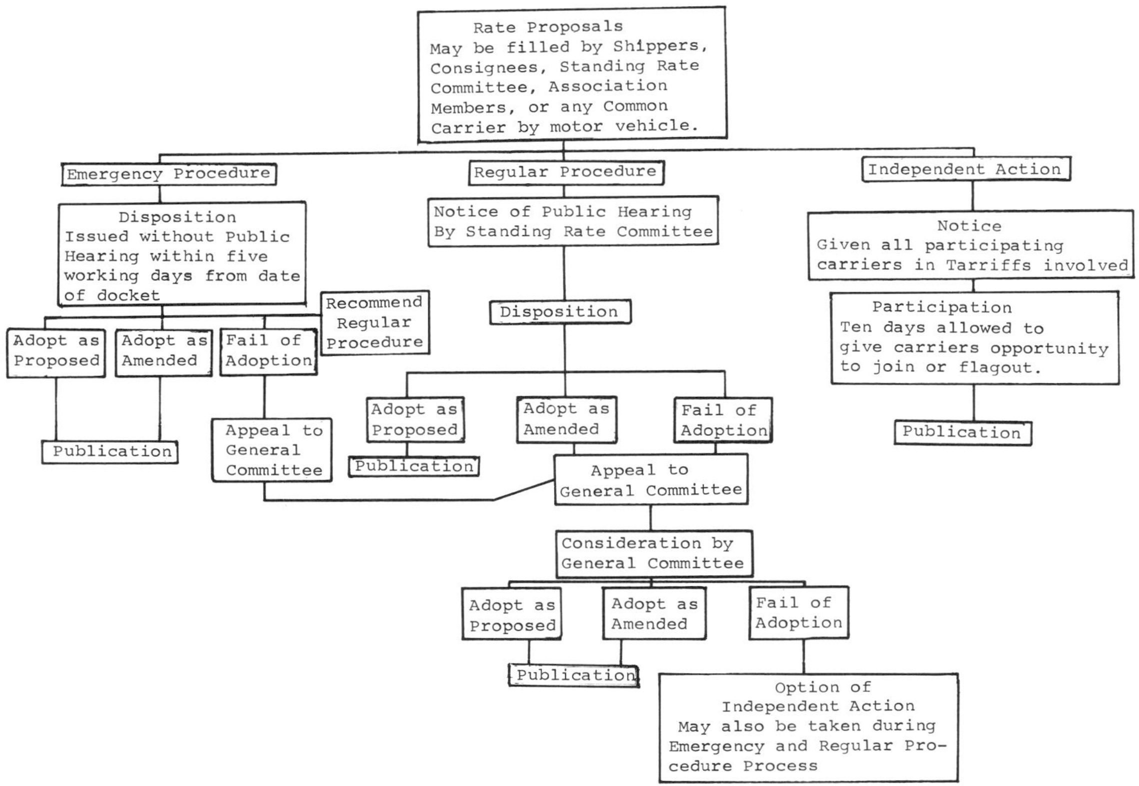

published by member carriers with which it disagrees. A recent study by Grant H. Davis and Charles S. Sherwood, however, conclusively demonstrated that a majority of independently published rates were not protested by bureaus, and considerable price sensitivity exists in the regulated segment of the transportation industry.[34]

Conference rate making is essential if through routes and joint rate proposals are to be processed in an orderly manner. Carrier managers in the rail and motor industries must be aware of all proposed changes to protect their firm's market position. By carefully analyzing docket bulletins for proposed modifications, carrier managers can support favorable dockets or strive to reject unfavorable proposals.[35] In short, management must be cognizant of any change that can potentially affect their firm's transportation markets.

As previously indicated, freight rates are published in tariffs that are important to the management team of any carrier because of their impact on commodity movements and profits. Perhaps one of the most significant marketing tools available to carrier managers is price. By increasing or decreasing price, carrier managers can affect the location of manufacturing concerns and influence the utilization of raw materials.[36] But it is imperative that carrier pricing specialists analyze in detail the effect of a transportation price increase or decrease and their customers' ability to shift or absorb any increase in price, since their geographical market size can be changed. This form of analysis represents the quintessence of carrier price strategy.

Fundamentally, there are four types of rate increases that carrier managers in all forms of transportation should be concerned with: general, specific, percentage, and flat, or some combination of each of these. In general rate increase, prices are raised on all commodities, while a specific increase pertains only to certain commodities. General increases tend to ignore transportation demand in an aggregate sense and frequently result in substantial diversions of traffic.[37] A percentage increase entails increasing a rate by a certain percentage, whereas a flat increase involves raising a freight rate by a flat amount.

Shippers of expensive commodities generally oppose percentage increases, and industrial shippers of inexpensive goods normally prefer flat increases. For example, if a shipper of color television sets is at present paying a freight rate of $10.00 per cwt., while a shipper of gravel pays $1.00 per cwt., a 10 percent increase would result in the television set rate being raised $1.00 and the gravel rate being increased only $0.10. Conversely, a flat increase of $0.10 per cwt. would increase the television set rate to $10.10 and the gravel rate to $1.10, resulting in a substantially disproportionate share being borne by the inexpensive goods.

Inflation and rapidly rising labor and capital costs have exerted upward pressure on carrier cost structures, and rates have been increasing during the past decade. Before seeking a rate increase, carrier managers should carefully analyze demand and supply elasticity for their customers' products. This analysis is important if the individual transportation firm is attempting to strategically develop a meaningful and viable price policy. Generally speaking, if a carrier's customers' final product has a relatively inelastic demand, any reasonable increase can be shifted to the ultimate consumer in the form of higher product prices. Other things being equal, of course, rates can be increased on this kind of traffic, whereas customers having elastic product demand (unless they have fixed cost, large profits, or excess capacity) normally cannot shift any increase in freight rates.

When possible, carrier managers should carefully evaluate their customers' supply of materials regarding any proposed rate increase. If a given customer has a relatively elastic supply, rate increases can be shifted to the ultimate consumer because the firm can react swiftly to changing market conditions. On the other hand, if the customer is faced with an inelastic supply, a given rate increase cannot be shifted.

One effective marketing strategy involving price that should be employed involves shifting a carrier's customers' geographical market area. For example, freight rates frequently represent the only significant difference in selling costs between two market areas. The price of shoes in Oklahoma City and Memphis is virtually the same from the same manufacturer located in Chicago. Other things being equal, a zone of indifference exists between the two cities as salesmen for the two business organizations seek to sell their wares in cities located between Oklahoma City and Memphis. If the delivered price of a pair of shoes includes a \$3.00 freight rate at the zone of indifference, the geomarket structure is shown in Figure 6.4.

By carefully examining his cost-revenue structure, a carrier can shift this zone through rate reductions. By reducing rates, for example, from Oklahoma City to intermediary points in commodity or exception tariffs to \$2.50, the zone of indifference can be shifted toward Memphis, or vice versa. Through his ability to set price, a carrier manager can directly influence a firm's location decision as well as expand its geomarkets. In short, carrier managers must employ price strategy to assist their customers' financial positions as well as to increase their own profit revenue situation.

SUMMARY

Price represents one of a transportation firm's important marketing variables and should be used in a strategic manner. Transportation pricing in the regulated segment of the industry is highly institutionalized. Even so, carrier managers should use conference

FIGURE 6.4

Effect on Geomarkets of Lowering Freight Rates

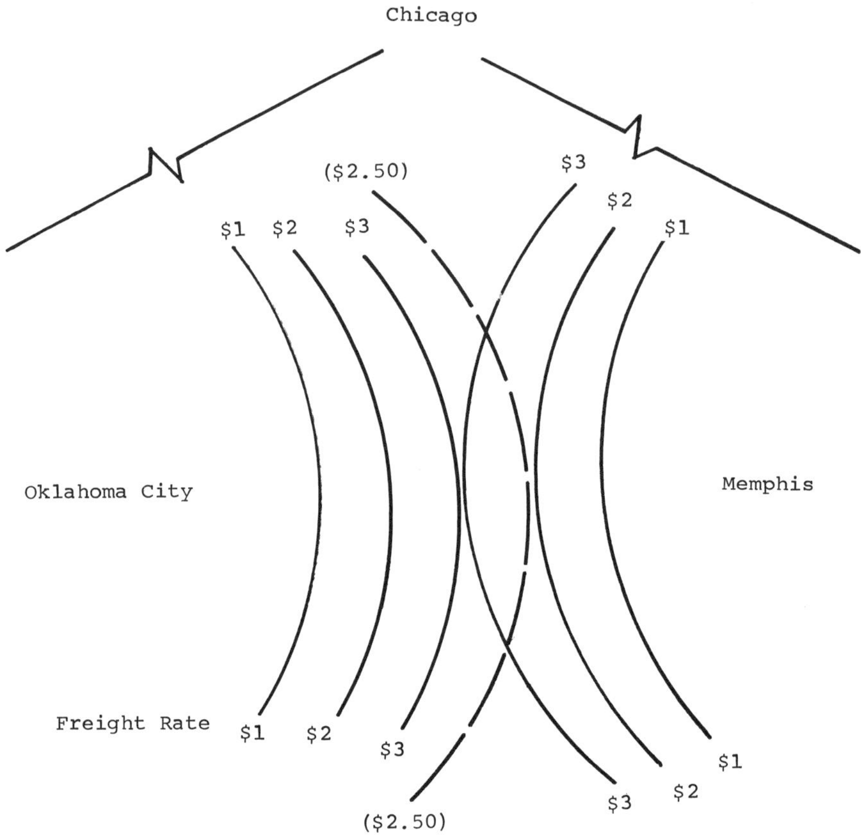

rate making procedures as part of an overall, well-developed marketing plan. We have developed here the economic theory of rate making and examined rate bureaus and geomarket price strategy. Carrier managers for all transportation firms should analyze their customers' price-shifting ability and geographical marketing territories in order to establish a realistic and meaningful price strategy. Further application of these concepts will be discussed in Chapter 9.

NOTES

1. 49, USC, sec. 1. Also, see Grant M. Davis and Alvin Swimmer, "A Methodological Approach for Evaluating Transportation Rate Increases," I.C.C. Practitioners' Journal, March-April 1973, pp. 308-25, for an in-depth probe of rate reasonableness.

2. 49, USC, sec. 5.

3. One analyst, in attempting to estimate the total number of freight rates in the United States, found 1,440,000 quintillion possible rates. See Herbert O. Whitten, "Why Freight Rates Must be Computerized," Modern Transportation: Selected Readings, 1st ed., Martin T. Farris and Paul T. McElhiney, eds. (Boston: Houghton Mifflin Co., 1967), pp. 316-26.

4. D. Philip Locklin, Economics of Transportation, 7th ed., (Homewood, Ill.: Richard D. Irwin, 1972), pp. 160-62.

5. One of the principal problems in transportation pricing evolves from the fact that the sales units and output units are separate. For an extensive discussion of output unit problems, see George W. Wilson, Essays on Unsettled Questions in the Economics of Transportation (Bloomington, Ind.: Foundation for Economic and Business Studies, 1962), pp. 31-78.

6. For some significant essays regarding the importance of demand elasticity to transportation pricing, see Merton J. Peck, "Competitive Policy for Transportation" in The Crisis of the Regulatory Commissions, Paul W. MacAvoy, ed. (New York: W. W. Norton and Co., 1970), p. 74; F. W. Taussig, "A Contribution to the Theory of Railway Rates," Quarterly Journal of Economics, vol. 5 (1891), p. 438; and Grant M. Davis and Linda Combs, "Some Observations Regarding Value-of-Service Pricing in Transportation," Transportation Journal, Fall 1974, pp. 1-12.

7. Grant M. Davis, "F.O.B. Terms--A Decision-Making Framework for Purchasing Management," Journal of Purchasing (February 1970), pp. 31-43.

8. George W. Wilson, "The Effect of Rate Regulation on Resource Allocations in Transportation," American Economic Review, May 1964, pp. 196-97, has a good discussion of this problem.

9. Davis, op. cit.

10. Grant M. Davis, "Managerial Techniques for Controlling Premium Transportation Charges," Journal of Purchasing, November 1971, p. 26; and Hugh S. Norton, Modern Transportation Economics, 2nd ed. (Columbus, Ohio: Charles E. Merrill, 1971), Chapter 5.

11. Dudley F. Pegrum, Transportation, 3rd ed. (Homewood, Ill.: Richard D. Irwin, 1973), Chapter 8 contains an excellent discussion of the problem of cost allocation.

12. James C. Nelson, Railroad Transportation and Public Policy (Washington, D.C.: The Brookings Institution, 1959), pp. 332-35; John R. Meyer, et al., The Economics of Competition in the Transportation Industries (Cambridge: Harvard University Press, 1959), p. 181; and Thomas G. Moore, Freight Transportation Regulation (Washington, D.C.: American Enterprise Institute for Public Policy Research, 1972), p. 52, to name a few of the critics of value-of-service pricing.

13. It is this feature of value-of-service rate making that many economists find objectionable.

14. David C. Nelson, "Demand Elasticity: Relevance to Railroad Ratemaking Philosophy," I.C.C. Practitioners' Journal, March-April 1972, pp. 375-85, poses this significant question.

15. In Charles A. Taff's Management of Physical Distribution, 5th ed. (Homewood, Ill.: Richard D. Irwin, 1972), Chapter 15, an excellent introduction to the complexity of establishing freight rates is presented.

16. Source: Glenn L. Shinn, Reasonable Freight Rates (Washington, D.C.: The Traffic Service Corporation, 1952), Chapters 6 and 8.

17. Kenneth V. Flood, Traffic Management, 2nd ed. (Dubuque, Iowa: Wm. C. Brown Co., 1965), pp. 29-39.

18. Specific types of tariffs are not examined in this chapter because of their highly technical nature. Carrier managers must be aware of how price strategies can be developed, not of tariff interpretation and construction.

19. Grant M. Davis and Phillip J. Taylor, "A Three Dimensional Approach for Locating Distribution Centers," in Papers and Proceedings (Washington, D.C.: Southern Regional Science Association, 1974), pp. 14-26.

20. G. E. Lowe, Practice and Procedure Before Rate-Making Associations (Washington, D.C.: The Traffic Service Corporation, 1967), pp. 10-62.

21. Considerable controversy existed between the two agencies for a number of years as an outgrowth of the Trans-Missouri Freight Association case in 1893.

22. 62 Stat. 479 (1948).

23. The right to exercise independent action is a condition precedent to receiving ICC approval.

24. 49, USC, sec. 5.

25. Ibid.

26. Charles A. Taff, Commercial Motor Transportation, 4th ed. (Homewood, Ill.: Richard D. Irwin, 1969), p. 352.

27. Lowe, op. cit.

28. The Central-Southern Bureau, for instance, publishes rates for motor carriers on freight moving between the Midwest and the South.

29. Trade Route 1, for example, involves water movements from U.S. Atlantic ports to East Coast South American ports. For a complete listing of all U.S. trade routes, consult ICC Dockets MC 56679, Sub 66; MC 136285, Sub 3; MC 136155, Sub 2, and MC 136230.

30. 46 USC 817 (a).

31. 49 USC 1373 (a) (c).

32. Charles A. Webb, "Reflections on the Report of Nader's Raiders," I.C.C. Practitioners' Journal, September-October 1970, pp. 943-48.

33. DOT emphasis is directed toward eliminating excess capacity in the rail industry and freeing entry into trucking, as well as changing rate rules.

34. Grant M. Davis and Charles S. Sherwood, Rate Bureaus and Anti-Trust Conflicts in Transportation: Public Policy Issues (New York: Praeger Publishers, 1975).

35. Lowe, op. cit.

36. Grant M. Davis and Stephen W. Brown, Logistics Management (Lexington, Mass.: D. C. Heath and Co., 1974), Chapter 7.

37. Locklin, op. cit., Chapters 16 and 17.

PART II

MANAGERIAL RESPONSES AND TECHNIQUES

Now that the five constraints faced by carrier management have been analyzed, our next task is to consider how carrier management responds to them. The chapters that follow consider the majority of the functions and techniques of carrier management.

In a very real sense, both responses and techniques are involved in this part. That is, each task or function is considered within the framework of the five constraints, and is therefore a response. At the same time, each task or function is discussed as a separate entity, and is therefore analyzed as a technique of carrier management.

CHAPTER

7

CONTROL AND ORGANIZATION

One of the primary concerns in carrier management is that of organization and control. In essence, there are two approaches to this subject. One concerns itself with the overall corporate structure and builds on the concepts of ownership noted in Chapter 5. The other concerns itself with internal organization and control within the corporate structure.

CORPORATE STRUCTURE

Some general comments about the overall corporate structure and its changing climate are in order before discussing the internal organizational structure of carriers. Although some of these developments were considered in the section on ownership patterns in Chapter 5, they can be reviewed here as examples of the importance of corporate structure.

One of the recent developments in the field of transport has been the formation of holding companies. This has been especially true in the case of railroads. Top management was primarily concerned with expansion into other areas in order to gain more flexibility in its operations. These holding companies have now initiated operations in such businesses as lumber, oil, steel, television and radio, and an underwear company. The inability to generate a high rate of return on investments in railroad operations prompted many such diversification efforts. There does exist a danger to the service performance of the railroad if subsidiary companies enjoy a higher rate of return and drain off needed capital from the rail operations.[1]

There have been a number of moves to allow one mode to own and operate in all modes. There is a great deal of interest in the area of common ownership, but, from a financial standpoint, there are mixed opinions.[2] The same holds true for customer service--especially for those companies shipping by several modes.

Size is important in the American business movement and mergers and acquisitions will more than likely continue to mold several companies into one large company. Business may possibly have some economies of scale in certain parts of the company, but more than likely, the problems created in structure and design that affect employees will offset many of the anticipated benefits.

Even though all railroad mergers have not been as financially successful as predicted, they will continue to occur in an effort to eliminate duplicate mileage and service. Motor carriers have been active in the merger and acquisition game, with varying degrees of success. Airlines have been less active but have enjoyed the same questionable success.

Ever present with the changing corporate structure are manpower needs. These assets are especially important in diversification efforts. Often these needs are ignored due to the overwhelming financial concerns.

Thus, a corporate structure exists, whose goals and aspirations affect the organizational structure; carrier management needs to be cognizant of this level of organization and control as well as of internal organizational structures; and, finally, carrier management needs to understand that both corporate structure and organizational structure blend into and affect one another.

ORGANIZATIONAL STRUCTURE

The organizational structure, like the larger corporate structure, develops over a period of time and has a great influence on corporate profitability. The organizational structure by itself is of little importance to the overall effectiveness of corporate profitability. A structure does mean different things to different people and can lead to the establishment of organizational relationships that may or may not be firmly developed over a period of time. Therefore, organizational structures should be designed not haphazardly, but with a great deal of concern and justification.

An organizational structure exhibits a great number of management activities. Among these are philosophy, centralization versus decentralization, decision making, various forms of internal controls, and the human (or dehumanized) aspects of management concerning supervisor relationships.

Form of Organization

The form of organization utilized by a transport firm is based on many things, including size, purpose, and philosophy of the company; the immediacy of decision making; and the general maturity of the firm. Probably the most important factor affecting the organizational structure is the management philosophy of the organizational structure.

General Organizational Philosophy

Transport firms vary considerably between and within modes in terms of their organizational philosophies. Organizational philosophy for a transport firm is firmly based on the management philosophies of the owners of the company, since they are the ones who can effectively exert influence on the management of the firm. Obviously, a single owner can do more in this regard, and do it faster, than 10 million minority shareholders.

A number of variables are involved in general organizational philosophy. These include management philosophy, delegation of authority, immediacy of decisions, maturity of the company, and industry and company appropriateness.

Management Philosophy. The way in which a management approaches the worth of a human being, the nature of the work, fringe benefits, authoritarian versus participative management, profit-center concept, and legal constraints, makes up a management philosophy. A management philosophy develops over a short period of time, and becomes firmly entrenched with the passage of time.

Individual personalities obviously play an integral role in developing transport management philosophies. Sometimes people and their ways of operating change over time, but a change in operating philosophy does not come easily.

One key aspect of management and organizational philosophy in any firm is the extent to which each management employee can realize his full potential as a manager and as an individual. The transport firm should allow these opportunities with the idea of achieving greater growth and profitability. Several factors are involved in the development of this talent; and include, in addition to the organizational philosophy, the leaders of management, the situations existing within the firm, and the individual himself.

Delegation of Authority. For an individual manager to achieve his full status as an effectively functioning manager, he must have both responsibility and the authority necessary to accomplish what he is responsible for. Carriers with a profit-center concept attempt to push both authority and responsibility to their lowest possible levels. Thus, a manager of a motor carrier terminal has full reign to succeed or fail, based on his own ability as a manager.

Decentralization of authority and decision making is an important part of a carrier's overall organizational philosophy. The extent to which delegation occurs is primarily determined by the quality of the available management and the situations in which it must conduct business.

Immediacy of Decisions. In many aspects of sales and operations, transportation firms are faced with decisions that must be made within a relatively short time span. Delegation of authority is valuable in this respect.

Some decisions, however, allow a longer time span, and can be made after a great deal of thought and consideration. The extent to which others are involved in the decision-making process will also affect the immediacy of the decision.

For example, the Japanese spend a great deal of time discussing, evaluating, and then deciding what the real question is, as opposed to Westerners, who concentrate entirely on the answer. To the Japanese, once the question is determined, the answer will fall into place accordingly.[3]

In matters relating to operating changes, terminal openings or closings, personnel changes, promotions, and general policy matters, it is best to involve more than one person in making the decision. By the very nature of these situations, a decision-making team may take considerable time in reaching the best corporate decision.[4]

Maturity of the Company. A young firm's organizational philosophies are usually not firmly established, and changes may readily occur. The same situation is also usually found in mature transport firms that are faced with financial crisis or general management stagnation.

The maturity of the firm can also be recognized by the advancement of employee benefit programs, training programs, and the existence of certain staff functions. All of these variables are a result of changing management and organizational philosophies. New management gains responsibility and feels it should exert both personal and professional influence on the future course the company will follow.

The various transport modes, in a historical perspective, are a living example of financial growth, employment, management changes, and other aspects of maturity.

Industry and Company Appropriateness. Even though management changes have been made as growth and development occur, the particular mode reflects a general organizational philosophy. A survey of organizational structure of railroads and airlines, for example, shows a larger number of staff and control functions that are not found in trucklines. This can be partially explained by the modal concerns for passengers as well as freight. It can also be expressed by other factors, such as total assets, profit margins, government subsidies, and ease of entry.

Line and Staff Form of Organization

Transport firms are organizationally structured along the same lines as most firms with both line and staff relationships. Even among the various modes, some of the same titles and functions are found, although not necessarily with the same reporting responsibility.

At the top level of the transport firm's organizational structure there is usually a corporate office structure that is concerned with the overall firm, and an officer and staff that heads up the entire operations of the firm. This corporate group usually exists whether or not that specific title is given. This is especially true in smaller companies where small numbers of managers are concerned with the progress of the total company.

The functional emphasis is visible in some firms at the top levels, but is quite difficult to observe from a purely structural point of view. An examination of the organizational structure characteristics of the various modes can help explain the nature of the line-staff structure.

Railroads. As we have noted, some railroads have organized as holding companies. This is sometimes known as "the industries approach," since the term "industries" appears in the title of the parent corporation. Obviously, many subsidiaries exist here, and many are quite large.[5]

In railroads not organized as industries and in the railroad subsidiary of industries, the internal organization typically contains four or five line and staff functions under a chief executive officer. A typical organizational structure is shown in Figure 7.1.

Under "marketing," the sales area is usually quite large, and is typically organized on a geographical basis, with district or state sales offices. Due to the interchangeability of equipment as well as the shipper's legal right to route rail cars, most railroads maintain sales offices "off-line." Hence, it is common to find sales offices and solicitors based and maintained at geographic locations some distance from the railway itself.

FIGURE 7.1

Typical Internal Organization of a Railroad

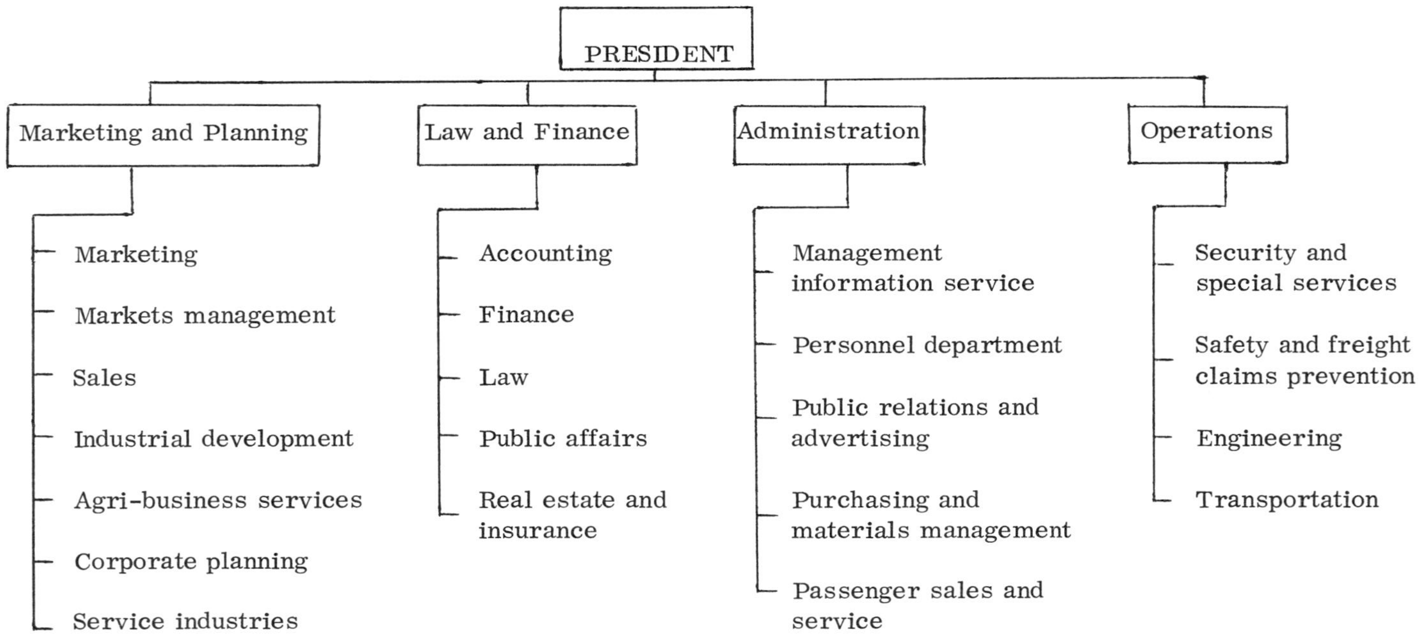

The various titles found in finance areas will vary according to the particular firm, and sometimes according to the level within the organization. For example, a finance officer may have a treasurer and a comptroller reporting to him.

The function of administration will vary greatly by railroad. Usually a number of staff departments are found under "administration," and it is common to find assistants to the president, public relations, advertising, labor relations, secretary, profit planning, purchasing and materials, taxation, and other departments. Many of these staff functions exist because the railroads are involved in so many areas of society, and because of the public visibility and regulatory emphasis placed on railroads.

"Operations" is the largest organizational area and normally includes all areas of transportation operation, including maintenance and engineering, as well as transportation itself. We will have more to say about the functions of operational management in Chapter 8, but it should be noted here that railroads have typically had a division type of operational organization. That is, the operating system is broken down geographically into divisions of a given size (originally in terms of the length of a normal journey or run of a freight train within a working day of 10 hours), and each division has its own level of supervision, such as divisional superintendent, divisional train master, or divisional maintenance.

It should be emphasized that some of the same internal organizational titles and functions will be found in other modes. However, because they came first, and because of their large corporate size, railroads have developed a more complete and complicated internal organization that most other modes of transportation.

Motor Carriers. Similar position titles are found in motor carrier organization charts, as illustrated in Figure 7.2. In the line structure are found such functions as operations, sales, finance (treasurer and comptroller), traffic, and maintenance.

Staff areas include administration, operating services, legal, assistant to the president, insurance and claims, training and personnel, industrial relations, real estate, purchasing, and planning.

Motor carriers appear to utilize the service of staff personnel less than the railroads or the airlines. This is due primarily to their size and availability of funds, rather than to their viewing the positions as unimportant. Of course, organization varies greatly among motor carrier firms.

Once again, operations involves the majority of the personnel, and in motor carriers this important function may be geographically structured, just as it is in railroads. While the term "divisions" may not always be found in motor carriers, it is common to group operations and terminal in a state or other geographic region under one supervisor.

FIGURE 7.2

Typical Motor Carrier Organizational Chart

President and Chief Executive Officer

- Vice President-Administration
- Vice President-Finance
- Vice President-Operating Service
- Executive Vice President-Operating Divisions
- Manager - Coca Cola Bottling Company, Battle Creek, Michigan
- Secretary and General Counsel — Legal Counsel
- Executive Secretary — Confidential Secretary
- Assistant to the President-Computer Services

Airlines. Airlines are more oriented towards passenger transportation than the movement of freight. This fact is generally reflected in their organizational structure, and it is common to find vice presidential offices involving safety, property and terminals, and marketing.

Line organizational areas in airlines include finance, maintenance and engineering, flight operations, marketing and sales, and ground operations. Airline staff offices include executive offices, industrial relations, public affairs, corporate development, investor relations, industry affairs, legal, and personnel.

Figure 7.3 presents a typical organizational chart of a major airline. Note that the operations area is broken down into three geographic divisions plus the important areas of maintenance and flight operations. The regional divisions are further broken down into separate line functions. Most of the staff functions are at the top level, with great attention given to the line functions in the field. Airlines, after all, primarily serve people and give great stress to the personalized nature of their service. Their public is made up of the millions of travelers with whom they deal directly during the year. Modes concerned with freight movement deal with inanimate objects (comfort is not an important factor in moving package freight, as it is in airlines, for example), and with a relatively small number of sophisticated buyers (traffic and distribution managers). These facts of transportation life are reflected in the organization of airlines.

Centralization and Decentralization

A very important part of a transport firm's management philosophy of controls and organization concerns the questions of centralization and decentralization. Deciding at what organizational levels to place the decision-making burdens has far-reaching effects on the firm's ability to operate at a profit, to attract and retain competent management, and to adopt new technology and concepts.

Size is an important factor in centralization and decentralization. Some firms are centralized in decision making when they are small, and become decentralized as they grow larger and require more specialized and complex abilities. Other firms tend towards more centralization as they grow larger, thus placing the company's future in the hands of a small group of managers in one location.

In order to fully understand the concepts of centralization and decentralization and their significance for transport firms, we will examine their definition, their advantages and disadvantages, the concept of limited decentralization, and the resulting effects of a specific course of action on managerial motivation.

FIGURE 7.3

Typical Airline Organizational Chart

- President and Chief Executive Officer
  - Executive Vice President and Chief Operating Officer
    - Eastern Division
      - Senior Vice President and General Manager
      - Vice President-Maintenance Services
      - Vice President-Property
      - Vice President-Marketing
        - Regional Vice President (4)
    - Central Division
      - Senior Vice President and General Manager
      - Vice President-Maintenance Services
      - Vice President-Property
      - Vice President-Marketing
        - Regional Vice President (1)
    - Western Division
      - Senior Vice President and General Manager
      - Vice President-Maintenance Services
      - Vice President-Marketing
        - Regional Vice President (3)
    - Maintenance Operations
      - Senior Vice President-Maintenance Operations
      - Vice President-Base Maintenance
      - Vice President-Engineering
      - Vice President-Maintenance Supply
      - Vice President-Maintenance Planning
    - Flight Operations
      - Senior Vice President-Flight Operations
      - Vice President-Eastern Division
      - Vice President-Western Division
      - Vice President-Flight Technical Services
      - Vice President-Flight Safety and Industry Affairs
      - Vice President-Flight Administrative Services
    - Vice President-System Operations Control
    - Vice President-System Personnel
      - Vice President-Personnel Services
    - Vice President-System Operations Services
      - Vice President-Facilities and Property
      - Vice President-Property
    - Vice President-System Marketing
      - Vice President-Advertising and Promotion
    - Vice President-Special Projects
  - External Affairs
    - Executive Vice President-External Affairs
      - Vice President-Industry Affairs
  - Corporate Planning
    - Senior Vice President-Corporate Planning
      - Vice President-Schedule Planning
  - Finance
    - Senior Vice President-Finance
      - Vice President and Treasurer
        - Assistant Treasurer
      - Vice President and Comptroller
      - Vice President-Purchasing
    - Vice President-Investor Relations
    - Auditor
  - Law
    - Senior Vice President-Law
      - Secretary of Corporation
      - Assistant Secretary

Source: Annual Report, United Air Lines, 1971.

Concepts Defined

Centralization means the putting together of a firm's decision-making process in one location or in one person; that is, a general office as opposed to field locations. For example, if each manager must go through a central person or office in order to purchase additional equipment, then we can say that equipment purchasing is centralized. On the other hand, if each branch location has the freedom to purchase its fuel locally, for example, we can say that fuel purchasing is decentralized.

The important point is that at either a centralized or decentralized location, someone must have the ability to decide among various alternatives. In the case of equipment purchasing, which is a complex technical area, it is probably most economical to have the expert make all the operating decisions. There are, however, less technical decisions that must be made and are still reserved for centralized decision making by a particular office or individual. This centralized decision making may even extend to outlays for company furniture, stationery, and promotional items for the field operation.

It many firms the line between centralized and decentralized decisions may be cloudy. Often a number of organizational levels exist between the branch manager and the vice president of operations, and decisions are made at each level. Some decisions, considered local ones, may require the approval of upper organizational levels before they are ultimately made. Other decisions, considered to be centrally made, can be made only after the consultation of a local branch manager.

It is difficult to specifically indicate which modes operate on a decentralized basis. Rather, one must analyze the type of decision to be made, such as purchasing, sales, operations, personnel, or acquisitions. It is common to find both centralized and decentralized decisions being made within all modes. In this regard, the personality and philosophy of the owners and managers will be reflected. It is safe to say that within each mode there will be striking differences in management philosophy and decision making.

Advantages and Disadvantages of Centralization

Advantages. The advantages of centralized decision making are often readily apparent. Normal results include more efficient management controls, quicker decisions, reduction of communication problems, and reduced costs (especially in purchasing).

By clearly pointing out that major decisions will be made by specific people, or in a specific location, the company management has established a process to be followed. It knows who or what department must account for certain expenditures or actions. By simply reducing the number of people involved in certain decisions, management places greater stress on certain individuals but does not make the decision-making process more manageable. Closer management controls in a transport firm will also be reflected in the organizational structure; the lines of responsibility, authority, and accountability; accounting controls; and the general regulatory basis under which the company must operate.

Centralization allows for decisions to be made within a short time span. Complex problems can demand and get a fast answer due to proximity of individuals and/or offices. Centralization does not force a transport firm to make decisions faster, but it does provide it with the ability to do so.

By operating on a centralized basis, the transport firm can reduce some of its communications problems, at least in the centralized location. The greater the number of management levels involved in decisions, the greater the probability of faulty communications that can ultimately affect the decision. It is also easier for one person at a centralized location to confer with other department heads for their input into the decision and get the answer from the top without burdening other levels.

A centralized function can sometimes mean a tremendous cost savings for a transport firm. By purchasing quantity, discounts involving millions of dollars annually may be available due to centralization. Equipment is expensive and can demand an annual budget ranging from a few million to hundreds of millions of dollars annually.

Disadvantages. There are also a number of disadvantages to centralized decision making. They fall more in the categories of management development, implementation of decisions, and communications.

Managers who have little opportunity to make decisions grow very slowly professionally. Decentralization allows a manager the chance to manage and develop his abilities in a corporate framework. It is difficult for a manager to truly develop if no decision-making responsibility is available. For the future, a firm should develop management talent to cope with expanding technologies, changing social conditions, and general management change within the firm. If a transport firm utilizes few people in decision-making capacities, its development of management talent is restricted.

Reduction of communications problems can be a disadvantage as well as an advantage. With decentralization, more people are involved in the decision-making process, and the risk of faulty communication is great. With centralization, few are involved, and they probably communicate very well in making decisions. However, with centralization there is a communications problem in that the majority of management is not apprised of current decisions, and usually hears about them through bulletins or company announcements. This may detract from the effectiveness of local managers, especially in dealing with customers, where information can affect their service requirements.

Effective delegation of authority goes with decentralization of decision making. This does not mean that the best decision will always be made, but it does mean that managers who are close to the problems will be involved in the decision-making process.

Limited Decentralization

In some transport firms it is possible to strike a happy medium and operate with a combination of centralized and decentralized decision making. Gaining effectiveness in decision making does not occur overnight, but comes only after philosophical and practical efforts have been made.

Some areas of the transport firm have a greater need for centralization, while others require decentralization. For example, in the areas of equipment purchasing, fuel procurement, and acquisition of computer equipment, specialists can be better informed. In the areas of sales and operations, on the other hand, it is possible to decentralize decision-making efforts to a greater extent.

Indeed, decisions made by air controllers, yard masters, and dock supervisors must be made on a local basis. Other decisions involving company policy will probably require going to a higher organizational level. This is not to say that unimportant decisions must be made on a centralized basis. Even though, from a transport firm's viewpoint, decisions do vary in their importance and effect on profits, all decisions are important to the person making them.

Managerial Motivation and Decentralization

The ability to motivate managers to achieve their full potential is one of the key elements in business success stories. Volumes have been written on the subject, but it still remains an enviable goal for many.

To allow a manager to attain his full potential, and at the same time achieve profitable growth, he must have a certain freedom of operation and decision making. Few individuals attain their full potential if they are boxed in organizationally, departmentally, or otherwise.

One way of pushing decision making further down the management ranks is through utilizing a profit-center concept. This practice is one of the many avenues that can be used to further motivate managers to both attain their full potential as managers and to contribute to the company's profitable growth.

Profit-Center Concept. A profit center can be defined as a work unit, or an easily definable group of work units, whose combined efforts can be financially and profitably evaluated. A terminal, region, division, or other field location that can be judged on a profit-and-loss basis is a good example of a profit center in transportation. Staff functions are difficult to place on a profit-and-loss basis, since they generate very little or no revenues and are constantly expending funds. In many cases, a part of the terminal profit-and-loss statement reflects administration costs incurred in a corporate headquarter location.

Advantages of Profit Centers. Profit centers, in a transport framework, have a number of motivational advantages for company management and may help managers achieve partial or full utilization of their management abilities. One of these motivational advantages is in delegation of authority and responsibility. With the profit-center concept, the local manager has the major decision-making responsibility for the profitable operation of his terminal. He can operate according to his own ability to control or partially control his operating environment. Within his range of authority and responsibility he has the feeling of running his own company.

The psychological advantages here are important. The manager feels the stress that coincides with his profit-center position. He may have more of a personal interest in effectively solving his local problems, and more pride in accepting praise for a job well done. There is also pride in the fact that his company has the confidence in him to allow him to run a profit center.

Another advantage is in the development of management talent. The profit-center concept allows more managers to make meaningful decisions, and thus the transport firm is developing its own management talent for future growth and expansion. Well-rounded management talent is maintained and enriched when decisions are concerned with all aspects of profitable operations, including labor, personnel, equipment, overtime, sales, office functions, revenue projections, and claims prevention. This example of management development is similar to the farm-club concept in professional baseball, where both the players and coaches build experience, and records, for future growth and responsibility.

A manager who is motivated to profitably manage a terminal may be managing several terminals in the future. Although he is receiving a very general education, he could possibly be able to fill a specialized staff role in the future as well. The profit-center concept, as an organizational device, produces profits, but its prime advantage to the transport firm is its role as a motivational variable for management action and growth.

Forms of Control

There are many management controls that affect the transport firm. Controls are both internal and external, and will vary from company to company and from one mode to another. Some of the forms control takes include ownership, organizational structure, regulation, accounting, and public consciousness.

Ownership

The owners of a transport firm will have a definite impact on the performance of the company. The ownership, whether widespread or limited, will determine policy and sometimes day-to-day decisions. Ownership philosophy regarding all aspects of management practice will permeate the firm. This impact will be noticeably evident in the financial transactions of the firm.

Organizational Structure

Earlier in this chapter we dealt with the forms of organization and how they can affect the firm. The extent of decentralization of decision making can also have ramifications for company action. The organizational structure itself is an important control function of ownership and/or management, and it also reflects their management philosophy.

Regulatory Controls

The transportation industry has a long history of regulatory controls, as we have described in Chapter 2. These controls affect all areas of the firm's operations. Indeed, we have called regulation a major constraint on management. Obviously, regulation is a form of control.

Accounting Controls

The ICC has accounting controls and requirements for reporting for all transport firms. The uniformity of reporting is most important for evaluation of financial performance and ability to perform shipper service requirements.

Each mode also has a number of internal financial controls that they observe daily to determine company profitability. These internal accounting controls are centered in profit figures and are composed of several cost variables. The variables will normally include terminal costs, line-haul costs, clerical and office costs, administration costs, maintenance costs, and passenger support costs. These cost categories and makeup will vary from one company to another and from one mode to another, but they do constitute one important form of control for decision-making purposes.

Public Consciousness

One form of control that is ever present in the transport firm is the public consciousness. The public has a major interest in a viable transportation system and has a watchful eye on efficiency. Carriers must meet shipper performance standards and satisfy passengers. All modes must be concerned about noise and air pollution (as well as other pollution effects), and safety standards are vitally important. The public image of a transport firm may merit thousands or millions of dollars in public relations efforts. The public's concern is one form of indirect control on the transport industry.

Span of Management

The span of management is a very important part of a transport firm's organizational framework. "Span of management" refers to the number of areas of responsibility a manager has in his job function. In most cases these job responsibilities are represented by various levels of management.

Management textbooks of the past attempted to use a rule-of-thumb number as the guideline for a manager to determine how many people should report to him. This rule-of-thumb usually varied from six to ten managers. Transport firms, as well as industrial firms, normally held to this rule, and many still do.

Later research and writing pointed out that the manager's own ability to manage and his other management characteristics are of pivotal importance in determining how many managers should report to him. The specific job functions and the immediacy of decisions were also felt to be important in this consideration.

For example, one transport manager may be capable of having 12 individuals report to him, while another has the ability to effectively work with only four individuals. A misplaced manager may have insurmountable problems if he has too many individuals reporting to him.

The span of management is significant for the transportation industry. All modes have been tradition-bound and are likely to have a number of ineffective managers who cannot work in their present span. These situations are found throughout the organizational structure. Talents are being underutilized as well, where managers have five individuals reporting to them when they can effectively handle more. The span of management may vary according to the specific organizational level in transport firms. The span may also vary between line and staff support functions.

A number of corporations have successfully flattened their organizational structure and drastically changed their span of management. In a recent example of pruning away management layers, one firm eliminated 10 jobs, from vice president on up, and cut salaried employment by 17 percent. In its present structure this firm now has 10 operating managers and 10 staff specialists reporting to the president and chief executive officer. The chief executive pointed out that the kind of people you surround yourself with has a great deal to do with determining how many people can report to any one man.[6]

Allied Managerial Concepts

There are a number of management concepts that are closely involved in span of management in a transport firm. We will indicate important concepts, and give a brief description of their significance.

Linking Pin

The linking-pin function basically stated is that the supervisor in one group is a follower in another group. While he must be effectively supervising a group of managers, he is also serving as a manager in another group.[7] A diagramatic presentation of the linking-pin concept is shown in Panel "A" of Figure 7.4. The reader should note that each group or triangle of functions reports to a "linking pin" who is a member of another group or triangle of managers higher up in the organizational structure.

Effective communications is an objective within span of supervision, and communications is also important in span of supervision. The leader must exert influence both upward and downward in the organization.[8]

The following characteristics of the linking-pin function are relevant for the transportation industry:

FIGURE 7.4

Management Concepts

PANEL A
LINKING PIN CONCEPTS

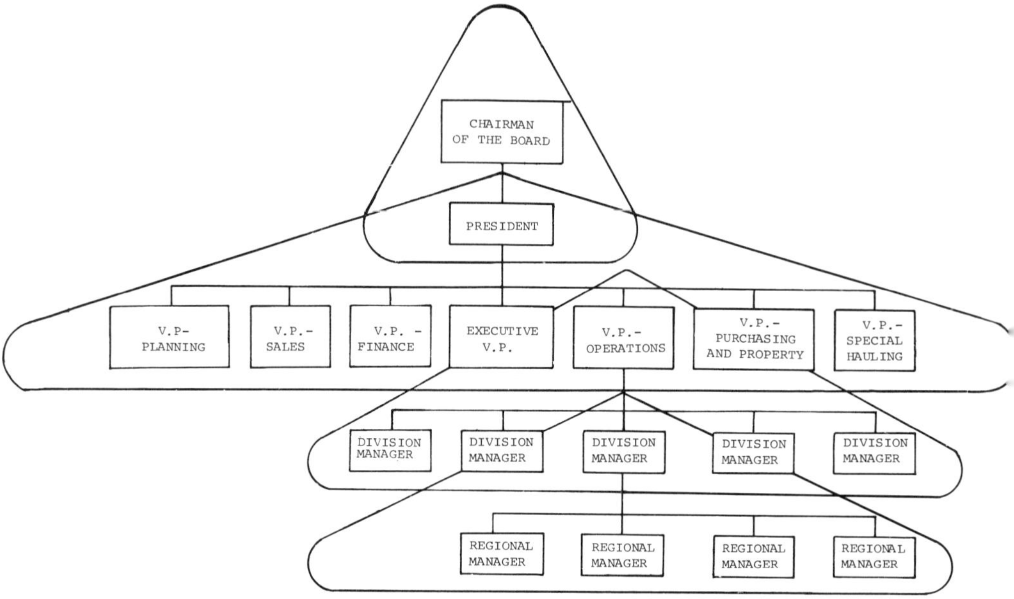

PANEL B
MAN-TO-MAN STRUCTURE

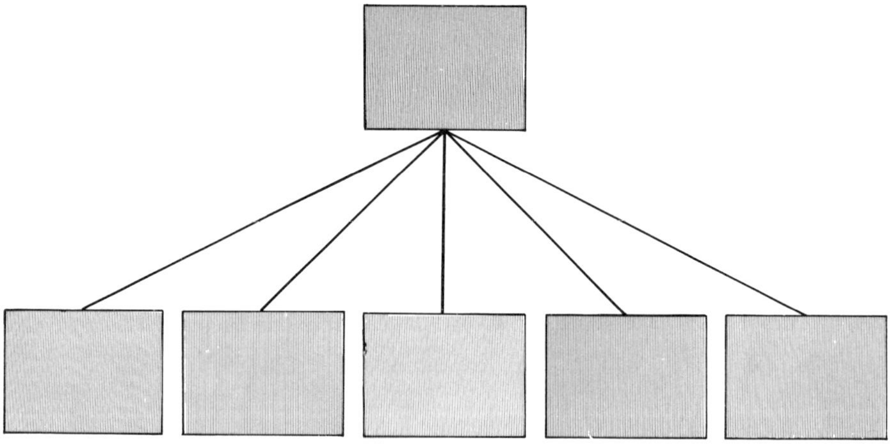

> If an organization is to derive the full benefit from its highly effective group they must be linked to the total organization by means of overlapping groups.
>
> The potential power of the overlapping group form of organization will not be approached until all of the groups of the organization are functioning reasonably well.
>
> The higher an ineffective group in the hierarchy, the greater the adverse effect of its failure on the performance of the organization. To help maintain an effective organization, it is desirable for superiors not only to hold group meetings of their own subordinates but also to have occasional meetings over two hierarchical levels. An organization takes a serious risk when it relies on a single linking pin or a single linking process to tie the organization together.[9]

Man-to-Man Organization Structure

In the man-to-man organization structure, the span of supervision is to and from specific individuals, and they are not considered a part of the work group.[10] A diagrammatic presentation of the man-to-man organization structure is shown in Panel B of Figure 7.4.

The major distinction between the linking-pin concept and the man-to-man structure is that the former deals with groups while the latter deals with individuals. The poor communicator can use the man-to-man structure, since he does not have to be concerned with a single work group, but rather with a number of individuals. It may not be possible for the transportation manager to convince his followers that they should work as a group. In this regard, the leader, the followers, and the situation will be the most important considerations.

Management by Objectives

The process of management by objectives is basically one whereby

> . . . the superior and the subordinate managers of an enterprise jointly identify its common goals, define each individual's major

> areas of responsibility in terms of the results expected of him and use these measures as guides for operating the unit and assessing the contribution of each of its members.
>
> . . . it is not an easy task to integrate the goals and objectives of all individuals with the goals of the organization. Yet it is not an impossible task. An approach to this problem which has been used successfully in some organizations in our cultures is a process called management by objectives.[11]

A transport manager has a good chance of being successful with his subordinates when using these techniques. Management by objectives allows him to successfully work with individuals and work groups on common objectives.[12]

Participative Management

Although participative management has proved to be a positive technique, transportation managers have not completely endorsed this approach to supervisory-subordinate relationships. A great deal of communicating and listening are involved in this process. It can be an effective method in a manager's relationship to his subordinates, since he can get to know each subordinate and his personal ideas and concerns, learn the abilities of each manager, and identify areas of improvement, while allowing them to participate in decisions that affect them.

Consensus Decision Making

Consensus decision making is concerned with group decisions involving total agreement or total disagreement by the entire group. The makeup of the decision-making group is obviously quite important, in that a number of individuals with varying qualifications will be focusing on one problem area. This approach to decision making in transport firms involves participative management, work groups, the linking-pin concept, and management by objectives.[13]

Consensus decision making is usually found at the top organizational levels of a firm. This does not mean that consensus decisions cannot be made at lower organizational levels. The transport firms using this method usually apply it to decisions in policy areas. Corporate goals and objectives, marketing strategy, serious personnel matters, the opening of a new terminal or territory, financial concerns such as a revolving credit agreement, new acquisitions, and top level promotions, are a few areas in which consensus decisions could be made. Day-to-day decisions, which must be made on the local level in order for a transport firm to continue to operate, will have to be made on a different (probably rigid) time span, and many are not of a policy nature.

One obvious question about consensus decision making is that of what happens if the group cannot reach a decision. The time frame for a decision is important. Policy decisions of long-lasting significance cannot be made on the spur of the moment, and usually require more time than daily operational decisions. A transport firm operating on this basis will normally not allow time to be a prime consideration in the decision to be made. It will then postpone making any decision until subsequent corporate actions change the opinion of the work group that has not agreed or disagreed up to that point. Hasty decisions in policy matters have usually proved unsatisfactory.

The span of management as a part of control and organization in a transport firm involves many aspects of management and decision making. The individual manager and his subordinates, as well as the conditions of the situation in which they must operate, are the prime variables in determining how many subordinates a manager can have. There are a number of management concepts that the leader must use, be aware of, and be a part of.

SUMMARY

The student of transportation must also be a student of management in order to be successful and effective. He must be able to know and understand management concepts and principles and then be able to apply them to his day-to-day business operations. Control and organization are two very important management concepts that are a part of, and are related to, many other concepts.

Forms of organization provide a philosophical basis from which to begin, as the owner, and manager, will spread their thoughts and ideas throughout the organization. They will also shape their philosophy on the basis of modal economic concepts and differences in operating procedures.

The extent to which decisions are pushed to lower organizational levels determines the extent to which managers are allowed to manage. Certain corporate functions may, at the same time, be performed more satisfactorily if they remain centralized.

The organization structure is a serious form of control in that it requires certain reporting procedures among the management ranks. Cost controls and corresponding reporting practices involve the accounting of a transport firm and also the communications efforts, since information must be utilized for many decisions. The nature of transportation as regulated causes other controls as well.

The span of supervision relates to control and organization, because it deals with the number of supervisors a manager can handle effectively. This ability is both corporate and individual--corporate, because of the company philosophy and structure, and individual, based on the leader and his own managerial abilities.

For a transport firm to operate on a profitable basis, it must be appropriately organized and controlled. This is indeed a delicate balance, and no one set of organizational structures and control mechanisms is appropriate for all transportation carriers or modes.

NOTES

1. L. L. Waters, "The Changing Structure of Transportation in the Remainder of the Century," Business Horizons, December 1970.

2. John L. Weller, "The Intermodal Transportation Company--Dream or Nightmare for Investors" (Remarks presented at the American Society of Traffic and Transportation Annual Meeting, Pennsylvania State University, September 10, 1971).

3. Peter F. Drucker, "What We Can Learn from Japanese Management," U.S./Japan Outlook, Fall 1971.

4. Jack J. Holder, Jr., "Decision Making by Consensus--The Experience at Yellow Freight," Business Horizons, April 1972, pp. 47-54.

5. For a visual representation of a typical "industries" organization in railroads, see the 1971 Annual Report of Santa Fe Industries, Inc.

6. "Kaiser Aluminum Flattens Its Layers of Brass," Business Week, February 24, 1973, pp. 81-84.

7. Rensis Likert, New Patterns of Management (New York: McGraw-Hill, 1971), p. 65.

8. Holder, op. cit.

9. Likert, op. cit.

10. Holder, op. cit., p. 51.

11. Paul Hersey and Kenneth H. Blanchard, Management of Organizational Behavior (Englewood Cliffs, N.J.: Prentice-Hall, 1969), p. 118.

12. George S. Odiorne, Management by Objectives (New York: Pitman Publishing Corp., 1970), p. 145.

13. Holder, op. cit., pp. 47-54.

CHAPTER

8

OPERATIONAL MANAGEMENT

Even though no one organizational structure is appropriate for all transportation carriers, every transportation carrier is organized in such a fashion that various work functions are performed. That is to say, specific managerial responsibilities for line-haul, concentration-dispersion, shipment service, vehicle service, interchange, and supportive staff functions, are normally assigned. The combination of these six essential activities constitutes the fundamental operations of air, motor, rail, water, forwarder, pipeline, and express carriers.[1]

Efficiency and productivity in transportation are dependent entirely on the success or failure in the performance of operational functions. It should be understood that the majority of transportation personnel will be involved in these operational undertakings. Moreover, these functions are the very basis of transportation itself. After all, it is the operational function that moves the freight and passengers and fulfills the essential role of transportation in the economy.

LINE-HAUL FUNCTION

One of a transportation carrier's principal activities concerns the line-haul function, that is, moving consignments from one point to another. This function, of course, creates place utility. From an operation-managerial perspective, dispatching carrier operators constitutes an important function of a firm's fast and efficient service. In the motor carrier industry, for example, over-the-road drivers are not allowed to operate for more than 10 hours, and then must have eight hours of rest.[2] Federal safety laws, administered by the Bureau of Motor Carrier Safety, not only pertain to placarding vehicles moving commodities and reflector configuration, but also deal with driver qualification, health, and laws of service. Driver logs must be maintained, and fixed-base operations require the geographic spacing of terminals in such a fashion that average speed enables drivers to reach their destinations within definite time constraints.[3]

Aviation line-haul activities consist of trips between cities. Some of these may be short trips, such as from Memphis to Little Rock, while others may be transcontinental routes, such as between New York and Los Angeles. Once more the dispatcher may be the manager here. In the airline industry, aircraft and pilot certification is rigorous, and high standards must be maintained to comply with FAA rules and regulations. FAA programs that affect line-haul aviation functions must be complied with. These requirements stipulate, first of all, regular maintenance programs for aircraft and component parts. Second, the agency maintains systems for recording aircraft, and a carrier cannot operate a craft without prior registration. Third, research and development are important FAA activities that affect carrier safety and reliability, and hence dependability. Fourth, the agency operates and maintains air navigation facilities--prerequisites to intercity travel by air. Finally, air space and air traffic management are supervised by the FAA. Without sophisticated air traffic control techniques, orderly air service would be virtually impossible. As an example of the effects of such operational regulations, in 1972, American Airlines pilots consumed their time allotment during the first 26 days of December, and, over the heavily traveled New Year's weekend, many flights were cancelled because of pilot shortage.

Line-haul operations in the domestic railroad industry are unique. That is, line-haul freight crews operate for eight hours or 100 miles, whichever comes first. Although controversial, this particular work rule requires spacing crews at fixed intervals along certain routes. Line-haul operations performed by both motor and rail carriers may entail stop-offs for partial loading and unloading or stopping-in-transit for milling, storage, and processing, in addition to the providing of specialized equipment.[4]

Water transportation carriers perform line-haul services through a variety of specialized equipment. Great Lakes carriers, for example, use package freighters and giant ore vessels in servicing their highly segmented and seasonal market. Intercoastal transportation firms use a variety of equipment, from tramp freighters to sophisticated LASH vessels. Inland water carriers, moreover, provide line-haul services in barges and other tow configurations.

Petroleum product pipelines provide dependable delivery of gasoline products. Line-haul movements are planned by placing high octane gasoline in the pipe followed by lower grade product. When diverted at destination to individual tanks, the interface between products is returned to the refinery for recooking.

Another important dimension of the line-haul function is the moving and preparing of the crews and individual operators. That is, the operations of motor, air, rail, and water transportation are dependent not only on labor and resource dictated schedules, but also on seasonal factors. Weather and other inclement conditions can directly affect line-haul operations, and operator preparation becomes important.

Communication constitutes yet another important segment of the line-haul module. Railroads and motor carriers use radios, telephones, and teletype instrumentalities for rapid and efficient communications. In the aviation industry, sophisticated communication systems using radar, omni, and radio navigation equipment are required for efficient and safe service.

CONCENTRATION AND DISPERSION FUNCTION

Consolidating and dispersing freight shipments and passengers is an important and pivotal operational function for transportation organizations. The speed and efficiency with which goods are concentrated and delivered from terminal areas substantially affects the overall profitability of any carrier operation. In the motor carrier industry, consignments must be picked up, transferred to line-haul trailers, unloaded onto delivery trailers at destination, and then unloaded at final destination.[5]

The key to increased productivity in all facets of freight transportation is handling. For several years, "pups" were employed by motor carriers to reduce aggregate handling costs.[6] Small detachable vans were used on regular pickup runs and all of the freight destined for the same city was loaded into the same van. At the terminal areas, pneumatic jacks were used to lift the vans, and a special frame was intersected for traveling to the destination terminal, where the pups were again placed on city tractors for delivery.

Approximately 70 percent of the freight handled by general commodity motor carriers is adaptable to special conveyer systems. The remaining 30 percent, of course, requires specialized equipment, such as fork lifts. After one major motor carrier recently constructed a highly automated break-bulk terminal in Kansas, productivity per man-hour increased from 1,800 to 3,600 pounds.

Primary concentration and dispersion activities in aviation freight focuses on containerization and automated handling systems, particularly for larger aircraft such as the Boeing 747 and the DC-10. Because airline freight rates are published from airport to airport, airlines rely primarily on local cartage operators and motor carriers for pickup and delivery service to and from the freight staging area. In this regard, productivity efforts concerning concentration and dispersion are the same as those previously discussed in the section dealing with motor carriers.

In the passenger side of air transportation, the concentration and dispersion function is carried on by the passenger himself. However, considerable labor is involved in the ticket-checking, seat arrangement, and reservation and luggage-handling portion of the air passenger movement.

Water transportation firms have witnessed a dramatic change in their concentration and dispersion activities. Rapid conveyor and air pressure loading and unloading systems are being installed rapidly. Innovations such as LASH and containerships have substantially increased maritime productivity during the past decade. Highly automated systems, moreover, facilitate the supertanker's success in the deep-water carrier industry.

In rail transportation, fully automated yards based on gravity systems are being installed for assembling and disassembling freight trains. Also, computer oriented scan systems are being employed to obtain exact train location status in order to better utilize equipment and hence increase productivity.[7] Although loading and unloading problems are experienced by rail carriers, shippers load and unload most rail consignments. Of course, the switching or spotting of cars is a part of the concentration and dispersion function.

One important problem confronting carrier managers responsible for the dispersion and concentration function is detention of equipment by shippers and receivers. This problem, of course, severely penalizes carriers. To reduce delays, rail, motor, and barge carriers maintain demurrage and detention tariffs that are designed to increase the release of equipment.

While the discussion above deals primarily with the modal, it should be emphasized that the concentration and dispersion function is often intermodal. Trucks are typically used to pick up and deliver freight over the city streets, while the line-haul movement may be by rail, water, air, or motor carrier. Buses, taxis and limousines, and private automobiles, once more using the city streets, provide concentration at, or dispersion from, air terminals and rail depots. With the exception of unit loads (such as carloads and bargeloads), most shipments experience intermodal concentration and dispersion.

SHIPMENT SERVICE FUNCTIONS

The shipment service function may be considered from two viewpoints--human shipments and freight shipments. In the area of passenger transportation, emphasis is placed on passenger services such as ticketing and reservations. Indeed, Amtrak has only recently started using confirmed reservation systems and accepting credit cards--a practice long employed in the for-hire airline industry. Sophisticated computer systems for passenger reservations have been in use for more than a decade in commercial air transportation. Although plagued by the ubiquitous no-show problem, severe criticism has been levied at the industry in the area of overbooking flights. Finally, motor bus ticketing has not changed in recent years.

Domestic intercity freight transportation is regulated for the most part, and must conform to various legal rules. One of the more important shipment service functions performed by regulated common carriers is establishing contractual arrangements through the use of bills of lading. These legal documents can be traced back to antiquity and were used during the course of normal business by early Mediterranean merchants.[8] A bill of lading is essentially a contract of carriage between carriers and shippers and serves three fundamental functions: documentary evidence of title, contract of carriage, and receipt for the goods.

Contractual terms varied substantially from carrier to carrier prior to 1916, because individual carriers issued their own bills of lading, and carriers frequently entered into special agreements to avoid liability. That is, if a shipment were destroyed or damaged on a joint movement involving two or more railroads, the claimant was forced to file a claim against each of the participating carriers. This ambiguity was corrected by the Carmack Amendment of 1906. Although liable under common law in most instances, the Bill of Lading Act of 1916 contained several exemptions. Lastly, the ICC can prescribe the exact form of bills of lading to be used by carriers subject to its jurisdiction.

There are five principal categories of bills of lading. The domestic uniform bill of lading can be either of a straight or an order variety. Not only does a straight bill of lading specify shipment from one consignor to one consignee, but it is also nonnegotiable. A straight bill, moreover, may be either a short or a long form. The former states that the shipper is familiar with all of the terms and conditions of carriage even though they are omitted from the contract, whereas the latter has the complete contract terms on the back of the document. Both forms, however, contain routings, shipper number, consignor, consignee, number of packages, article description, weight, and other pertinent information. Even though carriers are legally obligated to issue bills of lading, most large shippers provide their own forms.

An order bill of lading is normally issued when a supplier is concerned with a customer's credit or when the goods are shipped before they are sold. The principal difference between a straight and an order bill of lading is that the latter is negotiable. For example, when a vendor is undertain about a customer's financial ability, the original order bill of lading will be turned over to the consignee only when the amount of money stipulated on the invoice has been paid. A rail, water, freight forwarder, or motor carrier is prohibited from delivering an order to notify shipment until the original paid invoice and order bill of lading have been presented. Since the order bill is negotiable, the banking system can be used, and a draft can be drawn on the consigner's bank account. Should the original order bill be lost or not forwarded to the destination bank before the shipment arrives, the consignment can be delivered if the receiver can show title, or presents the carrier with a certified bank cashier check equal to 125 percent of the property value. Several restrictions against the use of order bills of lading exist.[9]

Order bills of lading are also used when goods are to be sold enroute. In this case, the shipper has the bill of lading made out to the order of himself. Upon sale of the goods, he merely endorses the order bill so that the consignee can claim the goods. Order bills facilitate the shipment of perishable goods in this manner and the carrier reconsigns (and sometimes diverts) the shipment to the new owner.

A uniform through export bill of lading is similar to the domestic uniform bill of lading; that is, the bill can be either straight or to order. This particular form of contract consists of three major segments: point of origin to port, port to port, and port to destination. Uniform through export bills of lading are restricted to Orient destined shipments moving through West Coast ports. Carrier managers must be aware, however, that all parties participating in the movement are not necessarily bound to the contract in the event that loss or damage is encountered.[10]

Another form of contract is the uniform livestock bill of lading. The major difference between this form of contract and the domestic uniform bill is that the consignor is not required to declare a financial value for the livestock. Also, in the absence of carrier negligence, no liability occurs in the event of losses or injuries due to overcrowding. Furthermore, the carrier is required to provide facilities for feeding, watering, and resting livestock after 28 hours of travel. The order bill form is not found here.

The last contract for transportation is a government bill of lading. This particular form is used by agencies of the federal government and their suppliers, and the terms and conditions are similar to those contained in commercial bills of lading. When entering into a government contract care must be exercised, because collect shipments cannot be accepted.

Although air carriers are not subject to the Bill of Lading Act, the services they perform must be published in tariffs, and reasonable rates charged. The uniform air bill is issued by the original carrier or industrial user. The conditions of carriage, moreover, are printed on the back of the bill. Air carriers limit their liability for loss and damage unless additional liability coverage is purchased.

Freight bills are documents issued by carriers and are important to carrier managers for a variety of reasons. These documents show weights, commodity descriptions, number of pieces, rate, route, revenue, interline divisions, and contract terms. They are also used to reject or support claims, and to gather customer account data. Freight bills issued by railroads and airlines are interchangeable, whereas freight bills used by motor carriers must be reissued by each carrier on interline shipments.

Claims for loss and damage to shipments represent the last facet of the shipment service functions. The principal causes of claims during 1971 were loss of entire package, partial package loss, improper handling, defective or unfit equipment, temperature failure, delay, theft, concealed damage, fire, and error of employee.[11] To combat claims, railroads participate in the Freight Claim Division of the Association of American Railroads, while motor carriers cooperate with the National Freight Claim Council of the American Trucking Association. Claims are harmful to customer relations and should be disposed of promptly.

Loss and damage claims must be filed with a carrier subject to the Interstate Commerce Act within 90 days. Standardized claim briefs filed with the carrier by the consignor or consignee give detailed information about the facts surrounding the claims. The following documents must accompany the claim brief: original paid freight bill (loss or damage notation must be signed by a carrier agent), original invoice or certified duplicate, and original bill of lading. In the event that the original bill of lading or freight bill is lost, a bond of indemnity can be used. Any dispute between carrier and customer that cannot be resolved falls within the jurisdiction of federal courts, and suit must be filed within three years of claim denial. However, Congress is debating the merits of transferring this authority to the ICC. In 1972, the ICC caused carriers subject to its regulatory powers to acknowledge the receipt of each loss and damage claim, investigate the claim promptly, and dispose of the claim within a specified period or explain to the claimant the reason for any delay.[12]

There are trillions of freight rates, thousands of freight tariffs, and millions of articles shipped, so rate errors are inevitable. Regulated carriers are required by law to charge the legal applicable rate at the time of shipment. If a carrier overcharges the shipper, he is required to refund the difference between the rate charged and the legal applicable rate. Conversely, when a carrier undercharges a customer, he is legally compelled to file an undercharge claim citing tariff authority for the claim.

Overcharge and undercharge claims are annoying and can cause friction between carriers and their customers.[13] There are three basic causes for overcharge and undercharge claims. First, shippers frequently misdescribe shipments. Second, articles requiring different classifications are often banded together. Third, consignors frequently route shipments via routes that are not applicable.

When a shipper files an overcharge claim, the brief must be accompanied by the original paid freight bill or a bond of indemnity; the original invoice, or a certified copy; the original bill of lading; and tariff authority. The statute of limitations for ocean and air carriers is two years, and for carriers regulated by the ICC, three years, except for REA Express, which is six months. Overcharge and undercharge disputes involving regulated surface carriers can be appealed to the ICC in the event that no settlement can be reached by the parties involved.[14]

Besides the matter of documentation and claims, other shipment service functions performed by carriers include routing, storage and elevation, and protection from the elements, theft, and damage.

VEHICLE SERVICE FUNCTION

The vehicle service function essentially involves maintaining and storing equipment, servicing tires, cleaning equipment, fueling vehicles, and repairing equipment. Federal safety laws require that motor tractors and trailers be inspected periodically and maintained. Rigorous tire laws, moreover, preclude excessive tire wear, and hence can increase carrier costs.

Rail carriers are also subject to rigorous safety laws regarding equipment. One common railroad problem involved "hotboxing," and most rail vehicle service programs are designed to eliminate this pressing problem. All types of rolling stock are periodically removed from service and repaired, or are subjected to preventive maintenance.

Of all the modes of transportation, air carriers are subject to the most rigorous vehicle maintenance programs. Not only is the basic air frame frequently examined for stress and wear, but equipment components such as radio engines, navigation equipment, and tires, are closely monitored.

The vehicle service function is extremely important to all carriers, because service dependability is a key selling point in transportation. In this regard, management failure to carefully maintain line-haul and pickup and delivery equipment frequently results in costly downtime and eventually decreased revenues and profits.

INTERCHANGE FUNCTION

The interchange function can be either intermodal or intramodal. Because carrier operating authority is frequently fragmented, transportation carriers of the same mode often join together to provide through service by means of joint routes and through routes. For instance, a rail shipment from Fayetteville, Arkansas to Los Angeles requires joint service between the Frisco and Southern Pacific companies. Due to complete standardization of rail equipment, boxcars interchange with ease. Furthermore, switching charges are usually absorbed and per diem charges employed to encourage the rapid return of equipment.

Air carriers also provide joint service, but seldom interchange equipment. Only recently, Eastern Airlines commenced flying Braniff equipment from Atlanta to Memphis, where a Braniff crew boards and continues the flight to Denver. Pan American and Delta Air Lines also interchange equipment on some flights. In general, however, equipment interchange is not widespread in aviation.

Interchange among motor carriers has not progressed as far as interchange in rail transportation, partially because of difficulties of equipment interchange and partially because of the segmented and competitive nature of the industry. State highway regulations on weight and length are far from uniform, and equipment standardization is not as easily attained as in rail transportation. Furthermore, it is common to have competitive routes among motor carriers, as noted in Chapter 4. Typically, motor carriers enter into interline agreements to provide LTL service to areas beyond their route authority, but this often involves transloading. Truckload shipments can often be interlined without transloading, and lease charges and per diem charges exist to facilitate the interchange function.

Intramodal interchange is also an operational function. In passenger transportation, the intramodal interchange between automobile, taxi or limousine, bus, airline, and train has already been mentioned as part of the concentration and dispersion function. If the journey continues to a distant point by another mode, the function is more one of interchange, however. The same is true with freight, and it is common for shipments to interchange from one mode to another at terminals and other points. Indeed, a large number of shipments will utilize two modes, and interchange is common.

SUPPORTIVE OR STAFF FUNCTIONS

The sixth and final area of operational management is concerned with supportive staff functions. Every transportation carrier organizes work along lines by which the work is performed. In order to carry out the line-haul function, the concentration and dispersion function, shipment service, vehicle service, and interchange, a series of staff functions is necessary. These include communications, record-keeping and accounting, purchasing and procurement, insurance, legal, property management, and real estate acquisition. These activities bear directly on the other functions, and the efficiency with which they are performed affects overall profitability.

In subsequent chapters, we will be concerned with other supportive staff functions such as marketing and sales, public relations and advertising, equipment selection, finance and credit, human relations-personnel training, labor relations and bargaining, and the location of transportation operations. These warrant special treatment, either because they affect so many areas of management and are universal to all managerial decisions, or because they are special decisions that are made infrequently but have long-run effects.

NOTES

1. Many of these functions can be subdivided. For an excellent discussion of functionalism in business, see Harold Koontz and Cyril O'Donnell, Principles of Management, 4th ed. (New York: McGraw-Hill, 1968), pp. 237-60.
2. William J. Hudson and James A. Constantin, Motor Transportation (New York: Ronald Press, 1958), p. 647.
3. For an example of driver constraints and spacing, consult Grant M. Davis and Stephen W. Brown, Logistics Management (Lexington, Mass.: D. C. Heath and Co., 1974), pp. 166-68.
4. An examination of the national rail car fleet reveals a substantial increase in specialized, assigned cars.
5. Truckload consignments are normally not transloaded.

6. Pups are small trailers that are linked together for over-the-road movements, where they are then referred to as "double-bottoms."

7. See Grant M. Davis, "The Freight Car Dilemma--A Problem of Contracting Capacity," I.C.C. Practitioners' Journal, November-December 1973, pp. 23-37, for a detailed discussion of industry efforts to increase freight car distribution efficiency.

8. Roy J. Sampson and Martin T. Farris, Domestic Transportation Practice, Theory and Policy, 3rd ed. (Boston: Houghton Mifflin Co., 1975), p. 279.

9. First, an order bill cannot be issued to a prepaid station unless authorized. Second, shipments stopped in transit cannot qualify for order bills. Third, air and express contracts exclude order ship rates.

10. Recourse is against the individual carrier.

11. Traffic World, June 1972, p. 25.

12. Jesse H. Merrell, "I.C.C. Issues New Claim Rules, Requests Authority to Settle," Transport Topics, February 28, 1972, p. 1.

13. For an excellent discussion of freight claims, consult Marvin L. Fair and John Guandolo, Transportation Regulation, 7th ed. (Dubuque, Iowa: Wm. C. Brown Co., 1972), pp. 100-15.

14. Claims can be subject to arbitration.

CHAPTER 9
CARRIER MARKETING

Transportation carrier marketing efforts are not directed toward selling a particular unit of output, such as a loaf of bread or an automobile, but instead focus on selling a service. This service sales unit, moreover, if successful, must be differentiated from services offered by competing carriers. Essentially, these services consist of speed, dependability, price, and flexibility.[1] Although the cost of transportation to industrial shippers is economically significant, service normally constitutes a carrier's most important sales and marketing variable. In an indirect way, we have already noted the importance of service by indicating the highly institutionalized nature of price change in Chapter 6 and the tendency to follow the path of least resistance on price changes in Chapter 2. In this regard, carrier marketing specialists should optimally develop pragmatic marketing strategies based on corporate resources and objectives, and stress the service aspects of their commodity.

To develop and implement meaningful marketing strategies, carrier marketers must possess a rudimentary familiarity with various techniques necessary to tailor a specific product to a market segment, by integrating price, promotion, and distribution. In this chapter, we will examine the areas of marketing concept, corporate objectives, environmental forces, market target selections, product strategy, market strategy, and price, promotion, and distribution.

THE MARKETING CONCEPT

"The market" is a nebulous concept when viewed alone. Applied to transportation carriers, "the market" consists of present and potential users of carrier services. Companies that have adopted the marketing concept analyze actual and potential customers' needs and tailor their services to those needs and wants. The emphasis is on the needs of the customer, not the needs of the carrier. While it is true that the regulatory environment tends to reduce or diminish a carrier's marketing efforts, firms that fail to adopt the marketing concept and give top priority to their customers' needs usually fail to optimize their revenue/profit goals.[2]

Figure 9.1 depicts an overview of the firm as a marketing system, as well as the strategic process of marketing. As indicated, the marketing objective of the firm may be to maximize profits or to gain a certain market share. Yet its specific objective is to tailor its product(s) to a specific market segment by integrating price, promotion, and distribution strategies.

Firm Objectives

When establishing corporate objectives, realistic appraisals of resource availability must be undertaken. For instance, if a motor carrier desires to reach a given revenue level at the end of a certain financial quarter, the carrier must obviously possess a sufficient number of tractors, trailers, and manpower to achieve this goal. If Delta Air Lines were to want to establish a load factor of 85 percent on all flights, then it would obviously have to have operating authority between city markets with sufficient growth potential to achieve this objective.

Three basic corporate objectives are profit maximization, certain market share, and specific profit goals.[3] Transportation firms desiring to achieve these objectives are faced with several significant contraints, such as route structure, a regulatory system, transportation competition, cost, and labor relations. In the railroad industry, a substantial amount of excess capacity is legally maintained. Rail management marketing and corporate objectives essentially focus on transporting bulk commodities in specialized equipment over long distances.[4] Two significant obstacles to achieving this objective are the common carrier concept, which we have discussed previously, and labor relations. Railroads are "affected with the public interest," and as such must provide rail service to all customers on the lines that it is authorized to serve.[5] This obligation is compounded because of the boxcar shortage problem and seasonal commodity movements.[6] As far as excess capacity is concerned, rail mergers require retaining acquired employees for specified periods of time or giving substantial severance pay--both of which are inordinately expensive.[7]

FIGURE 9.1

The Firm as a Marketing System and the Strategic Process of Marketing

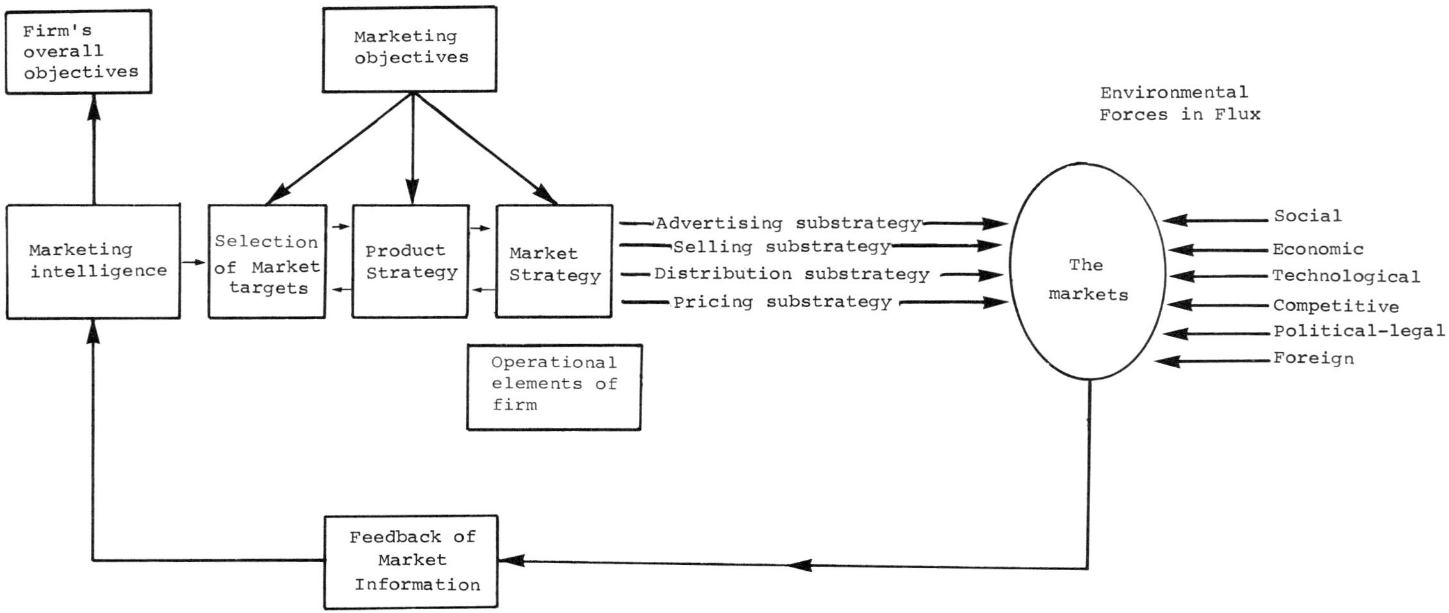

Source: George H. Downing, Basic Marketing (Columbus, Ohio: Charles Merrill Publishing Co., 1971), p. 61. Reprinted by permission.

Ambitious corporate objectives in the aviation industry are tempered by declines in profits and rising costs. These problems, moreover, were brought about by unchecked increases in labor, interest, and landing fee costs, coupled with the CAB's reluctance to permit airlines to raise rates.[8] Similar problems are found in the motor carrier, inland water, and pipeline transportation industries. In short, corporate and marketing objectives by transportation firms usually emphasize market share, steady dividend policy,[9] attaining revenue and operating ratio goals, or a steady growth rate.[10] These objectives, however, are fraught with constraints--including the five analyzed in Part One (Regulatory System, Transportation Competition, Route Structure, Ownership Pattern, and Pricing and Rate-making System).

Environmental Forces

Even though excellent and viable marketing strategies have been developed and implemented, there are certain cogent forces present in markets that cannot be influenced by the individual firm. In general, these can be called environmental forces. Carriers must be cognizant of these forces and evaluate their potential impact on their respective marketing plans and strategies. As depicted in Figure 9.1, changes in social, economic, competitive, legal, and foreign forces affect an organization's marketing program, and no control can be exerted by a carrier on these forces.

For example, social forces such as increased mobility affect the transportation service offerings beyond the scope and control of a carrier. Increased leisure time affects airline marketing programs, whereas technological innovations have reduced railroad market share. Legal and political forces may be aimed at nationalizing a portion of the rail system, and foreign competition has drastically reduced U.S. air and water traffic. However, the proper employment of marketing intelligence can minimize the impact of these forces. For this reason, carrier managers should always be attuned primarily to their customers' needs.

Selection of Marketing Targets

Carefully developed growth in terms of production and revenue frequently represents the major job of transportation carriers. Deciding when to add capacity, for instance, is a difficult task. Delta Air Lines, for example, added two additional DC-10s and several L-1011s in 1972 in anticipation of an upsurge in traffic, while other air carriers were holding steady.[11] Carrier marketing specialists must be aware of various indications of growth and sources of information pertaining to growth in their territory in order to assist in achieving their firm's objectives. Growth indicators include population, births, construction, assets, banking deposits, number of competing firms, and number of manufacturing firms and their types. Other significant indicators include the buying power index (BPI), the quality index (QI), and the index of sales activities (ISA).[12] When contemplating new or expanded operations, all of the factors regarding growth in a given market should be examined carefully.

Although state and civic organizations, such as development commissions, chambers of commerce, and university bureaus of economic research, may supply available data on trade and growth, the individual firm should be aware of other sources of data that are readily available. These include the following:

1. Census of Population, published by the Bureau of the Census, provides population changes by state, region, and standard metropolitan statistical area (SMSA).[13]
2. Census of Manufacturing, published by the Bureau of the Census, contains data pertaining to types of manufacture, employment, wages, value added, and other information, by SMSA.
3. Census of Transportation, published by the Bureau of the Census, provides information regarding travel and commodity movements.
4. Transportation Statistics in the United States, compiled by the ICC, contains earnings and cost data regarding regulated rail carriers, motor carriers, water carriers, pipelines, and freight forwarders.
5. "Sales Management Magazine" publishes an annual issue devoted to BPI, QI, and ISA, by SMSA.
6. Statistical Abstract of the United States, published by the Department of Commerce, furnishes an excellent compilation of statistical data.

Other specialized sources of data that can be employed for a given market target are available, but those enumerated above are the most widely used.[14] Carrier marketing specialists should ideally minutely analyze potential growth markets.

Gathering Marketing Data

When formulating carrier marketing decisions, various evaluations of market information should be used. The techniques for evaluation include marketing research, feedback, and sales reports. Marketing research, or the evaluation of the potential for new or expanded carrier services, can be conducted either internally or externally. Yellow Freight System, for instance, has a separate department concerned solely with market analysis. Most airlines and railroads maintain separate and distinct entities for research purposes, as noted in Chapter 7. The principal function of these organizations is to ascertain, identify, and measure certain environmental forces such as social, economic, technological, competitive, political, and foreign ones, over which the firm has no control, but which, in turn, influence existing and potential services.

As an example of the importance of marketing intelligence, after extensive market analysis, Southwest Airlines started offering a $10.00 one-way fare between Dallas and Houston and San Antonio. This fare is in force on the last night flight between the three cities. Although the bus fare between Dallas and Houston is only $9.95, Southwest's new fare is not only attracting new customers, but apparently is not diverting existing patronage from the regular $20.00 fare applicable during normal hour flights.[15]

Many firms turn to external sources for market research service. Many professional organizations, such as A. T. Kearney and Consultants of North America, are available for in-depth studies dealing with a diversity of subjects, from analyzing potential markets to productivity studies. Whether a carrier employs an outside marketing research firm or conducts its own research depends on many factors. First, if the carrier desires complete confidentiality, the research should be maintained within the firm. Second, if research is treated as a continuous, ongoing endeavor, internal research is perhaps less expensive than external. On the other hand, available evidence indicates that most businesses are reluctant to treat marketing research as a continuous process. Also, the final results of a marketing research program cannot always be measured quantitatively. Frequently, research conducted internally will be reported in such a fashion as to please the principal executive of an organization.[16]

A second approach for evaluating the several environmental forces in the marketplace involved feedback. This type of evaluated information can be gathered from salesmen, purchasing managers, and other employees. In the regulated motor carrier industry, city drivers are frequently the most active gatherers of marketing information regarding freight consignments. These carrier employees are familiar with shipping and receiving personnel and can usually solicit information pertaining to weekly and monthly tonnage and routes.

One of the primary uses of market intelligence data is for sales forecasting, which is the beginning of all budgeting by carriers. Sales forecasting is essentially an estimate of sales, in either dollars or physical units, for a specified future period under a proposed marketing program. Unequivocally, a good sales forecast is the most important single marketing planning tool and is the foundation for all carrier planning.

There are essentially two methods of sales forecasting available to carrier marketing specialists: the buildup technique and variable analysis. The buildup technique involves using estimates for various market segments from organizational units within the carrier entity. This technique simply involves soliciting forecasts from individual salesmen and other employees included in the carrier's sales program. After this feedback is aggregated, marketing research data on general factors is added. Finally, executive judgment is applied, and a sales forecast is made.

Variable analysis, however, is concerned with measuring the linear and statistical relationship of one or more variables and future sales volume.[17] Various readily available time series can be used and statistically significant relationships can be determined. Regression analysis represents the foundation for variable analysis. For instance, suppose that past sales volumes for a given carrier were plotted against the GNP. By applying various statistical techniques, a formula can be written that represents the relationship between sales volume and the independent variable of GNP. Since numerous forecasts of GNP are readily available, a carrier sales forecast can be found by applying the formula of the relationship between the two variables.

Other marketing research and forecasting techniques are also available. In practice, a forecast by the buildup technique can be used to check on and modify a forecast by the variable analysis technique, and vice versa. The important point is that sophisticated statistical forecasting techniques are available to make carrier sales forecasts.

Market Selection

Perhaps the most challenging task confronting carrier executives entails market selection. Airline marketing specialists are constantly seeking profitable routes and methods for differentiating their particular service offerings from those of other competing carriers. This same challenge also faces certificated and private motor carriers, railroads, freight forwarders, and water carriers. Indeed, during the market selection process, the carrier must tailor his product to a specific market segment.

The key to market selection is proper market segmentation, which involves differentiating service offerings by end use. Bus and rail passenger carriers and airlines have traditionally segmented their product on the basis of age, occupation, sex, geography, family size, education, social class, personality type, and family life-cycle.[18] These factors, of course, are essentially demographic in nature, and their overall marketing significance will vary from carrier to carrier and from market to market.[19] In the airline industry, factors such as family size, social class, occupation, and family life-cycle are important variables in market segmentation. Family fares are designed to encourage family travel, and their existence is predicated on changing family lifestyles that involve increased travel.[20]

The economic characteristics of the industrial goods market facing transportation carriers in the freight field is considerably different from those of passenger service. Industrial goods, of course, are those goods and services used in the production of other goods and services, and their basic economic characteristics are that their demand is derived and relatively inelastic.[21] The essential market characteristics, moreover, are that there are fewer buyers and sellers, there is a geographic concentration of buyers, their average sales unit is larger than that of consumer sale, that reciprocity is widely practiced, and the purchaser is normally a professional.

Segmenting the industrial market by carrier should emphasize final use by industry. For example, manufacturing markets should be segmented on the basis of steel manufacturers, textile producers, tire concerns, and so forth. The broad classification, moreover, can be subdivided by specific product line and along geographic lines. Some motor carriers, such as Arkansas Best Freight, Yellow Freight System, and Jones Truckline, have established special commodity divisions to transport certain industrial commodities. One important constraint to industrial market segmentation is route structure and operating authority. Unless a regulated carrier can receive broad, unrestricted authority, the ability to effectively segment a given industrial market will be virtually impossible to attain.[22]

The ability of a carrier manager to effectively segment passenger and freight markets is a prerequisite to a carrier's financial success. If markets are properly segmented (or selected), a transportation firm can effectively tailor its service offering to the industrial segment, and any market strategies relating to distribution, pricing, and promotion can also be tailored to these segments.

CARRIER PRODUCT STRATEGY

The domestic transportation industry's basic product is fast, dependable, and efficient service. In the freight sector of the market, service focuses on speed, cost, and reliability, while considerable personal attention is frequently required in the passenger market. Nevertheless, service, together with an ability to satisfy customer needs and wants, is the product of transportation carriers. For example, a recent survey conducted by New York University revealed that 49 percent of the respondents selected airlines on the basis of convenient schedules.[23]

Most products have life-cycles. From its birth to its death, a product exists in different stages and in different competitive environments. The ability of a product to adjust to these changing environments determines to a considerable degree how successful its life will be.[24] Product life-cycle is shown schematically in Figure 9.2. The time frame for each stage varies widely, ranging from a few weeks in women's fashions, to several years in electronic parts, to several decades in capital equipment and locomotives. Also, when new uses are found for a product, the cycle starts once again.

FIGURE 9.2

Typical Product Life-Cycle

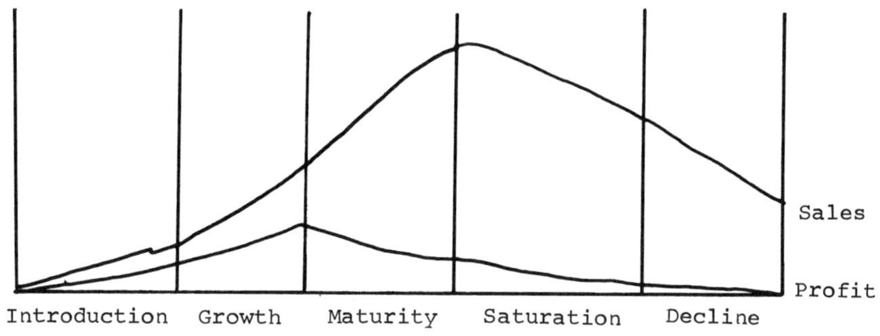

The four stages, as applied to transportation, are usually characterized in the following manner:

1. Introductory stage. New products, such as airline family fares, are initially focused on a limited core market. Product modifications are frequent, distribution is limited, and demand is cultivated. Selling cargo blockspace is an example of an aviation service at present in the introductory stage.

2. Growth stage. Not only do sales increase vigorously, but the increase takes place at an increasing rate. New competitors enter the market, profits are substantial, and selective demand is created. United Parcel Express' small package offering represents a service in the growth stage.

3. Maturity stage. Sales increase, but at a decreasing rate; emphasis is on service differentiation; and overall profits decline. An example of a carrier service in this stage is Poolcar or Pooltruck.

4. Saturation stage. Although the number of competitors decreases during this stage, dealer strength becomes a major competitive tool. Services such as stop-offs and transit privileges can be classified as being in the saturation stage.

5. Decline stage. The fundamental economic characteristics of this stage are the same as for the introductory stage. Rail passenger service is an example of a carrier service in the decline stage.

The significance of product life-cycle to carrier managers is simple--marketing strategies and plans should vary by stages. That is to say, each stage optimally requires a different marketing plan.

Although service is the market offering of a transportation firm, there are basically four different product strategies available for use. First, product differentiation can be employed. This strategy requires creating real or imagined differences in services. Differentiation of services, of course, constitutes the true product strategy between transportation carriers. TWA emphasizes the seating configuration of DC-10s, rail carriers stress dependable and inexpensive freight service, and motor carriers promote speed as the principal differences in service.

The second product strategy is product adjustment. Frequently, carrier service offerings must be modified as a result of technology, competition, or market changes. An example of these changes is deferred air freight, a service provided by combination carriers for several years that entailed delayed delivery of air freight and rates competitive with surface modes.[25] Increased speeds by land carriers resulted in the delay period being reduced considerably.

Eliminating a product represents a third and major product strategy. The favorable dimension of product elimination includes profit contributions, poor quality product removal, available use of new resources, and demand. On the other hand, the unfavorable aspect is tradition. For the most part, railroads are eliminating passenger service because of excessive losses and revenue drains,[26] but the tradition of rail passenger service has resulted in delays in eliminating substantial portions of the service.[27]

The final product strategy involves new service decisions. New product (service) ideas usually emanate from customers, research and development, competitors, technology, channels, the sales force, and company executives, from both within and outside the firm. Double-bottom trailers and package express are relatively new carrier services derived from changing competition and advances in technology.

In summary, a transportation carrier's only product is service. However, this service represents the only justification for a carrier's existence. These services, moreover, have definite life-cycles that require different product strategies and plans. Lastly, product adjustment is frequently essential because of changes in competition, technology, and other market conditions.

MARKET STRATEGY

After a transportation carrier has selected its markets, product offering, and marketing objectives, it must resolve several questions. How can the product best be sold to potential customers? What pricing policies should be developed? How can potential customers be informed of the merits of the product? Marketing strategy attempts to answer these questions.

There are four basic marketing strategies available for carrier management use. Fast and efficient movement of goods represents the principal marketing strategy that should ideally be developed by a transportation company. When dealing with actual and potential customers, carrier management should stress the overall importance of volume control and avoiding premium transportation charges for his customer.[28] Volume control is significant to an industrial shipper when sizable distribution costs are present, intricate production scheduling is required, and complicated distribution channels exist. Volume control consists of the shipper's merely buying FOB origin and selling FOB destination.[29] This enables the firm to select a given carrier and prescribe the route to be used. By emphasizing its ability to facilitate volume control by shippers through providing efficient, safe, and reliable carriage, a carrier can develop and implement this viable marketing strategy.

Avoiding premium transportation outlays on the shipper's part constitutes a second marketing strategy available for carriers. When specifying various forms of transport on a priority basis, any excess transportation charges incurred can be properly identified and allocated.[30] Carrier marketing specialists should work closely with shippers and receivers to explain the need and importance of implementing priority-based transport decisions. In this manner, carrier service can be emphasized as a marketing strategy.

Carrier managers must stress the transportation features of logistics systems as a marketing strategy. By demonstrating to the shipper the importance of high customer service standards, carriers can develop a marketing strategy centered on minimizing shipper inventory carrying cost and expanding customer service standards. Air carriers, for instance, are not able to compete with surface modes in terms of rates. However, the industry has successfully shown many industrial shippers that freight is only one dimension of landed cost and, by employing air freight, inventory investments can be reduced substantially.[31] Lost sales by shippers brought about by stockouts can be prevented by fast, efficient, and dependable transport service. In this regard, the rail industry commits certain parts of its fleet to specific shippers in order to facilitate shipping needs, which clearly is an effective marketing strategy.[32]

The final carrier marketing strategy involves basic storage or warehousing. This strategy entails demonstrating to a potential customer that financial resources can be conserved by using the carrier as a form of rolling warehouse. In effect, the transportation carrier becomes an integrated part of the customer's physical-logistics system. When implementing this particular strategy, care must be exercised to make certain that all affiliated cost reductions are correctly identified and revealed to the customer.

PRICE, PROMOTION, AND DISTRIBUTION

Having developed corporate objectives and marketing strategies, three additional variables must be integrated in such a way as to tailor the product offering (service) to a specific market segment. Because of economic regulation, the ability to integrate these variables is somewhat limited; nevertheless, an attempt should be made.

Price

As previously indicated, regulated transportation carriers must publish reasonable rates through institutional means. Even though rates are controlled, many carriers have demonstrated ingenuity in pricing decisions. Airlines, for example, have pioneered in group fares, and are now acquiring resort areas, which allows them to sell a complete packaged tour that includes both airline fare and accommodations.[33] Motor carriers, moreover, have been innovative in regard to certain weight items, while railroads have experimented with unit trains and incentive rates based on weight. But any pricing strategy must be used in conjunction with other marketing variables.

Promotion

Two schools of thought exist with respect to transportation promotion--direct sales effort, and indirect sales effort and advertising. While almost all carriers rely primarily on direct customer contact for promotion, a considerable amount of advertising takes place. Some carrier executives contend that media advertising is not effective because they are offering services that are regulated, routes that are fixed, and prices that are identical. Therefore, these managers focus most effort on direct sales.[34]

Arkansas Best Freight conducts an extensive, ongoing advertising program designed not only to acquire traffic, but to upgrade the traffic profession. It advertises in a number of magazines, including *Fortune*, *Traffic World*, *Business Week*, and *Transportation and Physical Distribution Management*. Their top management believes that the program has been successful.

Regulated air carriers engage extensively in advertising. For example, American Airlines recently introduced Flagship Express Service between Chicago and New York and advertised it extensively. Features of this service include early boarding, nine special entrees available on request for the dinner flight, and the fact that passengers can write their own tickets.[35] United Air Lines, on the other hand, advertised its experimental "live in-flight happenings," which includes guitar players, caricaturists, and wine tasting experts. This service was limited to Tuesdays, Wednesdays, and Thursdays aboard DC-10 equipment on New York-California flights during the summer months. This promotion was designed to attract family groups, increase midweek traffic, and compete with American's piano bars aboard their 747s.[36]

Other forms of transportation rely primarily on direct sales. In short, promotion is used to inform actual and potential customers about the service offered.

FIGURE 9.3

Channels of Distribution to Consumer

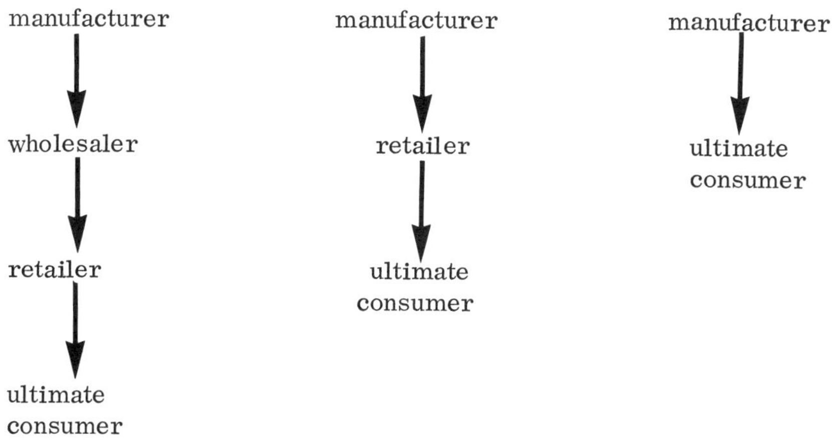

Industrial Goods Channels of Distribution

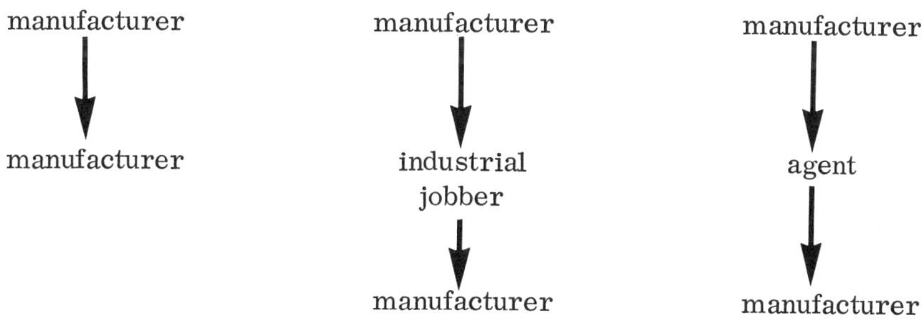

Source: Compiled by the authors.

Distribution

A channel of distribution is merely the path that legal title takes as it flows to the ultimate consumer. Channel can be simple--direct from the manufacturer to the ultimate consumer, or complex--from manufacturer to jobber, to retailer, to the ultimate consumer. Buying channels, moreover, are simply the reverse of distribution channels. Figure 9.3 depicts several representative channels.

Channels are important to carrier marketing specialists because transportation represents the cement that binds a channel together.[37] When marketing transport services, transport should be demonstrated as the binding force holding warehousing, procurement, inventory, customer service, and scheduling together in one system. Carriers should sell their transport service on the basis of its being an integral part of their customer channels.

SUMMARY

Marketing carrier services are significant to transportation firms. Although functioning in a regulated environment, firms should adopt the marketing concept of giving primary concern to the customer's needs. Also, the key to a successful carrier marketing program is to tailor a service to a market segment by integrating price, promotion, and distribution. Most successful freight marketing programs focus on establishing their firms as an integral component of their industrial shippers' buying and distribution channels.

NOTES

1. Other factors, such as common control, could be included, but for the most part these are representative.

2. E. Jerome McCarthy, Basic Marketing, 3rd ed. (Homewood, Ill.: Richard D. Irwin, 1968), Chapter 2.

3. James H. Donnelly, Jr., James L. Gibson, and John M. Ivancevich, Fundamentals of Management (Austin, Texas: Business Publications, 1971), Chapter 4.

4. Grant M. Davis, "The Freight Car Dilemma--A Problem of Contracting Capacity," I.C.C. Practitioners' Journal, November-December 1973, pp. 23-37.

5. Roy J. Sampson and Martin T. Farris, Domestic Transportation Practice, Theory and Policy, 3rd ed. (Boston: Houghton Mifflin Co., 1975), Chapter 7.

6. See John Richard Felton, "Freight Car Shortages: The Problem and Some Proposed Solutions," *Nebraska Journal of Economics and Business*, Spring 1972, p. 43; Edward Rastatler and John W. Snow, "Car Hire Changes and Railroad Car Shortages," in *Transportation Research Forum* (Oxford: Richard B. Cross, 1970), pp. 115-23; and Grant M. Davis, "An Analysis of the Propriety of Transferring Car Service Functions to the U.S. Department of Transportation," *I.C.C. Practitioners' Journal*, May-June 1970, p. 558, for an in-depth evaluation of the impact of car shortages on rail marketing programs.

7. For an in-depth evaluation of several deterrents to rail consolidation, see Leonard A. Lecht, *Experience Under Railway Labor Legislation* (New York: Columbia University Press, 1955), Chapters 4 and 7.

8. W. V. Henzey, "Is Nationalization Inevitable?" *Airline Management and Marketing*, January 1971, pp. 20-23.

9. Available evidence suggests that firms have a tendency to emphasize stable dividends even though earnings may fluctuate considerably. For a substantiation of this observation, consult R. Murray Havens, John S. Henderson, and Dale L. Cramer, *Economics* (New York: Macmillan Co., 1966), pp. 432-33.

10. Yellow Freight System, for instance, attempts to grow at whatever growth rate GNP experiences each year. In 1972, GNP increased 15 percent.

11. R. Slawsky, "New Delta Airlines," *Airline Management and Marketing*, June 1972, pp. 33-35.

12. See the section on "Some Location Techniques" in Chapter 15 for the formulas for computing BPI, QI, and ISA. All three indices must be used in conjunction with other means, such as market and size.

13. An SMSA is an integrated economic and social unit consisting of a substantial population nucleus. It must contain a core city of 50,000 or more inhabitants or an adjacent city with which it has a combined population of 50,000. An SMSA includes the central city's county and any adjacent counties that are socially and economically integrated with the central city. For an example of how this statistical concept is used in marketing efforts, see Exhibit 16, Dockets No. MC56679, Sub 66; MC13628 5, Sub 3; MC136155, Sub 2; and MC1366230, before the ICC.

14. Other sources, for example, would include *Thomas' Register of Manufacturers* (New York, Thomas Publishing Co.).

15. "Southwest's $10 Fare Attracts Travelers," *Aviation Weekly*, July 3, 1972, p. 33.

16. Walter B. Wentz and Gerald I. Eyrich, *Marketing Theory and Application* (New York: Harcourt, Brace and World, 1970), pp. 478-79.

17. Frank J. Charvat and W. Tate Whitman, Marketing Management (Boston: D. C. Heath and Co., 1964), p. 138.

18. For an extended analysis of product life cycle, consult Chester R. Wasson, Product Management (St. Charles, Ill.: Challenge Books, 1971), Chapter 1.

19. Chester R. Wasson, "How Predictable Are Fashion and Other Product Life-Cycles?" Journal of Marketing, July 1968, pp. 36-43.

20. Charles S. Murphy, "Airline Prosperity Is Not Simple" in Passenger Transportation, ed. Stanley C. Hollander (East Lansing, Mich.: MSU Business Studies, 1968), pp. 306-15.

21. See Donald V. Harper, Price Policy and Procedure (New York: Harcourt, Brace, and World, 1966), pp. 42-48, for an excellent discussion of the characteristics of the industrial market.

22. ICC policies, for instance, stress the impact of any new service on existing carriers, a policy that frequently deters implementing new marketing strategies. For an example of ICC policy on carrier marketing strategy, see Arrow Trucklines, Inc., Docket No. MC-121060, Sub No. 8.

23. K. G. Norodick, "What Motivates the Consumers' Choice of an Airline?" Journal of Retailing, Spring 1972, pp. 30-39.

24. Grant M. Davis and Stephen W. Brown, "Physical Distribution Strategies and the Product Life-Cycle: Infusing the Time Element" (Paper presented before the Southern Marketing Association, Houston, Texas, November 8, 1973).

25. This service was designed to increase load factors during off-peak hours.

26. Robert W. Harbeson, "The Rail Passenger Service Act of 1970," I.C.C. Practitioners' Journal, March-April 1971, pp. 330-39.

27. For an in-depth evaluation of passenger service capacity and delays, see U.S., Congress, Senate, National Transportation Policy (Washington, D.C.: Government Printing Office, 1961), pp. 60-66.

28. Grant M. Davis, "F.O.B. Terms--A Decision-Making Framework for Purchasing Management," Journal of Purchasing, February 1970, pp. 31-38.

29. Ibid., p. 44.

30. Grant M. Davis, "Managerial Techniques for Controlling Premium Transportation Charges," Journal of Purchasing, November 1971, pp. 24-37.

31. Grant M. Davis and Stephen W. Brown, Logistics Management (Lexington, Mass.: D. C. Heath and Co., 1974), Chapter 1.

32. Costs are frequently high because of empty return movements. Also, consult "Rail Transportation Technology" in Readings

in Physical Distribution, 2nd ed., ed. Hale C. Bartlett (Danville, Ill.: Interstate Printers and Publishers, 1970), pp. 318-28.

33. Braniff, for example, owns Braniff Place in New Orleans, and United Air Lines controls Western Motels.

34. In short, the only differentiating element is the salesman.

35. "American Has New Flagship Plan," Advertising Age, May 8, 1972, p. 22.

36. "Strolling Guitarists, Wine Tasting Part of United's New Happening," Advertising Age, July 17, 1972, p. 2.

37. Consult Louis W. Stern, Distribution Channels: Behavioral Dimension (Boston: Houghton Mifflin Co., 1969), for an inclusive marketing view of channels.

CHAPTER

10

PUBLIC RELATIONS AND ADVERTISING

Transport firms are concerned about their acceptance by the public and they use a number of techniques to convince it that they are providing an important service to society. A number of alternatives are available for shippers and passengers who purchase transport services, and their choice can be influenced by carrier advertising, public relations, and public service. Additionally, for carriers that are publicly owned, it is desirable for the firm to have a favorable public image.

A good public image may also be helpful in attracting management talent to transport firms. Profitable carriers generally have more fringe benefits available to employees and more opportunities for advancement than less profitable ones. A greater capacity to serve customers and the opportunity to grow within a general industrial framework by providing new services can be appealing to potential managers. Even though such firms may not spend many dollars for paid advertising, their actions with customers and the public creates an image that speaks louder than words.

A number of methods of working with the shipper and with the public are available to attract additional revenues. Carriers not only must convince the shipper of their availability, but must follow through with good performance when the opportunity arises. Advertising of availability, points served, and other services has often proved successful. Public relations and promotions within the carrier and shipping industry, as well as in the local community, have also often proved successful in attracting additional revenues.

Advertising is expensive and carriers must be careful to weigh potential revenue and profit return against cost outlay. There is no general rule of thumb giving the percentage of revenue that should be allocated to advertising, and these outlays differ substantially among modes. Each carrier must decide the degree of advertising efforts and the corresponding amount it is willing to spend.

This chapter will consider types of advertising and public relations efforts of carriers. Such programs have many component parts, and judging their results by marketing and cost objectives is a difficult task. A successful advertising and public relations program is a total program. Segmented advertising, and public relations programs that are not firmly based in a workable practical philosophy, will be ineffective.

TOTAL PROGRAM CONCEPT

A total advertising and public relations program is one in which a company first assesses its own operating philosophy and how this philosophy can best be communicated to the public. Steps must then be made to implement the program.

Operating philosophies are concerned with marketing programs and strategies, efforts toward maintaining customer service standards, emphasis on cost controls, types of line-haul equipment utilized, fleet maintenance programs, employee benefit programs, employee promotional programs, the degree of involvement, public responsibility, public versus private ownership, the relationship to the federal and state governments, and so on.

Once the philosophy of the carrier has been established, the next task is to communicate these concepts to the public, employees, and customers. Different advertising modes and public relations efforts will have to be utilized, and transport firms must be aware of the effectiveness of each.

A total program involves total philosophical and practical operating programs, total use of advertising and public relations, and total emphasis to the public, employees, and customers. Many transport firms utilize only segments of their operating philosophy when communicating through various media. Every company has positive and negative attributes, but realistic and practical approaches are necessary.

Emphasizing total advertising and public relations does not imply that all communication modes should be used. Obviously, depending on the particular carrier, some channels of communication will be more effective than others. Discretion must always be used. It is possible that advertising themes may not be synthesized, and if this results, problems could occur.

The operating philosophy will generally determine the degree of public, employee, and customer emphasis in transport advertising and public relations. If a company deals very little with the general public, then their concern may be primarily with the user--the shipper. When the primary user is the general public, then the orientation must be cognizant of this fact. If employees are an important part of a corporate philosophy, then good employee benefits, activities, and company publications should be emphasized.

A total program of advertising and public relations should be firmly based in philosophy and be directed toward the public, employees, and customers.

MEASURING THE EFFECTIVENESS OF ADVERTISING

The effectiveness of carrier advertising and public relations is only partially evident in terms of revenue fluctuations from year to year. Advertising, by itself, has very little to do with a change in movement of goods from one mode to another. Such items as price, delivery time, claims ratios, and other variables are of primary significance with regard to both intermodal and intramodal transportation competition. All factors must be considered, including economic characteristics and inherent economic advantages, when evaluating revenue changes.

It is difficult to measure carrier advertising effectiveness in the transport industry. There are many factors affecting freight and passenger movements that complicate obtaining a true measure of advertising success. For example, if a man were planning on taking his wife on a trip from New York to Las Vegas for a New Year's Eve vacation, he would normally have a limited time, and would thus fly on the most convenient airline. Price would not be a factor in his choice, since regulation and competition force the fares to be similar. Customer service would be an important factor, as well as schedules, equipment, and convenience. Advertising that stresses these factors may be highly effective, whereas advertising stressing price would be ineffective.

By the same token, let us assume a shipper must move a 500-pound engine from Detroit to Dallas within 24 hours. He would pay the larger expense to move it by air to satisfy a customer, when he would normally have moved the engine by motor carrier. Under these circumstances, price is unimportant. Space, place, and time utility continue to play important roles in shipper distribution decisions, and advertising that stresses these factors can be effective.

Conversely, price may at times be a major factor. When an industrial shipper moves large quantities of goods on a regular basis, a decrease in price may very well cause him to switch carriers. Advertising stressing price can be effective in such cases.

Shipper and passenger choice turn on many variables. Advertising that stresses one variable may be effective under certain conditions and ineffective under other conditions. Customer requirements and their constraints cause freight and people to move in the most practical and objective way. It is the job of advertising to inform the shipper and passenger about the variables he might consider. Since these factors are constantly shifting, there is no way to objectively measure the effectiveness of a given advertising campaign.

OBJECTIVES OF CARRIER ADVERTISING

Carrier advertising is primarily designed to increase sales--either passenger or freight. The carrier modes utilize diverse programs in this respect with rail, air, and motor being the prime advertisers in the transportation field. Due to the type of commodities moved, carrier advertising has been specifically directed toward certain segments of the shipping public, toward the public in general, and toward their own employees.

A modal approach is best suited for a critical look at the objectives of carrier advertising.

Rail Transportation

Increasing sales is not the only objective of the railroads. Due to a heavy burden of legislation, the railroads have directed some of their efforts toward attracting public sympathy for their aims. The more usual objective of attracting shippers is also involved. A survey of railroad advertising indicates that it has four objectives: freight identity, community and industry status, projection of company goals, and communication of information to shippers.

A great deal of railroad advertising is directed toward the modern freight capabilities of the railroads, recent innovations, and modern management techniques. In effect, the railroads are attempting to establish a new identity and shed their past image, which was often associated with passenger service. An attempt to increase status in the community and industry is also involved. The rail image within the shipping public is very important and efforts are being made to see that this image is maintained. Some advertising portrays the company employees as people who are concerned about their jobs, their community, and their country. Somewhat allied to status as an objective is the projection of company goals. Here the railroads have the objective of showing the shipping public that carrier goals are important and consistent with national goals. Finally, the objective of informing the shipper is important. Railroad companies attempt to inform their shippers that they are stable and financially sound. They also want to point out that their rates are attractive, their hardware is the very best, their routes are the shortest, and they are concerned about industry's future through their interest in initiating industrial developments and other real estate projects affecting the shipper and the local population.

Air Transportation

While the railroad appeal is directed primarily toward the traffic manager, the airlines are concerned with passengers, not freight. Air freight is important and growing rapidly, but it is still a sideline compared to the movement of the public. A survey of airline advertising indicates that it has four objectives: to emphasize their personal service, to encourage travel in general, to emphasize the physical attractiveness of their equipment, and to emphasize specific destinations.

First, in an attempt to emphasize personal service, airline advertising stresses the number of people available to assist the passenger in air travel. Employees are featured in many of their ads, particularly physically attractive employees, who are always ready to serve the passengers' needs. Second, ads attempt to encourage travel in general. In their competition for a larger share of the air travel market, airlines encourage people to travel for business or pleasure and to develop creative reasons for air travel, and thus develop new markets (and revenues) for air transportation. Third, emphasis on the physical attractiveness of their equipment is found. The type of equipment flow seems important to the public, and is thus utilized in advertisements. Leg room, comfortable seats, attractive surroundings, and reliability are emphasized. In addition to equipment, the terminals are shown as attractive to the traveler. Further, maintenance and safety receives some attention in advertising for the airlines. Fourth, airlines tend to emphasize specific destinations. The attractive attributes of each city served by the route structure is noted. Accommodations, new and different sights and experiences, tours, special events, and so forth are given attention.

Motor Transportation

Motor carrier advertising is directed primarily toward the traffic manager and strives to attract his business. Generally, advertising tries to assist the sales force by supplying some additional tools and informing shippers of services available. The objectives of motor carrier advertising are to stress route structure, speed, flexibility, and reliability.

Route structure is stressed by promoting through service or one carrier service to important points. When new route authority is obtained, a carrier will heavily promote this fact. Secondly, speed of delivery is stressed. While the airlines have a rapid delivery time, they are expensive. At more competitive rates, motor carriers claim to be faster than rail and water carriers. The image of speed is sometimes even contained in the carrier's name. Thirdly, flexibility of motor carrier service is emphasized. Personal door-to-door pickup and delivery anywhere that a street or road exists is an attribute of motor carrier service that is often pointed out. Finally, due to the poor image of the past, some effort has been made to stress reliability and stability.

ADVERTISING IMPACT

Carrier advertising aimed at the shipper has an indirect impact. This is due primarily to the technical knowledge of the shipping clerk or traffic manager, restrictions to specific routes, delivery requirements, personal friendships, and the lack of time to read all the advertising. On a day-to-day basis, shippers are dealing with carriers and can readily measure the quality of service being provided. By virtue of their experience and tenure with a company, traffic managers can also provide a historical evaluation of carrier service and performance by the various modes.

The carrier sales representative usually maintains frequent contact with the shipper and provides an information source on a much more personal basis than does carrier advertising. Even though shippers have a close working relationship with carriers, they are also aware of carrier advertising in publications. These ads do have an effect in the sense that they are aesthetically pleasing, reinforce the sales contact, and provide a basis of conversation for both the shipper and the carrier representative. It is not uncommon for a shipper to specifically inquire as to why a carrier does not advertise in certain journals or to ask for more information on a given service.

Advertising may have more impact on the public in general. One main goal may be to inform the public, as well as shippers, regulatory officials, and congressmen, about the legislative proposals the carriers are supporting. These advertisements are sometimes looked upon as paid political ads rather than carrier advertisements, of course.

An example of this type of expenditure for advertising is the elaborate program sponsored by the motor, rail, and water interests supporting the Surface Transportation Act of 1971. The appeal to the various carrier publics was for specific legislation and not for increasing the shipper's or public's use of any particular mode.

While most of the advertising expenditures in this regard have been made by the railroads, other carriers also have acute regulatory needs. The American Trucking Association has sponsored numerous campaigns on both a state and national level to support an increase in size and weight of trucks and trailers. The airlines have attempted to gain support in their air fare battles with nondomestic carriers through advertising and public relations programs.

TYPES OF ADVERTISING BY CARRIERS

A wide use of media is utilized by carriers in their advertising efforts, including television, radio, periodicals, newspapers, and trade journals. Carriers also expend large amounts of money each year for on-site customer entertainment and promotion.

Railroads and Airlines

The railroads and airlines make use of almost every media in their advertising efforts. In addition to television, radio, periodicals, newspapers, and trade journals related to their specific mode, they also utilize ad agencies and special interest publications such as *Export*, *Import*, and *Food*. Outdoor advertising (billboards) and direct mail are also used.

Both railroads and airlines utilize their industry associations extensively. However, they also rely heavily on their own companywide efforts, which tends to personalize their advertising message. In addition to nationally oriented messages, the railroads and airlines have specific advertising efforts aimed at local terminals and their marketing programs.

Motor Carriers

Motor carriers utilize their industry association, the American Trucking Association, intensively in their television advertising efforts. Additionally, a number of industry publications, journals, and newspapers are used. Some motor carriers also advertise extensively in industry publications and trade journals (as opposed to industrywide ads).

Radio and newspaper ads and direct mail efforts are utilized less extensively by the motor carriers than by the railroads and the airlines. Some motor carriers do use an advertising agency, but, again, fewer than the railroads and airlines. There are many more trucklines than rail or airlines. As a result, many are quite small and utilize none, or very little, of their financial resources for advertising. Due to the extent of their capitalization and small profit margins, many tend to rely solely on their past working relationships with shippers and hire very few sales representatives.

The majority of all carrier advertising efforts takes place in the rail, air, and motor industries. Most water carriers and pipeline companies expend few advertising dollars on a national or regional basis. When they do advertise it is usually in the local area of operation and is aimed at a specific group of customers.

Customer Promotion and Entertainment

By far the greatest amount of promotional and advertising dollars is spent on direct customer promotion and entertainment. It is in this area that the competition for shipper revenues is reflected. The carrier sales representative has a more direct and personal relationship in this area than in advertising efforts.

Within modes, carrier salesmen have been known to go to extravagant lengths to secure the business of specific accounts. In some cases they must be willing to outbid competitors within their mode, as well as competitors in other modes. Because of the intense personal contact, questions are occasionally raised regarding the ethics of these sales efforts. The shipper is usually quite involved with the salesmen and should share in whatever questions are brought forth regarding ethics.

PUBLIC RELATIONS

It is often difficult to specifically determine where advertising ends and public relations begins. A campaign may have elements of both, and confusion can easily occur. Public relations is sometimes confused with publicity, promotion, or propaganda as well, but the terms are not synonymous. Advertising is the act of purchasing space or time with the goal of increasing revenues. Publicity is communication in action, and generally involves obtaining space or time in the media without having to purchase it. Promotion is the commercial application of advertising or publicity or both, while propaganda is the political application of advertising or publicity. Public relations makes use of publicity, but it is a much broader concept and it has been defined as "building and holding good will," "doing good and getting credit for it," "winning the respect of one's community," and "putting one's best foot forward." Public relations includes the overall conduct of an organization plus telling its story. Publicity is the act of telling.[1]

Public relations activities are both inside and outside the firm and are designed to enhance the firm's goodwill among the various publics associated with the firm. Public relations activities are sometimes looked on as indirect advertising, since freight revenues (sales) can sometimes be generated. Corporate philanthropy can also result in some benefits to company employees in the local community. One should not feel that every corporate public relations activity must always end in positive results, for sometimes negative feelings can be avoided by good public relations.

Public Service and Community Relations

Shippers and carrier employees are usually involved in a wide variety of community activities. Like other professionals, they are sometimes involved in political activities, school boards, service clubs, churches, urban renewal, and other economic and social concerns in the community. It is not uncommon to find carrier representatives holding state legislative positions or mayoral and other elected political offices. These same representatives are normally expected to treat their carrier position as their first priority and their elected position as an extracurricular activity. Community activities such as the United Appeal and cancer drives involve many carrier representatives. YMCA and YWCA, as well as Junior Achievement, involve carrier representatives with programs for children of all ages.

Again, the important point is that carrier representatives be involved in these activities because it benefits both the company and the individual. It also brings them into close contact with many shippers.

Company Publications

Publications within a firm can be a very useful public relations device on an in-house basis. The purpose of most transport carrier publications is to provide a means for communicating information about the company to the employees, to provide general information about employees to the firm, and to make employees feel more an integral part of a growing firm. These purposes will naturally vary according to the firm's management philosophy. Publications can be aimed at three specific groups: all employees, specific employee groups, and those outside the firm.

All Employees

Publications aimed at all employees cover general items of interest within the company, regardless of their organizational stature, sex, or union affiliation. One usually finds a variety of publications in this category, ranging from newspaper to magazine formats. Some publications are expensive to produce and may cover more of the conceptual, social, and philosophical aspects of transport as opposed to the practical, day-to-day methods of running a terminal. News items about employees are prevalent in some publications that are mailed to all employees. Some companies diversify their publications for all employees by having a news item publication dealing with peripheral aspects of business. Mailing dates are coordinated so that each publication will complement the other.

Specific Employee Groups

It is not uncommon to find in-house publications aimed at specific employee categories, such as managerial and supervision, sales operations, engineers, pilots, or drivers. These publications can concentrate on the specific items of interest and concern to that particular employee segment. Employees in all firms tend to associate with the part of the business in which they work. It thus stands to reason that they will be more interested in information concerning their area of activity than information of a general nature. In some cases a terminal or office facility will employ enough people to merit a publication solely for the employees at that location. For example, some company headquarters locations have a weekly publication with news and information for that specific location. Items ranging from promotions, want ads, and information about the Christmas dance to the cafeteria's weekly menus may be covered.

Those Outside the Firm

It is common for transport firms to continue sending company publications to their retired employees. There also may be special mailings to members of the board of directors. Some firms mail their company publications to all shareholders, while others even mail to select customers. Publications that are widely distributed to those outside the transport firm should reflect this fact through their content. Shareholders and customers are concerned about financial, marketing, and service developments in which they can see a self-interest or professional interest. General employee items of news and information are usually of little interest to them.

Media Relations

A good working relationship with the news media is usually of benefit to any firm. There are times when special announcements, financial reporting, and other items of general public interest need to be effectively written and released on a timely basis. We have defined this as publicity. A firm that has a good working rapport with the media will usually get better coverage on such publicity items than a firm that has a poor working relationship. Transport firms that advertise extensively will generally have established this rapport as a result of a long business association with the news media, and can often place such communications relatively easily.

Another good reason for developing a strong media relationship is that it is better to have the media working with you than against you. Obviously, advertising and news releases alone will not establish a good rapport. It takes a personalized contact and interest, not unlike a sales representative's working relationship with a customer.

AMOUNT DEVOTED TO PROMOTION

How much of the sales budget should be devoted to promotion? This is a difficult question to answer. Several theories are prevalent regarding the firm's optimum expenditures for promotion within the firm. The amount of expenditures may also fluctuate from year to year due to specific program design or the company's financial standing, and thus a specific percentage would be meaningless. The expenditures may also increase and decrease according to the promotion programs being utilized.

Even though transport firms are aware of the competition's advertising and promotional efforts, there is no general rule-of-thumb percentage of sales that should be devoted to advertising and promotional efforts. Transport firms react very sensitively to a change in their overall revenues, and generally revenue changes will drastically affect expenditures within the firm. Some modes--especially trucking--react more quickly than others.

It should also be noted that some large firms do very little, if any, national advertising, and allocate expenditures through areas of promotion. This does not mean that they spend more or less than other firms on their programs as a whole. The extent of advertising programs, media utilized, length of the program, specific market concentration, and other factors drastically affect promotional budgets. Firms in the process of mergers, acquisitions, going public, or changing their usual corporate identity may have greater promotional expenditures than firms not enjoying similar successes or failures.

The size of total revenues must obviously be considered when discussing the percentage of sales devoted to promotion. The actual dollar outlay for some larger firms may be quite high but may still reflect a small percentage of sales. On the other hand, smaller firms may allocate a large percentage of sales to promotion that actually results in fewer total dollars. For example, of the top 50 transport firms in the United States ranked on a revenue basis, the majority are railroads and airlines--19 and 17, respectively, in 1972.[2] The railroads and airlines do spend more dollars for advertising and promotion than the other modes. However, it is likely that, with their large revenues, their percentage of sales devoted to advertising and promotion would be quite small.

A close relationship of profits to promotional expenditures does not seem to exist. This is particularly true on the downside. Only a state of bankruptcy eliminates the promotional expenditures altogether. In order to attract revenues, usually in the form of paying customers, the airlines must continue their advertising efforts. The railroads, since they more specifically deal with bulk commodities, are more likely to reduce their promotional budgets under financial crisis. The motor carriers do not seem to spend the actual dollars or the percentage of sales on advertising that the railroads and airlines do, and motor carriers are also quick to reduce these expenditures when the profits begin to decrease. If it could be said that promotional expenditures are effective in increasing revenues, this policy might be self-defeating.

It still remains evident, however, that there exists no hard rule of thumb regarding the percentage of sales that should be devoted to advertising and promotion. A total marketing strategy, emphasizing the promotional budget as only one variable, is of importance to specific companies and specific modes.

Considering specific promotional expenditures, the sales expense for field salesmen is an important part of the total promotional budget. This expense reflects the most direct customer contact by the transport firm. In many companies the sales expense (customer entertainment and promotion) is reflected as a percentage of sales for that local office. For example, at small terminal facilities the sales expense will normally be a larger percentage of sales than at the larger terminal. The same is true for a new terminal trying to attract business. Firms that do little or no advertising will normally allocate a sizable budget for sales expense.

Transport firms generally feel that such expenditures are well spent because of the importance of the salesman in creating customer relationships. These expenses are often not part of the total advertising and promotional budget since they are concerned with specific customers in specific marketing territories. The advertising and promotional budgets are concerned more with the total corporate image and projecting the generalized customer and the generalized public, while sales expenses are often aimed at a specific customer.

The advertising and promotional efforts, while very closely related to the marketing efforts, may sometimes be found organizationally under a corporate administrative office. When this situation exists there may be a lack of communication and coordination and thus a fragmented, rather than a synthesized, program results.

SUMMARY

Although there is some question as to the degree of effectiveness of carrier advertising, such activities do serve as an important part of a carrier's marketing program. Each mode orients its promotional programs to its respective publics and customers. In some cases the customers are obviously the same, and thus there is likely to be considerable duplication in advertising and sales emphasis.

Carriers generally use a variety of advertising efforts. As an industry, the railroads and the airlines appear to make the widest use of advertising media, with the trucking industry falling into third place. Each mode uses its respective industry association extensively in advertising, lobbying, and promotional efforts.

In addition to advertising, a wide variety of public relations methods are used to appeal to customers. Many of these public relations activities are not only helpful to the carrier and sales and service efforts, but may also provide personal and professional development for the individual carrier representative. Intracompany publications and other employee-related activities play an important role in public relations within the firm.

The proper amount that should be devoted to advertising and promotion by carriers is debatable. Exact information is, in many cases, confidential and specifically related to the total marketing program of the individual carrier.

The one ingredient that will ultimately determine the importance and effectiveness of an advertising and public relations program is the degree to which these efforts are integrated into a total marketing program.

NOTES

1. Martin T. Farris and Roy J. Sampson, _Public Utilities: Regulation, Management and Ownership_ (Boston: Houghton Mifflin Co., 1973), Chapter 15.

2. "Table of the Top 50 Largest Transportation Companies," _Fortune_, July 1973, p. 131.

CHAPTER

11

EQUIPMENT SELECTION

One of the most important decisions confronting transportation carrier managers is equipment selection. Not only is the selection process in itself important, but equipment should optimally be acquired that is capable of performing specified functions. Delta Air Lines, for example, would not procure DC-9 equipment for its New York-Los Angeles runs. On the other hand, an over-the-road tractor-trailer would not be purchased for use in city pickup and delivery service.

Rolling stock represents a sizable financial investment for carriers and should be carefully analyzed for end use, route, future and present tonnage, technological change, and safety regulation. It should also be emphasized that equipment has a long life and, therefore, carriers must live with an equipment decision for a number of years. Carrier managers, moreover, must resolve the lease-or-buy dilemma facing most carriers.

Closely related to equipment selection is maintenance and repair. Because of stringent federal and state safety laws, equipment should ideally be maintained in such a fashion that downtime is minimized. This, of course, implies a need for some form of systematic maintenance program in order to assure adequate levels of equipment availability.

The discussion of equipment can be considered in three parts: net investment in transportation; types of equipment used by railroads, motor carriers, airlines, and water carriers; and maintenance programs and federal safety laws, as they relate to carrier maintenance and acquisition programs.

NET INVESTMENT IN TRANSPORTATION EQUIPMENT AND FACILITIES

In order to sustain orderly growth and increase productivity, adequate levels of investment in equipment and facilities must be attained by carrier managers. Indeed, failure to pursue proper fleet replacement programs usually results in costly downtime, deteriorating service, lost revenue, and customer diversion. In this regard, carrier managers should ideally plan equipment expansion to provide adequate transport capacity when passenger and freight ton-miles are expected to increase.

Some idea of both the magnitude of, and the change in, transportation investment can be gained from Table 11.1. The value of private investment in transportation equipment and facilities in 1968 has already been noted in Table 1.10. However, here we are principally interested in the change that took place between 1960 and 1968.

The largest percentage increase was experienced by commercial airlines as they continued to re-equip with jet aircraft during this period. The largest absolute increase involved highway and related uses. Railroads, while expanding in total net investment, incurred the smallest increase. Water carriers actually decreased in net investment during this period. Overall change in net investment in equipment and facilities was 56 percent for the eight years, or approximately 7 percent per year.

Considerable care must be used with these data, however. First, no adjustment has been made for inflation, and while inflation in the 1960s was less severe than in the 1970s, it must be realized that the 7 percent overall increase in net investment may be inflated because of the decrease in the value of the dollar. Second, facilities are included in these figures. For carriers, this includes such things as terminals. For manufacturers, this includes factories and plant increases. Indeed, it could be questioned whether equipment manufacturers and dealers, service stations, repairs, and garages should be included at all. Finally, no attempt is made to measure efficiency or technology. While we still consider this factor indirectly in the next section, the reader should realize that new equipment may be technologically superior to the equipment it replaces, and may actually produce more transportation per dollar invested. Also, better use of existing equipment and facilities may cause a decrease in investment.

TYPES OF TRANSPORTATION EQUIPMENT

When acquiring equipment, carrier executives must attempt to obtain rolling stock designed to perform efficiently. When speed limits were reduced to 55 miles per hour because of the energy crisis,

TABLE 11.1

Changes in Net Investment in Privately Owned Transportation Equipment and Facilities, 1960-68 (millions of dollars)

	1960	1968	Percent of Change
Air carriers			
Commercial	2,565	7,965	
General	556	1,747	
Total	3,121	9,712	211.1
Equipment manufacturers			
Motor vehicles and equipment	9,512	17,625	
Other than motor vehicles	5,954	13,652	
Total	15,466	31,277	102.2
Highway			
Automobile	61,715	97,569	
Truck and trailer	8,467	17,568	
Bus	300	439	
Dealers, service stations	5,396	9,117	
Repairs, garages, etc.	1,653	3,041	
Total	77,531	127,734	64.7
Oil pipeline	2,600	3,842	47.8
Railroad	30,537	31,748	4.0
Transit (includes municipally owned)			
Bus and trolley	2,055	2,442	
Bus	408	510	
Total	2,463	2,952	19.8
Water carrier	3,011	2,930	-2.8
Grand total	134,729	210,195	56.0

Source: Compiled from Transportation: Facts & Trends, 10th ed. (Washington, D.C.: Transportation Association of America, October 1973), p. 28.

tractor-trailers manufactured to cruise at 65 miles per hour suffered diminished efficiency. Conversely, equipment should not be procured that has a performance level that vastly exceeds the power to move goods. Also, factors such as terrain and road conditions directly and indirectly affect a carrier's equipment selection process. Some idea of present types of equipment used by railroads, motor carriers, airlines, and water carriers, and equipment changes, will illustrate these points.

Railroads

Because of the economic characteristics of the domestic railroad industry, substantial amounts of capital investment in the form of facilities and rolling stock are required. Table 11.2 reflects railroad capital expenditures between 1952 and 1971. The variable nature of capital expenditures reflects earnings, while the declining investment level in railway and structures since 1966 is a direct result of reduction in excess capacity, which in turn indicates a declining number of boxcars and equipment.

During 1973, railroads moved 4.4 million carloads of coal, 1.9 million carloads of metallic ores, 1.6 million carloads of grain, and 1.4 million carloads of chemicals and allied products.[1] To move these commodities, together with 18 million other carloads, the domestic rail industry used 27,461 diesel electric units and 1,710,659 freight cars. Table 11.3 reflects the rail industry's rolling stock for 1953, 1963, and 1971. As indicated, significant declines occurred for plain box, refrigerators, gondolas, hoppers, and miscellaneous cars. These reductions essentially provide insights into rail marketing strategy, that is, moving bulk commodities for long distances in equipment specifically designed for and assigned to a particular industrial user.[2]

Most diesel electric units are manufactured by General Motors and are subdivided into switch engines, line-haul engines, and multipurpose engines. One carrier, Seaboard Coast Line, recently ordered 15 additional motors for additional tractive effort (MATEs) from General Electric to expand motive power units from two to three engines. These units increase both utilization and flexibility of locomotives because the companion power units simplify starting trains in addition to enhancing performance at higher speeds. General Electric, moreover, has estimated that the elimination of an extra locomotive unit through the use of a MATE can result in a 40 percent reduction in maintenance costs on drag applications.[3]

TABLE 11.2

Yearly Capital Expenditures by Railroads, 1952-73
(in dollars)

Year	Total	Equipment	Roadway and Structures
1952	1,340,912	935,090	405,822
1953	1,259,797	857,893	401,904
1954	820,246	498,726	321,520
1955	909,521	568,202	341,319
1956	1,227,857	821,357	406,500
1957	1,394,705	1,007,749	386,956
1958	738,036	479,680	258,356
1959	818,002	567,546	250,456
1960	919,154	663,490	285,664
1961	646,425	427,130	219,295
1962	832,938	593,369	239,569
1963	1,043,788	784,874	258,914
1964	1,417,263	1,139,683	277,580
1965	1,630,687	1,303,602	237,084
1966	1,952,805	1,554,223	398,581
1967	1,522,478	1,148,381	374,097
1968	1,186,979	818,720	368,259
1969	1,509,394	1,088,712	420,681
1970	1,351,439	993,095	358,344
1971	1,177,627	863,517	314,110
1972	1,215,581	847,623	367,958
1973	1,342,000	892,690	449,448

Source: Yearbook of Railroad Facts (Washington, D.C.: Association of American Railroads, 1972), p. 56, for 1952 to 1971; Statistics of Railroads of Class I in the United States (Washington, D.C.: Association of American Railroads, 1974), for 1972 and 1973.

TABLE 11.3

Serviceable Cars, Class I Railroads, 1953, 1963, 1971

Serviceable Cars	1953	1963	1971
Plain box	645,675	509,443	327,475
Equipped box	47,952	65,145	162,577
Refrigerators	95,747	86,262	94,365
Gondolas	276,826	215,360	176,329
Hoppers	531,762	408,002	375,192
Covered hoppers	31,302	69,742	130,192
Flat	44,528	52,457	70,905
Other	79,854	63,384	46,853
Total	1,753,645	1,469,795	1,384,046

Source: Interstate Commerce Commission, Annual Report for Fiscal Year Ended June 30, 1972 (Washington, D.C.: Government Printing Office, 1972), p. 23.

Containerization requires standardized, flexible vans and represents an area where additional equipment is being purchased. Trailer-on-flat-car (TOFC) represents the rail growth market and Mini-Bridge has increased domestic demand for additional trailers.[4] This market has an estimated potential of 1.8 million tons. When acquiring containers for this growing market, rail carriers have four advantages: rail/water transportation user costs are competitive with all water costs, capital investment costs are lower, they have an expanded revenue base, and they have lower freight rates.[5]

When transporting manufactured goods, rail carriers are using damage-free (DF) cars. Specialized equipment such as rack cars and tank cars are normally assigned to specific shippers. The investment criteria for this type of equipment acquisition are based on anticipated tonnage and growth of the individual user.[6]

Technological innovations are important factors to be considered during the equipment selection process.[7] The Department of Transportation began a six-month Turbo Train experiment on February 7, 1972, on a route over the mountains from Washington, D.C. to Parkersburg, West Virginia. The experiment included braking and speed tests.[8] The Santa Fe Railroad, moreover, has modified the configuration of cars used in high-speed service between Chicago and Los Angeles. Lastly, the USSR contends that it successfully tested a rail car powered by an aircraft jet engine and the test revealed that conventional rails on reinforced concrete ties "readily withstood" speeds of 155 miles per hour.[9]

Motor Carriers

Motor carrier operations are essentially classified as common carriers, contract carriers, private carriers, brokers, and exempt carriers. The rolling fleet, moreover, consisted of over 20 million trucks and buses during 1972.[10] The fleet provided 22.2 percent of the intercity freight ton-miles and 2.07 percent of intercity passenger-miles in 1971,[11] and traveled on 3,730,082 miles of streets and highways.[12]

Because of the diversified nature of motor carrier operations, different equipment is used for different tasks, such as tank trucks, sand and gravel trucks, general commodities trucks, flat beds, and refrigerated trailers. Charles A. Taff explains the basic scenario for equipment selection as follows:

> A basic starting point is to make a detailed study of the carrier operation. Different equipment will be used for an over-the-road operation than will be used for local. Equipment requirements will vary also for a short-haul carrier and for pickup and delivery operations for the over-the-road carrier. Road conditions should be considered also, the terrain, and the maximum grades, as well as other physical factors affecting the operation, such as temperature.[13]

Other factors, of course, include engine size, tire wear, and any specialized equipment dictated by terrain or other operational factors.

Substantial research by truck manufacturers has been undertaken to develop a turbine engine. A power unit of this type would be desirable due to its lower maintenance and operational costs as a result of fewer moving parts and fuel economy. Ford Motor Company is currently testing a turbine powered truck and will market a limited number of units.

Technological innovations in motor transportation are important because of rapidly increasing labor costs. One important equipment innovation is double bottoms or "pups." The two trailers reduce handling cost and permit more carefully planned loadings. Another innovation similar to double bottoms is the detachable trailer of 20-foot length that can be pneumatically switched from city pickup trucks to over-the-road rigs. One principal constraint in selecting motor carrier equipment is state laws concerning length, width, and height. Table 11.4 shows these constraints as they existed in 1974. Many states have length limitations that preclude using cost-saving devices such as double bottoms. It should be noted, however, that the change in federal laws in late 1974 allows for more flexibility in this regard, especially on the interstate system.

Aviation

Excluding general aviation, for-hire air carriers are classified as trunk line, local service, or air taxi operators.[14] Equipment used by these carriers will vary by routes, passenger and freight density, and financial resource availability. Table 11.5 shows aircraft in service by U.S. scheduled airlines for 1963, 1968, 1972, and 1973. This table illustrates the increase in jet and turbo-prop-type equipment and the phasing out of conventional propeller-type planes during the 1960s (jet and turbo equipment are so designated). Analysis of the table will also help the reader appreciate the massive investment in re-equipment that has been undertaken by U.S. airlines as they entered the Jet Age.

America's first jet airliner to enter service was the Boeing 707-120, on December 20, 1957. The initial commercial flight was made by Pan American on October 26, 1958, from New York to Paris. The aircraft has a wing span of 130 feet, 10 inches, it is 144 feet, 6 inches long, and weighs 258,000 pounds. It is powered by four JT3D-3 turbofans generating 18,000 pounds of thrust. The plane is capable of speeds of up to 600 miles per hour, and can range more than 3,000 miles. Similar craft were designed by Convair and McDonnell-Douglas. Delta, Pan American, TWA, Northwest, Continental, Eastern, Western, and National use this aircraft on long-distance, high-volume routes.

Intermediate-range routes, from 1,000 to 1,700 miles, are normally served by medium-range jetliners, such as Boeing 727s and Convair 990s. More than 750 Boeing 727s are at present in service, making this the most widely used airplane. A 727 can transport a payload of up to 179 passengers, cruise at a speed of 600 miles per hour, and fly up to an altitude of 42,000 feet. Medium-range aircraft are used on routes such as Detroit-Dallas and Dallas-Phoenix.

Four categories of aircraft are available for use in shuttle or short-range routes. Boeing manufactures 737s capable of transporting up to 107 passengers, and McDonnell-Douglas produces DC-9s in four versions that can accommodate from 90 to 125 passengers.

TABLE 11.4

Height, Weight, and Length Restrictions on Trucks by States, 1974

State	Height (ft)		Weight (lbs)		Length (ft)		Number of Trailers	
	13-6	Other	73,280	Other	65	Other	Doubles	Triples
Alabama	X		X			55		
Alaska	X			100,000		70	X	
Arizona	X			76,800	X		X	
Arkansas	X		X		X		X	
California	X			76,800	X		X	
Colorado	X			75,200	X		X	
Connecticut	X			73,000		55		
Delaware	X		X		X		X	
District of Columbia		12-6		70,000		55		
Florida[a]	X			138,271		110	X	
Georgia	X		X			55	X	
Hawaii	X		X		X		X	
Idaho		14		105,500		70		X[b]
Illinois	X		X		X		X	
Indiana[a]	X			127,400		98	X	
Iowa	X			72,634		60	X	
Kansas[a]	X			130,000		105	X	
Kentucky	X		X		X		X	
Louisiana	X		X		X		X	
Maine	X		X			56.5		
Maryland	X		X		X		X	
Massachusetts[a]	X			127,400		98	X	
Michigan[a]	X		Limited to 11 axles		X		X	
Minnesota	X		X		X			
Mississippi	X		X			55	X	
Missouri	X		X		X		X	
Montana	X			105,500	X		X	
Nebraska	X			95,000	X		X	
Nevada	none			76,800		70		X[c]
New Hampshire	X		X			55		
New Jersey	X		X			55	X	
New Mexico	X			86,400	X		X	
New York[a]	X			127,400		108	X	
North Carolina	X		X			55		
North Dakota	X		X		X		X	
Ohio[a]	X			127,400		98	X	
Oklahoma	X			90,000	X		X	
Oregon	X			76,000		75		X[c]
Pennsylvania	X		X			70		
Rhode Island	X		X			55		
South Carolina	X		X			55		
South Dakota	X		X		X		X	
Tennessee	X		X			55		
Texas	X			72,000	X		X	
Utah		14		130,000		108		X
Vermont	X		X			55		
Virginia	X			70,000		55		
Washington	X			76,000		70	X	
West Virginia	X		X			55		
Wisconsin	X			73,000		55		
Wyoming		14		101,000		75	X	

[a]Toll roads only.

[b]Length for triple trailer here is longer than normal limit--98.

[c]Length for triple trailer here is longer than normal limit--105.

TABLE 11.5

Aircraft in Service by U.S. Scheduled Airlines, 1963, 1968, 1972, 1973

Manufacturer	Model	1973	1972	1968	1963
Boeing	B707 (jet)	315	337	380	133
	B720 (jet)	44	56	134	104
	B727 (jet)	710	662	516	-
	B737 (jet)	134	134	66	-
	B747 (jet)	109	106	-	-
Convair	240	-	1	3	49
	340/440	6	7	46	153
	580/600 (turbo)	129	135	148	-
	880 (jet)	37	41	41	46
	990 (jet)	-	-	9	19
Lockheed	Constellation	-	-	-	40
	Super C' stell	-	-	-	111
	Electra (turbo)	19	19	86	117
	L-382B (turbo)	1	3	9	-
	L1011 (jet)	48	17	-	-
McDonnell-Douglas	DC-3	-	2	14	197
	DC-4	-	-	-	14
	DC-6	3	3	7	217
	DC-7	-	-	15	164
	DC-8 (jet)	207	227	217	104
	DC-9 (jet)	335	329	260	-
	DC-10 (jet)	86	59	-	-
Other		177	257	349	144

Source: Air Transport 1974 (Washington, D.C.: Air Transportation of America, 1974), p. 17.

In normal operations, all versions of the DC-9 can take off on a 600-mile flight with 50 passengers and baggage from a runway of less than 5,000 feet and make two intermediate stops without refueling. These aircraft are used extensively by most airlines for short-range flights.[15] Convair 580s and Martin 600s are turbojets used in "feeder" operations by such carriers as Frontier, Southern, and North Central.[16]

One interesting innovation in short-range equipment involves short take-off and landing (STOL) equipment. The dominant design limitations in the development of STOLs are a ride control system for smooth flights and noise reducers. Tests are currently being conducted toward achieving a comfortable flight system.[17] However, payloads are such that commercial firms have refrained from actively encouraging the introduction of STOLs.[18]

In an attempt to achieve operating economy and reduce capacity strains on the airway system, high-density aircraft were introduced into commercial service in 1969 and 1972. The Boeing 747 jetliner can carry up to 490 passengers in all-economy seating, or 365 passengers in mixed class configurations. The aircraft cruises at 625 miles per hour with an operating range of 4,000 miles. Also, more than 150 of these aircraft have been sold to foreign and domestic carriers. Two additional wide-body jetliners now in service are the DC-10 and L-1011 produced, respectively, by McDonnell-Douglas and Lockheed. Both aircraft are new generation wide-bodied, flexible-range trijet transports designed to accommodate from 250 to 345 passengers. These two aircraft are used extensively in high-density markets, but their range and seating arrangement flexibility provide alternate uses by airline managers. Nevertheless, some delivery problems on the L-1011 were encountered by air carriers during the early 1970s.[19]

Water Carriers

Equipment used by water carriers consists basically of deep-water equipment used for maritime service and on the Great Lakes, intercoastal, and coastwise routes; and shallow-water craft used on rivers and inland waterways and on intracoastal waterways (connecting rivers, canals, channels, and bays protected from the open sea) found along most of the Atlantic and Gulf coasts. There are approximately 1,849 companies actively engaged in commercial operations on the domestic waterways, and 185 of them are certified by the ICC. The 1,849 carriers use 17,527 dry cargo barges and scows with a total cargo capacity exceeding 19,710,605 tons, 3,420 tank barges with a cargo capacity of 7,486,718 tons, and 4,278 towboats and tugs with aggregate horsepower exceeding 4,302,333.[20]

While there are deck barges, carfloats, and scows with capacity carrying loads ranging from 350 to 1,350 tons, equipment selection essentially is a function of water velocity, channel depth and width, dock facility, and time of year. Most commodities transported on the inland waterway system are sand and gravel, steel, grain, and similar bulk commodities.[21]

Two recent innovations involving domestic and deep-water maritime operations are the LASH and SEABEE (Sea--barge) systems.[22] LASH and SEABEE are essentially intermodal systems in which barges are floated into and from a vessel without extensive handling. The mother ship may have an overall length of 820 feet and a dry cargo capacity of 20,263 long tons, which means that 1,498 standard 20-foot containers can be accommodated.[23] SEABEE, now in service between Gulf points and Europe, can transport 1,800 containers or vehicles.[24]

During recent years, Great Lakes tonnage constituted approximately 40 percent of total tonnage generated by domestic water carriers.[25] Principal bulk commodities transported are iron ore, bituminous coal, limestone, petroleum products, and cement. Nonbulk commidities moved include automobiles, trucks, buses, and related parts. Two types of vessels now operating on the Great Lakes are bulk carriers and package freighters. Bulk cargo capacity normally is 25,000 deadweight cargo-tons, and package freighters have cargo capacities of 2,500 deadweight tons. These same two equipment types are used on both coastwise and intercoastal carriers.

MAINTENANCE PROGRAMS AND SAFETY REGULATIONS

Reliability of equipment and rolling stock is essential to the successful operation of any transportation venture. Closely affiliated with equipment reliability are variable maintenance programs designed to prevent accidents and downtime. Given the amount of private investment in transportation equipment, maintenance activities should be ongoing, continuous projects in order to effectively achieve carrier goals and objectives.

During periods of financial setbacks, some carriers have demonstrated a propensity for deferring maintenance outlays on rolling stock and right-of-ways, which in turn results in accidents and profit drains. Also, all carriers, both regulated and nonregulated, that operate their vehicles in interstate commerce, must comply with federal safety laws such as OSHA (Occupational Safety and Hazards Act) and those enforced by the DOT. These safety laws obviously affect maintenance.

Railroads

Financial outlays for maintenance of way and equipment in railroad transportation operations usually constitute 50 percent or more of total rail operating expenses. Table 11.6 shows maintenance expenditures of railroads for selected years from 1929-73. The reader should note both the massive sums involved and the substantial increase over the years.

TABLE 11.6

Maintenance Expenditures and Transportation Expenditures of U.S. Railroads, Selected Years, 1929-73 (thousands of dollars)

Year	Maintenance of Way and Structures	Maintenance of Equipment	Transportation
1929	855,355	1,202,912	2,079,954
1939	466,831	765,935	1,417,794
1947	1,212,096	1,558,011	3,476,433
1957	1,430,504	1,913,015	4,094,780
1967	1,287,834	1,867,788	4,186,049
1973	2,041,588	2,535,084	5,901,391

Note: Outlays for maintenance of way and equipment plus expenses of operation account for 90 percent of operating expenses.

Source: Association of American Railroads, Yearbook of Railroad Facts (Washington, D.C.: Association of American Railroads, 1974), p. 16.

Although most rail carriers pursue continuous maintenance programs, such as periodic track and ballast replacements, locomotive overhauls, and boxcar repair, many of their programs are required by federal law. Since the Rail Safety Act of 1970, the FRA's Bureau of Railway Safety exercises jurisdiction over all areas of rail safety, such as track maintenance and inspection standards, equipment standards, and operating practice standards.[26] The bureau also regulates safety standards for locomotives, safety appliances, and power brakes--items that are principally involved with quality maintenance programs.[27]

To administer its safety functions, the Bureau of Railroad Safety is subdivided into five divisions: hazardous materials, engineering and accident analysis, locomotive safety, general safety, and signals and train control.[28] A geographically dispersed field staff, moreover, supplements the bureau.

During fiscal year 1972, various divisions of the bureau inspected 87,124 locomotives and 821,132 freight cars, and more than 11,000 locomotives and 82,063 freight cars were found to have defective safety appliances. Signal complaints during 1972 focused on sand and rust on rails, relay failures, open circuits, broken apparatus, weather failure, obstruction, and connection errors.[29] In short, these federal requirements directly affect a rail carrier's maintenance program.

Airlines

Because of the total control of aviation maintenance functions through the certification processes of the FAA, aviation maintenance expenditures are costly. Further, these expenditures tend to fluctuate considerably with respect to the wide-body jets. Ascertaining exact maintenance expenditures for this equipment has been difficult to determine due to insufficient usage of these new planes to compute cost; the extensive modification of engine and airframe on Boeing 747s, DC-10s, and L-1011s; the substantial number of avionics systems, which adds a new dimension to maintenance costs; and smaller airlines (such as Braniff) that may contract maintenance and overhaul work to major operators of wide-bodied jets.[30] Maintenance expenditures on all types of equipment are difficult to ascertain due to the way in which airlines segregate costs.[31] However, equipment maintenance is rigorous because of federal safety standards.

The FAA enforces federal aviation safety laws that result in strenuous testing, certification, and high maintenance standards for both commercial and private air carriers.[32] As required by the Federal Aviation Act of 1958,[33] the agency must (1) regulate air commerce in such a manner as to best promote its development and safety and fulfill the requirements of national defense; (2) promote, encourage, and develop civil aeronautics; (3) control the navigable airspace of the United States to the advantage of civil and military users; (4) consolidate navigation research and development; and (5) develop and operate a common system of air traffic control and navigation for both military and civil aircraft.[34] To carry out its function, the FAA issues and enforces rules, regulations, and minimum standards pertaining to the manufacture, operation, and maintenance of aircraft, in addition to certifying the airworthiness of aircraft and airmen. Also, airports served by airlines regulated by the CAB must be certified by the FAA. This agency, moreover, performs flight inspection of air navigation facilities in the United States.[35] In short, air carrier maintenance programs are dictated by certification standards promulgated by the FAA.

Motor Carriers

Although only interstate motor carriers and buses are subject to federal safety laws, most states have patterned their safety regulatory statutes after the federal provisions. These provisions, moreover, directly affect maintenance programs administered by carriers. The Bureau of Motor Carrier Safety of the DOT's Federal Highway Administration is responsible for administering motor carrier safety laws at the federal level. Principal safety functions of the bureau include (1) inspecting records maintained by interstate motor carriers; (2) conducting periodic inspections of motor carrier vehicles, either enroute or on the carrier's premises; (3) removing vehicles from service when found imminently hazardous; (4) investigating accidents; and (5) reporting violations.[36]

One of the major problems small carriers face in pursuing viable maintenance programs is finance. Most smaller carriers are family owned and operated and are frequently confronted with serious cash flow problems, and hence tend to defer maintenance.[37] Cummings Engine Company, on the other hand, is offering a pay-as-you-go engine repair or maintenance contract to small carriers. The program is tailored to the carrier trade-in cycle, and if the owner's contribution at the end of the contract period exceeds expenses, 50 percent of the surplus will be returned. Cummings' executives foresee this service as an incentive to follow a preventive maintenance schedule.[38]

Water Carriers

Domestically operated water carriers usually pursue maintenance schedules provided by equipment manufacturers on both power plants and barges. This equipment normally needs only periodic annual service, but every five to ten years it must be overhauled and keels must be carefully checked for corrosion or structural failure. Managerial scheduling of these maintenance programs depends on such factors as demand, time of year, and excess capacity.

The Coast Guard is the principal federal agency administering maintenance safety laws in water transportation. Merchant Marine safety falls within the purview of the Coast Guard and this program primarily consists of the following activities: inspecting and regulating vessels and related equipment to provide protection for crews, cargo, and passengers; licensing, regulating, and protecting the rights of Merchant Marine personnel; approving plans for constructing, altering, and repairing vessels; approving vessel equipment and appliances; investigating and reviewing marine casualties and acts of incompetency or misconduct; relating to international bodies and the maritime industry; documenting vessels; and publishing vessel registers.[39] To the extent that equipment must comply with both comprehensive and specific regulations, maintenance programs must be continuous and vigorous.

SUMMARY

Carrier management must strive to accurately select equipment for use in its operations that is suitable for a given operation. Equipment selection, moreover, represents a major management task because of the sizable financial investment in rolling stock. Ongoing maintenance programs are prerequisites to financial success in the transportation industry because of the need to avoid downtime and lost revenues. Also, federal safety laws administered by various agencies within the DOT influence the degree and level of maintenance expenditures by carriers.

NOTES

1. Yearbook of Railroad Facts (Washington, D.C.: Association of American Railroads, 1974), p. 28.
2. Grant M. Davis, "The Freight Car Dilemma--A Problem of Contracting Capacity," I.C.C. Practitioners' Journal, November-December 1973, pp. 23-37.
3. "MATEING Time Again for SCL," Railway Age, June 12, 1972, p. 50.
4. For an excellent analysis of equipment needs for Land-Bridge and Mini-Bridge, where the United States serves as a model for management from Europe to Asia, see W. P. Mano, "Rail Freight Transportation--World Concept" (Papers and Proceedings, 14th Annual Southwest Transportation Seminar, University of Texas, El Paso, Texas, February 20, 1970).
5. "Mini-Bridge and its Health," Railway Age, May 29, 1972, p. 29.
6. "Commoditrain: Running Again," Railway Age, May 29, 1972, p. 16; and "PC; ATSF: A Bridge Team," Railway Age, August 28, 1972, p. 13.

7. "Survival Through Technology," *Railway Age*, September 11, 1972, pp. 39-42.

8. "Turbo Train Heads for the Hills," *Railway Age*, February 14, 1972, p. 12.

9. "U.S.S.R. Has Real Jet-Powered Trains," *Railway Age*, May 8, 1972, p. 22.

10. U.S. Bureau of the Census, *Statistical Abstract of the United States: 1973* (Washington, D.C.: Government Printing Office, 1973), p. 548.

11. Ibid., p. 538.

12. See Table 1.6.

13. Charles A. Taff, *Commercial Motor Transportation*, 4th ed. (Homewood, Ill.: Richard D. Irwin, 1969), p. 98.

14. Included within the classification of general aviation are all private aircraft not operated by certified carriers.

15. "United Cities Gain on Commuter Route," *Aviation Weekly*, June 12, 1972, p. 30.

16. These carriers essentially bring passengers to large hubs for passage to other points, via truckline carrier, for the most part.

17. D. A. Brown, "Public Acceptance Key to STOL," *Aviation Weekly*, March 6, 1972, pp. 21-23.

18. E. H. Kolcom, et al., "Firm Short-Haul Transport Design Near," *Aviation Weekly*, June 5, 1972, pp. 56-57.

19. D. Watkins, "TWA Confident on L-1011 Despite Snags," *Aviation Weekly*, June 19, 1972, pp. 27-30.

20. *Big Load Afloat* (Washington, D.C.: American Waterways Operators, 1973), p. 3.

21. U.S. Corps of Engineers, *Water-borne Commerce of the United States, Domestic Deep-Sea and Lakewise Traffic* (Washington, D.C.: Government Printing Office, 1973).

22. K. Taylor, "Containerships: Australia's Lost Infant," *Fleet Owner*, June 15, 1972, pp. 86-89.

23. *Big Load Afloat*, op. cit.

24. Ibid., p. 47.

25. See note 22.

26. For legislative background concerning this bill, see Grant M. Davis, *The Department of Transportation* (Lexington, Mass.: D. C. Heath & Co., 1970).

27. U.S. National Archives and Records Service, *United States Government Manual: 1973/74* (Washington, D.C.: Government Printing Office, 1974).

28. Federal Railroad Administration, *Department of Transportation News* (Washington, D.C.: Department of Transportation, February 20, 1968), pp. 2-4.

29. U.S. Department of Transportation, Sixth Annual Report (Washington, D.C.: Government Printing Office, 1972), p. 207.

30. M. S. Yaffee, "Cost of Maintenance Still Fluctuating," Aviation Weekly, October 23, 1972, pp. 70-78.

31. See "Two and Three Engine Aircraft, Hourly Cost," Aviation Weekly, July 17, 1972, p. 34; and "Four Engine Aircraft, Hourly Cost," Aviation Weekly, July 10, 1972, pp. 32-33.

32. For an analysis of aviation safety results, see Grant M. Davis and Martin T. Farris, "Federal Transportation Safety Programs--Misdirected Emphasis and Wasted Resources," Transportation Journal, Summer 1972, pp. 5-17.

33. Public Law 85-726, 85th Cong., 2nd sess., 1958.

34. Ibid.

35. United States Government Manual: 1973/74, op. cit., p. 356.

36. Consult Grant M. Davis, "Federal Highway Safety Programs--Organizational Disunity," Journal of Alabama Academy of Science, January 1971, pp. 54-63, for an evaluation of the bureau's activities.

37. "Smaller Fleets' Money Problems," Fleet Owner, February 1972, pp. 168-69.

38. "Cummings Control Repair Program and Recondition Rebuilt Components," Fleet Owner, December 1971, p. 165.

39. United States Government Manual: 1973/1974, op. cit., p. 354.

CHAPTER

12

FINANCE AND CREDIT

The American money market is a diverse subject consisting of numerous sources. Like any other resource, money flows into areas where the largest returns are earned. The domestic transportation industry must compete with other industries for capital sources. Unfortunately, some segments of the industry have suffered inordinate losses and hence encounter difficulty when attempting to secure funds for either current expenditures or capital outlays.

Transportation carrier managers should be familiar with several dimensions of finance in order to better accomplish goals and objectives, because scarce financial resources must be allocated among competing projects within the firm. In this chapter, five important aspects of financial management as they relate to carrier management will be examined. These are capital expenditure programs, rate levels, sources of funds, lease-or-buy decisions, and federal finance regulation.

CAPITAL EXPENDITURE PROGRAMS

Due to the substantial investment frequently required in transportation facilities, systematized procedures and programs should ideally be developed to assist management in making investment decisions. Capital expenditure programs in general, and carrier management specifically, should be a continuous, ongoing search for profitable projects. However, capital budgeting and planning is not used by many firms. Even though capital expenditure programs vary from firm to firm, and from industry to industry, certain common elements should be present in these programs. The essential components of any capital investment program are as follows:

1. A continuous search for profitable investment opportunities.[1] A pragmatic capital expenditure program must provide for a perpetual quest for profitable investment opportunities, both within and outside the firm. Capital expenditures should not be approached on a spasmodic, random basis.

2. Measuring the worth of the project. An investment can be justified on a combination of both economical and financial grounds. Serious problems, however, can occur when deciding on the proper measuring methodology, such as present value or discounted rate of return.

3. Long-range capital forecast. Capital expenditures require long-range planning. If the objective of the organization is to capture a certain share of the market by 1985, and physical capacity must be expanded to accommodate the expansion, then capital expenditure requirements must be well known in advance. It is possible that, in some instances, long-range capital plans may conflict with the long-range objectives of the business enterprise.

4. Maintaining a short-run capital budget. To adequately evaluate a proposed expenditure, the venture should be incorporated into a one-year budget. This action will enable management to determine the monetary impact and contribution of the project, in addition to measuring its effect on other capital items.

5. Screening and selection. By establishing and ranking investment alternatives on the basis of priority (descending returns), only the more profitable projects will be considered for selection. Cash flows and cash available for capital expenditures also play major roles in the screening and selection process.

6. Regulating authorized capital expenditures. Controls must be formulated and implemented to avoid expending excessive sums on a given project. Indeed, rates of return are computed on planned investments, and spending in excess of the sum authorized for an asset of a program diminishes the effectiveness of a company's capital expenditure program. The Convair Division of General Dynamics failed to exercise this principle of capital budgeting during the late 1950s and subsequently encountered serious financial difficulties.

7. Post-mortems. To insure the quality of estimates associated with capital expenditure activities, post-mortems should be conducted. Should an investment prove unprofitable, management should locate and identify why a variance occurred between estimated and actual earnings.

8. Withdrawal and disposal. When a value of future earnings declines beneath the market value of an asset, strong consideration should be directed toward withdrawing and disposing of the asset.

9. Capital accounts and procedures. Special forms and procedures should be adopted and maintained for capital acquisitions if an effective and efficient operation is to be achieved.

10. Economics of capital budgeting. A basic understanding of the capital budgeting concept, together with knowledge regarding the time value of money, is a prerequisite for all capital expenditure programs.

RATE OF RETURN AND INVESTMENT ANALYSIS

When planning for capital acquisitions, forecasts should be made regarding the estimated life of the asset and its projected value. Management decisions associated with capital budgeting and procurement normally are related to buying or leasing equipment, expansion of plant and physical facilities, and replacement of existing assets. In order to correctly solve problems affiliated with these decisions, rates of return and cost of capital for alternative investment opportunities should be computed.[2]

In a static sense, a rate of return is simply the ratio of annual revenues to original cost. Suppose that an asset that costs $1 million generates annual receipts of $100,000. The rate of return is 10 percent. Figure 12.1 shows the various components that together determine a static rate of return. As shown, the earnings ratio is determined by dividing profits by sales, whereas turnover is computed by dividing sales by capital employed. Other causative relationships are also depicted in Figure 12.1.

The rate of return represented in Figure 12.1 would be theoretically sound provided it represented an investment in a permanent, nondepreciating, nonappreciating asset that generated a continuous, constant stream of dollar earning--an investment that simply does not exist in most instances. The static rate of return is unrealistic because it ignores the time value of money. In other words, at various time intervals, the value of a dollar fluctuates, and the common denominator for comparing different times and values is the interest rate.

A dollar next year is different from a dollar today. Suppose that money is invested at 8 percent interest. If $1.00 is invested, it will be worth $1.08 next year, and even more the following year. In financial terminology, this process is referred to as compounding. Conversely, discounting involves moving from the future to the present. Thus, at 8 percent interest, $1.08 has a present value of $1.00. This process can be, and is, extended many years into the future. From this discussion, it should be obvious that the rate of return on the investment is the rate of interest, which equates the present value of the cash return on the investment to the present value of the cash outlays associated with the investment.

FIGURE 12.1

Schematic Calculation of Financial and Investment Ratios

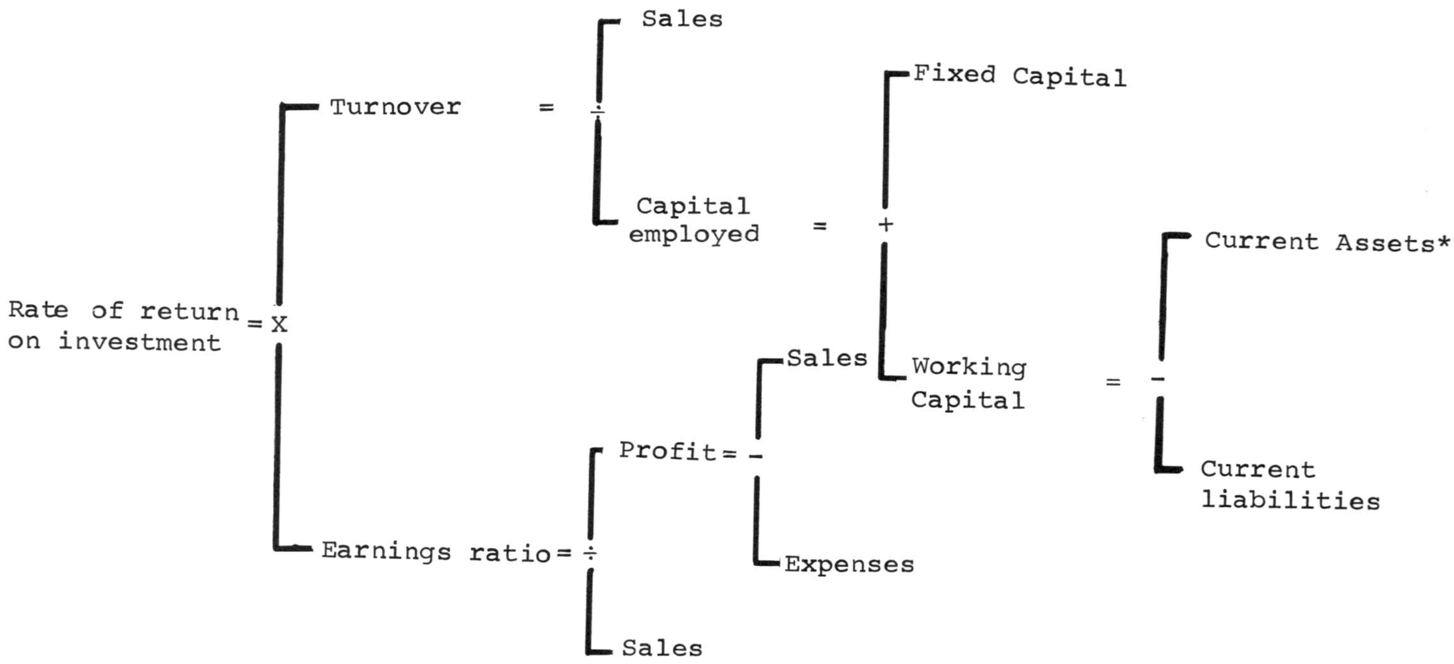

Source: U.S. Small Business Administration, Computing Rate of Return on Assets: Guides for Profit Planning (Washington, D.C.: Government Printing Office, 1960), p. 44.

Investment Analysis

To illustrate the concept of present value and rate of return in the investment selection process, we will compare the following three alternative investment possibilities:

1. An opportunity exists whereby the firm can expand its trailer fleet by an additional 20 vehicles. This investment will require a monetary outlay of $20,000, but will provide incremental revenues of $2,000 annually for five years. Also, the life of the investment is five years, with no salvage value. Transportation costs will be reduced $4,000 annually for five years, if this investment is made.

2. The firm is provided with an opportunity to purchase 10 used railroad flatcars at a total cost of $25,000. This equipment has a service life of five years with no scrap value. Not only will the purchase of the flatcars increase incremental revenue $4,000 annually, but transportation costs will also be lowered $1,000 each year.

3. Ten fork lifts are available for purchase to be used in terminal operations. The total investment cost is $5,000, with the equipment possessing a service life of five years and no salvage value. This particular investment will augment incremental revenues $1,000 each year and simultaneously reduce handling costs $1,000 annually.

For demonstration purposes, the estimated lives of the three assets are identical--five years. Notice that investment opportunity number one requires a capital expenditure of $20,000. This outlay generates incremental revenues of $2,000 annually for five years, while simultaneously reducing transportation cost outlays by $20,000 over the five-year period.

From an analytical point of view, carrier managers would be vitally interested in cash flows generated by the three projects under consideration. Table 12.1 represents both gross and net cash flows that would be generated if the firm described in investment opportunity number one were to expand its trailer fleet. To compute gross cash flow in year one, incremental revenues are added to the cost savings resulting from acquiring the 20 trailers. However, gross cash flow is subject to corporate income taxes, in this instance of 52 percent. (Investment tax credits have been ignored in these examples). Thus, net cash flow for each year is $2,800 to $14,400 for the life of the investment. In investment opportunity number two, purchasing the flatcars would produce an annual net cash flow of $2,400, and a cumulative net cash flow of $12,000, as indicated in Table 12.2. Table 12.3 shows earnings generated from acquisition of 10 fork lifts by the firm described in investment opportunity number three. Net cash flow for this investment is $960, with a five-year total of $4,800.

TABLE 12.1

Gross and Net Cash Flows Generated from Investment Opportunity Number One (dollars)

	Year One	Year Five	Total
Incremental revenue	2,000	2,000	10,000
Cost savings	4,000	4,000	20,000
Gross cash flow	6,000	6,000	30,000
Taxes (52 percent)	3,120	3,120	15,600
Net cash flow	2,880	2,880	14,400

Note: Investment tax credits are not included.

TABLE 12.2

Gross and Net Cash Flows Generated from Investment Opportunity Number Two (dollars)

	Year One	Year Five	Total
Incremental revenue	4,000	4,000	20,000
Cost savings	1,000	1,000	15,000
Gross cash flow	5,000	5,000	25,000
Taxes (52 percent)	2,600	2,600	13,000
Net cash flow	2,400	2,400	12,000

Note: Investment tax credits are not included.

TABLE 12.3

Gross and Net Cash Flows Generated from
Investment Opportunity Number Three
(dollars)

	Year One	Year Two	Total
Incremental revenue	1,000	1,000	5,000
Cost savings	1,000	1,000	5,000
Gross cash flow	2,000	2,000	10,000
Taxes (52 percent)	1,040	1,040	5,200
Net cash flow	960	960	4,800

Note: Investment tax credits are not included.

The data presented in Tables 12.1, 12.2, and 12.3 are inadequate for decision-making purposes because the time value of money has been ignored. For management decision purposes, the present value of income streams generated by each of the three investment opportunities is more meaningful. As previously indicated, present value is merely the discounted rate of return of the investment. The following formula is used to compute present value:

$$P_r = \frac{A_1}{(1+i)} + \frac{A_2}{(1+i)^2} + \ldots \frac{R_n}{(1+i)^n} + \frac{S}{(1+i)^n}$$

P_r = present value

i = interest rate, or cost of capital

$A_1 A_n$ = cash inflow after taxes during years 1, 2, 3...n

S = salvage value of the asset in year n

n= life of the asset

This formula is employed when comparing investment values with the supply cost of an asset. Stated another way, when present value exceeds investment costs, the investment is desirable.

Using the present-value formula to solve complex problems can be cumbersome. For example, assume that the cost of capital for the three investment proposals is 10 percent. Applying the present-value formula to investment opportunities one, two, and three results in the following:[3]

Investment one: $P_r = \frac{\$2,800}{(1.10)} + \frac{\$2,800}{(1.10)^2} + \frac{\$2,800}{(1.10)^3} + \frac{\$2,800}{(1.10)^4} + \frac{\$2,800}{(1.10)^5}$

Investment two: $P_r = \frac{\$2,400}{(1.10)} + \frac{\$2,400}{(1.10)^2} + \frac{\$2,400}{(1.10)^3} + \frac{\$2,400}{(1.10)^4} + \frac{\$2,400}{(1.10)^5}$

Investment three: $P_r = \frac{\$960}{(1.10)} + \frac{\$960}{(1.10)^2} + \frac{\$960}{(1.10)^3} + \frac{\$960}{(1.10)^4} + \frac{\$960}{(1.10)^5}$

An easier method for computing present value is to use a table of present values. Table 12.4 shows net cash flow for investment opportunity number one. By referring to the table of present values in Table 12.5, the present value can be determined.[4] To use the present-value table, turn to the column marked 10 percent and read downward for five years--0.909, 0.826, 0.756, 0.683, and 0.621, and multiply the net cash flow by the discount rate. Note that the present value of the net cash flow for investment opportunity number one in Table 12.4 is $10,922.60, not $14,400. Table 12.6 reflects the present value of investment opportunity number two, which is $9,196 rather than $12,000. Lastly, the present value of investment opportunity number three, illustrated in Table 12.7, is $3,638.90, and not $4,800.

TABLE 12.4

Discounted Cash Flow of Investment Opportunity Number One Using Present-Value Tables (dollars)

	Net Cash Flow	x	PV Ratio*	Present Value
Year one	2,880	x	.91	2,635.80
Year two	2,880	x	.83	2,390.40
Year three	2,880	x	.75	2,160.00
Year four	2,880	x	.68	1,950.80
Year five	2,880	x	.62	1,785.60
	14,400			10,922.60

*Assuming a 10 percent discount rate.

TABLE 12.5

Present Value of One Dollar

Periods Until Payment	1%	2%	4%	6%	8%	10%	12%	14%	15%	16%	18%	20%	22%	24%	25%	26%	28%	30%	35%	40%	45%	50%
1	0.990	0.980	0.962	0.943	0.926	0.909	0.893	0.877	0.870	0.862	0.847	0.833	0.820	0.806	0.800	0.794	0.781	0.769	0.741	0.714	0.690	0.667
2	0.980	0.961	0.925	0.890	0.857	0.826	0.797	0.769	0.756	0.743	0.718	0.694	0.672	0.650	0.640	0.630	0.610	0.592	0.549	0.510	0.476	0.444
3	0.971	0.942	0.889	0.840	0.794	0.751	0.712	0.675	0.658	0.641	0.609	0.579	0.551	0.524	0.512	0.500	0.477	0.455	0.406	0.364	0.328	0.296
4	0.961	0.924	0.855	0.792	0.735	0.683	0.636	0.592	0.572	0.552	0.516	0.482	0.451	0.423	0.410	0.397	0.373	0.350	0.301	0.260	0.226	0.193
5	0.951	0.906	0.822	0.747	0.681	0.621	0.567	0.519	0.497	0.476	0.437	0.402	0.370	0.341	0.328	0.315	0.291	0.269	0.223	0.186	0.156	0.132
6	0.942	0.888	0.790	0.705	0.630	0.564	0.507	0.456	0.432	0.410	0.370	0.335	0.303	0.275	0.262	0.250	0.227	0.207	0.165	0.133	0.103	0.033
7	0.933	0.871	0.760	0.665	0.583	0.513	0.452	0.400	0.376	0.354	0.314	0.279	0.249	0.222	0.210	0.198	0.178	0.159	0.122	0.095	0.074	0.059
8	0.923	0.853	0.731	0.627	0.540	0.467	0.404	0.351	0.327	0.305	0.266	0.233	0.204	0.179	0.168	0.157	0.139	0.123	0.091	0.068	0.051	0.039
9	0.914	0.837	0.703	0.592	0.500	0.424	0.361	0.308	0.284	0.263	0.225	0.194	0.167	0.144	0.134	0.125	0.108	0.094	0.067	0.048	0.035	0.026
10	0.905	0.820	0.676	0.558	0.463	0.386	0.322	0.270	0.247	0.227	0.191	0.162	0.137	0.116	0.107	0.099	0.035	0.073	0.050	0.015	0.024	0.017
11	0.896	0.804	0.650	0.527	0.429	0.350	0.287	0.237	0.215	0.195	0.162	0.135	0.112	0.094	0.086	0.079	0.066	0.056	0.037	0.025	0.017	0.012
12	0.887	0.788	0.625	0.497	0.397	0.319	0.257	0.208	0.187	0.168	0.137	0.112	0.092	0.076	0.069	0.062	0.052	0.043	0.027	0.018	0.012	0.008
13	0.879	0.773	0.601	0.469	0.368	0.290	0.229	0.182	0.163	0.145	0.116	0.093	0.075	0.061	0.055	0.050	0.040	0.033	0.020	0.013	0.008	0.005
14	0.870	0.758	0.577	0.442	0.340	0.263	0.205	0.160	0.141	0.125	0.099	0.078	0.062	0.049	0.044	0.039	0.032	0.025	0.015	0.009	0.006	0.003
15	0.861	0.743	0.555	0.417	0.315	0.239	0.183	0.140	0.123	0.108	0.084	0.065	0.051	0.040	0.035	0.031	0.025	0.020	0.011	0.006	0.004	0.002
16	0.853	0.728	0.534	0.394	0.292	0.218	0.163	0.123	0.107	0.093	0.071	0.054	0.042	0.032	0.028	0.025	0.019	0.015	0.008	0.005	0.003	0.002
17	0.844	0.714	0.513	0.371	0.270	0.198	0.146	0.108	0.093	0.080	0.060	0.045	0.034	0.026	0.023	0.020	0.015	0.012	0.006	0.003	0.002	0.001
18	0.836	0.700	0.494	0.350	0.250	0.180	0.130	0.095	0.081	0.069	0.051	0.038	0.028	0.021	0.018	0.016	0.012	0.009	0.005	0.002	0.001	0.001
19	0.823	0.686	0.475	0.331	0.232	0.164	0.116	0.083	0.070	0.060	0.043	0.031	0.023	0.017	0.014	0.012	0.009	0.007	0.003	0.002	0.001	
20	0.820	0.673	0.456	0.312	0.215	0.149	0.104	0.073	0.061	0.051	0.037	0.026	0.019	0.014	0.012	0.010	0.007	0.005	0.002	0.001	0.001	
21	0.811	0.660	0.439	0.294	0.199	0.135	0.093	0.064	0.053	0.044	0.031	0.022	0.015	0.011	0.009	0.008	0.006	0.004	0.002	0.001		
22	0.803	0.647	0.422	0.278	0.184	0.123	0.083	0.056	0.046	0.038	0.026	0.018	0.013	0.009	0.007	0.006	0.004	0.003	0.001	0.001		
23	0.795	0.634	0.406	0.262	0.170	0.112	0.074	0.049	0.040	0.033	0.022	0.015	0.010	0.007	0.006	0.005	0.003	0.002	0.001			
24	0.788	0.622	0.390	0.247	0.158	0.102	0.066	0.043	0.035	0.028	0.019	0.013	0.008	0.006	0.005	0.004	0.003	0.002	0.001			
25	0.780	0.610	0.375	0.233	0.146	0.092	0.059	0.038	0.030	0.024	0.016	0.010	0.007	0.005	0.004	0.003	0.002	0.001	0.001			
26	0.772	0.598	0.361	0.220	0.135	0.084	0.053	0.033	0.026	0.021	0.014	0.009	0.006	0.004	0.003	0.002	0.002	0.001				
27	0.764	0.586	0.347	0.207	0.125	0.076	0.047	0.029	0.023	0.018	0.011	0.007	0.005	0.003	0.002	0.002	0.001	0.001				
28	0.757	0.574	0.333	0.196	0.116	0.069	0.042	0.026	0.020	0.016	0.010	0.006	0.004	0.002	0.002	0.002	0.001	0.001				
29	0.749	0.563	0.321	0.185	0.107	0.063	0.037	0.022	0.017	0.014	0.008	0.005	0.003	0.002	0.002	0.001	0.001	0.001				
30	0.742	0.552	0.308	0.174	0.099	0.057	0.033	0.020	0.015	0.012	0.007	0.004	0.003	0.002	0.001	0.001	0.001					
40	0.672	0.453	0.208	0.097	0.046	0.022	0.011	0.005	0.004	0.003	0.001	0.001										
50	0.608	0.372	0.141	0.054	0.021	0.009	0.003	0.001	0.001	0.001												

TABLE 12.6

Discounted Cash Flow of Investment Opportunity Number Two Using Present Value Tables (dollars)

	Net Cash Flow	x	PV Ratio*	Present Value
Year one	2,400	x	.91	2,184.00
Year two	2,400	x	.83	1,992.00
Year three	2,400	x	.75	1,900.00
Year four	2,400	x	.68	1,632.00
Year five	2,400	x	.62	1,488.00
	12,000			9,196.00

*Assuming a 10 percent discount rate.

TABLE 12.7

Discounted Cash Flow of Investment Opportunity Number Three Using Present Value Tables (dollars)

	Net Cash Flow	x	PV Ratio*	Present Value
Year one	960	x	.91	873.60
Year two	960	x	.83	796.80
Year three	960	x	.75	720.00
Year four	960	x	.68	652.80
Year five	960	x	.62	595.20
	4,800			3,638.90

*Assuming a 10 percent discount rate.

The Discounted Rate of Return and the Cost of Capital

The cost of capital can be defined as the minimum rate of return necessary to induce a firm to invest. The discounted rate of return is the rate of discount which, when applied to future cash flows, will equate their sums to the asset's supply price. The formula for computing the discounted rate of return is as follows:

$$C_r = \frac{A_1}{(1+r)} + \frac{A_2}{(1+r)^2} + \frac{\ldots A_n}{(1+r)^n}$$

If r>i (return greater than interest), the investment is financially desirable. Applying the formula to our three hypothetical opportunities indicates that all three investments are desirable.

Finding the discounted rate of return is primarily a question of trial and error. Suppose a firm does not know the discounted rate of return. How does it locate the rate? Experimentation is required. Table 12.8 illustrates the trial use of a 2 percent discount rate in an attempt to discover the true discount rate. Turning to the present value table (Table 12.5), add the values in the 2 percent column for the five years involved, which total $4.71. Multiplying this amount times the three investment opportunities produces results of $13,564.80, $11,304.00, and $4,521.60, respectively. Obviously, 2 percent is too low, and thus a higher rate should be experimented with until an appropriate rate is found.

TABLE 12.8

Trial Use of a 2 Percent Discount Rate in Three Hypothetical Investment Opportunities (dollars)

	Net Cash Flow	x	PV Ratio*	Present Value
Investment one	2,880	x	4.71	13,564.80
Investment two	2,400	x	4.71	11,304.00
Investment three	960	x	4.71	4,521.60
				29,390.40

*4.71 = .98 + .96 + .94 + .92 + .91.

Other Measures of Profitability

Two additional techniques of analysis should be employed when evaluating capital expenditure projects. These are payback index and profitability index (PI). Payback measures the number of years necessary to recoup the original investment, after taxes but before depreciation. Profitability indexes reveal the desirability of investing in a given project. The two formulas are expressed as follows:

$$\text{Payback} = \frac{\text{Net investment}}{\text{Net cash flow}}$$

$$\text{PI} = \frac{\text{Cash flow (PV annuity)} + \text{Salvage (PV single payment + others)}}{\text{Net Investment}}$$

While payback reveals the number of years necessary to recover the original investment, PI is concerned with the overall profits associated with an investment. A PI$>$1 is favorable whereas a PI$<$1 should be avoided.

To illustrate the application of payback and PI, suppose that the management of Jones Trucklines is studying the feasibility of purchasing and installing a new automated conveyor system in one of its major terminals. Data affiliated with the system is represented in Table 12.9. Notice that installation of the new conveyor system will produce a net cash flow of $23,400. Total net investment, moreover, is $128,000, because of an increase of $8,000 in working capital required for purchasing the conveyor system. Accounting depreciation is $100,000 for the equipment's estimated 10-year life ($128,000, less scrap and working capital).

TABLE 12.9

Cash Flows and Net Investment in a Hypothetical Conveyor System (dollars)

Net income before taxes and depreciation	36,800
Taxes (cash outflow)	13,400
Net cash flow	23,400
Investment in conveyor equipment	120,000
Working capital	8,000
Net additional total investment	128,000*
Scrap	20,000
Less working capital	8,000
Accounting depreciation data	100,000
Service life of 10 years - depreciation	10,000

*Concerned with this amount in decision.

Jones' management is concerned with determining the number of years required for the investment to be retired as a result of new cash flow. This would be determined in the following manner:

$$\text{Payback} = \frac{\text{Net investment}}{\text{Net cash flow}}$$

$$\text{Payback} = \frac{\$128,000}{\$\ 23,400}$$

$$\text{Payback} = 5.47 \text{ years}$$

Even though 5.47 years is a relatively short period, a PI should be constructed. Assume that Jones has a corporate policy that requires a 15 percent rate of return on all internal investment. Using the present value tables (Table 12.5), turn to the 15 percent column and add the PVs for years 1 through 10, which total 5.019. The salvage and working capital, however, are recovered in year 10, so use the PV for a single payment in year 10, or 0.247. Having gathered the essential data, PI is computed as follows:

$$\text{PI} = \frac{\text{Cash flow (PV annuity)} + \text{Salvage (PV single payment + others)}}{\text{Net investment}}$$

$$\text{PI} = \frac{\$23,400\ (5.019) + 20,000\ (0.247) + \$8,000\ (0.247)}{\$128,000}$$

$$\text{PI} = .9716$$

Inasmuch as $.9716 < 1$, acquiring the automated conveyor system would be an undesirable investment, if Jones truly seeks a 15 percent return on all internal investments. Interestingly, if accelerated depreciation is used rather than straight-line, this project has a $\text{PI} > 1$. Similar results are obtained if federal investment tax credits are calculated and used.

For another example of payback and PI, suppose that Frontier Airlines is interested in acquiring new fork lift equipment for its freight operations. By purchasing new equipment, the firm can avoid a $4,400 maintenance outlay, but income tax liability will increase. Table 12.10 illustrates cost data associated with the carrier investment decision. As indicated, net investment is $21,200, and the annual depreciation charge is $2,120. Table 12.11 reflects net cash flow for the investment, which is $4,120. Depreciation, in this situation, functions as a tax shield, and Frontier's net investment is shown in Table 12.12. Payout in this case, is the maintenance outlay avoided plus the increase in income taxes. With respect to this fork lift investment, suppose Frontier's management desires to earn, as a matter of policy, 12 percent on all internal capital expenditures. Payback is computed as follows:

$$\text{Payback} = \frac{\$23,000}{\$\ 4,400}$$

$$\text{Payback} = \text{five years}$$

On the other hand, the profitability index is as follows:

$$PI = \frac{\$4,120\ (5.32) + \$4,000\ (0.322)}{\$23,000}$$

$$PI = 1.06$$

This, of course, is a profitable acquisition, since PI>1.

TABLE 12.10

Depreciation of Hypothetical Fork Lift Investment
(dollars)

Fork lift equipment	24,000
Service and delivery	1,200
Total investment	25,200
Salvage	4,000
Net investment	21,200
Annual depreciation charge (10-year life)	2,120

TABLE 12.11

Gross and Net Cash Flow Generated from
Hypothetical Fork Lift Investment
(dollars)

Cash flow after depreciation but before taxes	4,000
Less taxes	2,000
Net savings after depreciation and taxes	2,000
Add depreciation	2,120
Net cash flow	4,120

TABLE 12.12

Net Investment in Hypothetical Fork Lift Investment
(dollars)

Equipment	24,000	
Service and delivery	1,200	
Total	25,200	
Outlay avoided	4,400	
Net investment	20,800	Payout
Increase in income taxes	2,200	
Net investment	23,000	

Nomographs

On many occasions, a need develops for quick and accurate calculations regarding the feasibility of a capital expenditure project. Nomographs are graphs that enable one to use a straightedge to relate the numerical value of a dependent variable when the values of two or more independent variables are known. Nomographs are predicated on the following formula:

$$\text{Percent of return on investment} = \frac{\text{Annual gross returns} - \text{Annual depreciation charge}}{\text{Gross capital investment} = \dfrac{\text{Annual depreciation charge}}{2}}$$

Basically, nomographs are valuable because of their speed and ease of use.

Although somewhat limited in application, nomographs can be used in transportation when considering capital expenditure programs.[5] To illustrate the application and worth of nomographs, consider the following three examples.

1. Assume that construction of a small freight terminal requires a gross investment of $6,000. The terminal is estimated to have a depreciable life of 15 years, and annual incremental income generated by the asset is anticipated to be $2,000. What is the rate of return?

The nomograph used to find the correct rate of return is presented in Figure 12.2. Locate the reference point R and place a straightedge on the $6,000 investment and the $2,000 return. At this point, by drawing a line from R through the anticipated 15-year life span, the rate of return is located at about 24 percent.

FIGURE 12.2

Nomograph on Hypothetical Terminal Investment

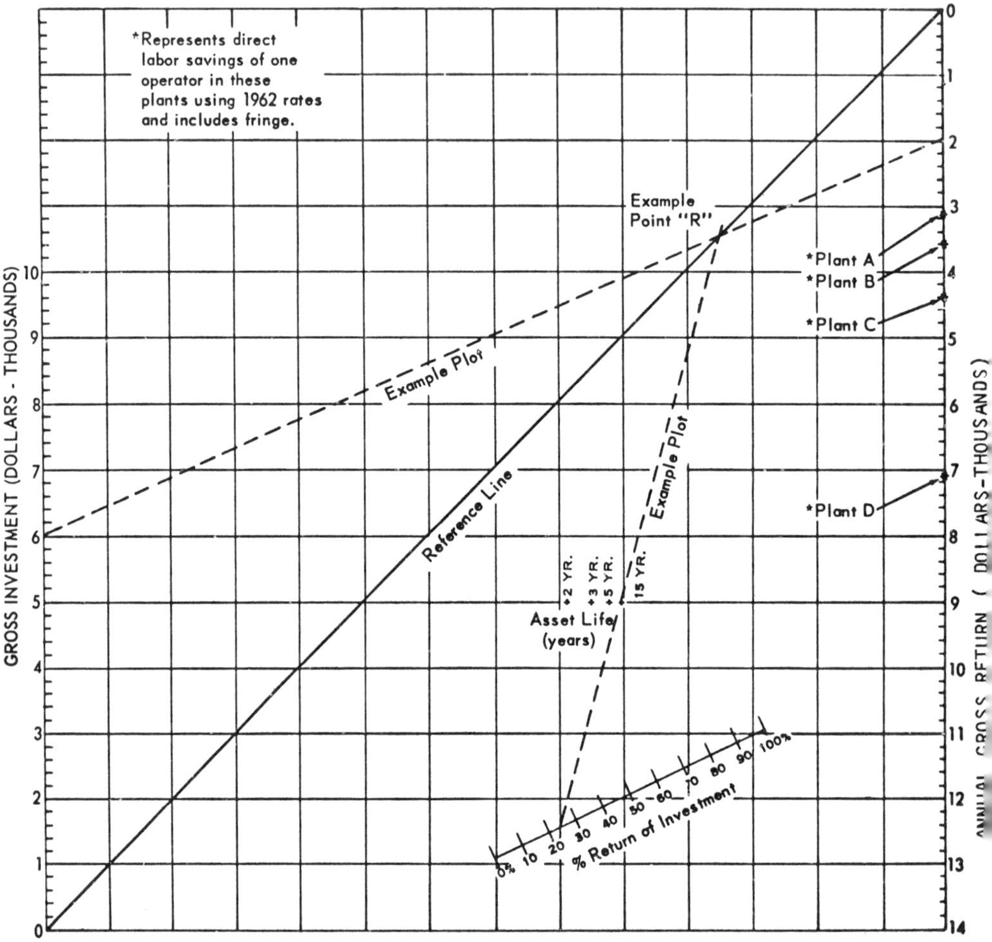

Note: 1. This graph can be used for larger values than scale by moving decimal point (on both scales).

2. Does not consider working capital needs, start-up costs (including off-standard variance), rearrangement expense, tool amortization or other nonrecurring operating expense needed for the project.

3. Based on straight line depreciation.

4. As a rough estimate this graph can be used for percentage return of first year or subsequent years.

Source: Leslie R. Greene, "Useful Tools for Estimating Economic Justification," The Engineering Economist, vol. 8, no. 3 (Spring 1963), p. 34. By permission.

2. Assume that Arkansas Best Freight has an opportunity to acquire four fork lifts for $10,000. The estimated equipment life is 10 years, and the investment represents a 10 percent rate of return. What should the annual savings be in order to justify this investment?

The nomograph to be used is illustrated in Figure 12.3, which is more detailed than the first nomograph. Using this nomograph, find the point where the 10 percent curve intersects the 10-year vertical line. By reading horizontally to the left, a worth value on Scale W is obtained of 6.25. At this point, take a straightedge and connect 6.25 with the equipment cost of $10,000, located on Scale C. By extending the straightedge to the intersection with Scale C, the savings is located. In this case, the annual savings is $1,625.

3. Suppose that United Parcel Service (UPS) is considering purchasing a new truck for $10,000, which in turn will produce a $4,000 annual savings for the firm. While it is obvious that the payback period is 2.4 years, what would the capital recovery period be if UPS' internal investment policy requires a 30 percent rate of return?

Again, refer to the nomograph in Figure 12.3. Using a straightedge, connect the $4,000 savings per year with the investment outlay on Scale C of $10,000. Extending the straightedge to Scale W, the value 2.5 is obtained. Reading horizontally to the right, the 30 percent curve is located. Dropping down vertically, the payback period is seven years.

Investment Comparisons

On the surface, one investment opportunity often appears more desirable or more profitable than another. This superiority is often an illusion. Table 12.13 demonstrates the need for in-depth analysis of capital expenditure projects. As indicated, two investments of equal amounts are being evaluated. Investment number one, however, has an expected life of one year and will provide a gross rate of return of 30 percent, as compared with 20 percent for investment opportunity number two. Nevertheless, when the present value of the two investments is computed at 15 percent, note that investment one's profitability is $261,000, not $300,000; on the other hand, investment two has a present value of $458,000. Lastly, investment one has a PI of 1.26, whereas investment two's is 1.46. In summary, when confronted with two or more investment alternatives, an in-depth analysis is in order.

FIGURE 12.3

Nomograph on Hypothetical Fork Lift Investment and New Truck Investment

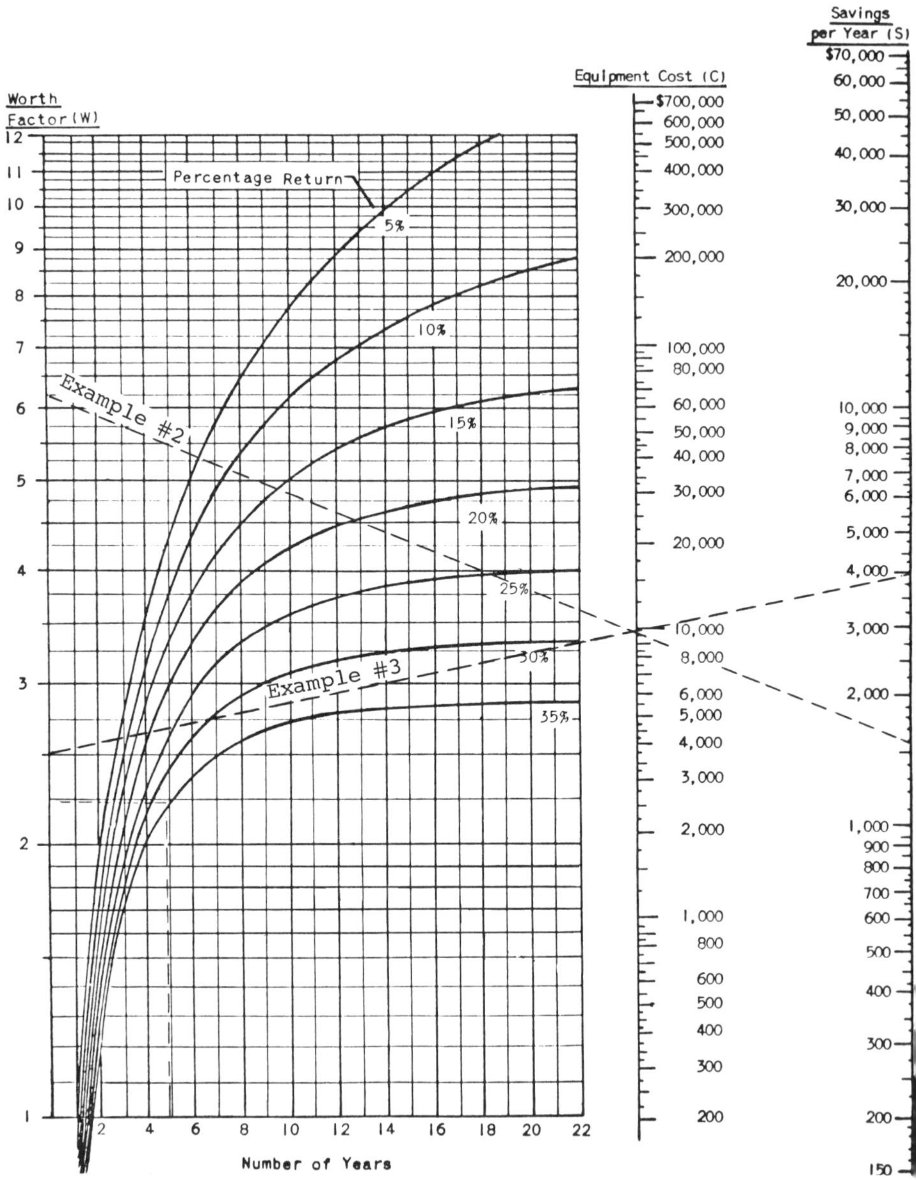

Source: Philip A. Scheuble, Jr., "How to Figure Equipment Replacement," Harvard Business Review, vol. 33, no. 5 (September 1955), p. 85. By permission.

TABLE 12.13

Comparison of Two Investment Opportunities

	Investment Opportunity Number One	Investment Opportunity Number Two
Investment	$1,000,000	$1,000,000
Annual earnings	300,000	200,000
Expected life	one year	three years
Return on investment	30 percent	20 percent
Profitability at 15 percent rate	$1,261,000	$1,458,000
Profitability index	1.26	1.46

Pro Forma Income Statements

Careful and in-depth planning are prerequisites to success in any business venture. Pro forma means projected or anticipated, and a pro forma income statement reflects what management anticipates will occur in the future. The value of pro forma income statements is that they assist the business enterprise in attaining its objectives. Without a statement of objectives, numerically expressed in pro forma income statements, management might conceivably fail to do its utmost toward increasing profits or expanding dividends. Also, the pro forma income statement requires interaction among all segments of a firm, which, in turn, stresses coordination.

Suppose that Federal Barge Line's management is studying the possibility of capital expenditures associated with the following investment opportunities A, B, and C, of $1,500, $2,000, and $1,800, respectively, for different time periods.

A. A $1,500 investment in specialized materials-handling equipment will reduce total costs associated with handling shipments from $500 to $200 annually. Moreover, the investment will increase income generated by $1,000 for a two-year period.

B. An investment of $2,000 in bracing equipment will not only reduce costs from $900 to $600 annually, but will also produce additional income of $1,500 for a period of three years.

C. Incremental revenues are anticipated to increase $2,500 annually for a two-year period as a result of an investment in equipment that totals $1,800. This investment will reduce outlays from $2,000 each year to $1,500.

For investment purposes, management should be concerned with incremental revenue only.

The carrier's management is interested in projecting the impact and the results of the proposed investment alternatives on revenues. Table 12.14 shows pro forma process over the years involved. Note that only opportunity B still generates an incremental revenue in 1974. Examining the three investment alternatives on a composite basis reveals that opportunity B is the most profitable, which is shown in Table 12.15. However, these data are incorrect, since future earnings have not been discounted. In the lower part of Table 12.15, however, gross incremental income is somewhat different, when the present value of the three streams of income is computed.

TABLE 12.14

Pro Forma Income Statement Investment Alternatives, 1972, 1973, 1974 (dollars)

	Opportunity A	Opportunity B	Opportunity C
1972			
Sales increase*	1,000	1,500	2,500
Transport gross margin	1,000	1,500	2,500
Less transport outlays	200	600	1,500
Gross income	800	900	1,000
1973			
Sales increase*	1,000	1,500	2,500
Transport gross margin	1,000	1,500	2,500
Less transport outlays	200	600	1,500
Gross income	800	900	1,000
1974			
Sales increase*	0	1,500	0
Transport gross margin	0	1,500	0
Less transport outlays		600	
Gross income	0	900	

*Assuming no installation expense.

TABLE 12.15

Composite and Discounted Pro Forma Income Statement
Investment Alternatives, 1972, 1973, 1974
(dollars)

	Sales Increase*	Transport Gross Margin	Less Transport Outlays[b]	Gross Incremental Income
Opportunity A	2,000	2,000	400	1,600
Opportunity B	4,500	4,500	1,800	2,600
Opportunity C	5,000	5,000	3,000	2,000
Discount at 15 Percent				
Product A	1,630	1,630	326	1,304
Product B	3,435	3,435	1,374	2,061
Product C	4,075	4,075	2,395	1,680

*Assuming no installation expense.

[b]Transport outlays also discounted at 15 percent for applicable years being considered.

Benefits available to management from using pro forma income statements are evident. Not only should transportation capital expenditure programs be carefully evaluated, but their impact on future revenues, costs, and profits should be evaluated. Furthermore, changes in balance sheet items resulting from acquisition of capital assets should also be projected and analyzed.

RATE LEVELS

Regulated rail, motor, water, air, and pipeline carriers are limited in the aggregate amount of revenues that they can earn by law, as we noted in Chapter 2.[6] That is to say, rates of return and operating ratio levels are established and administered by federal agencies such as the ICC, CAB,[7] and Federal Power Commission. The absolute level of aggregate and individual rates is important because it determines carrier profits, which in turn influence sources of funds and capital assets.[8]

Numerous elements of value must be considered when ascertaining a transportation carrier's rate base or fair value on which earnings are permitted.[9] These include the following:

1. Auxiliary, or overhead construction cost

Labor	Interest
Materials and supplies	Brokerage and bond discount
Transportation	Organization
Injuries and damages	Engineering
Insurance	Contingencies
Legal expenses	Incidentals

2. Tangible items of value

Used and useful land	Buildings
Equipment	Working capital

3. Intangible items of value

Franchise value	Favorable contracts
Going concern value	Patent rights[10]
Goodwill	

In short, these items constitute value, which in turn is reflected in the rate base. As we noted in Chapter 2, the exact statistical weight given these items is a matter of considerable judgment. This is particularly true with items in category three.

Rail carriers and pipelines have substantial amounts of fixed costs and their overall carrying levels are controlled through the mechanism of rates of return. For instance, if Colonial Pipelines' property valuation devoted to the public is $1 million, and the industry is permitted a 7 percent rate of return by the ICC, any continued earnings exceeding $70,000 would result in a governmental order to reduce rates.[11] Industries with large fixed costs are more apt to be regulated in this fashion. Air carrier rate levels--although most air carrier costs are variable--are also regulated by means of rates of return. The CAB permits the industry to earn an average of 11 percent rate of return,[12] which is composed of a weighted average of debt and equity.[13] The concept of a "zone of reasonableness" was noted in Chapter 2.

Short-run costs of motor carriers, barge lines, and bus companies are mostly variable, so a rate-of-return control device for industry earnings is not applicable. In this segment of the transportation industry, an operating ratio is employed as an earnings standard because of the predominance of variable costs. The ratio is expressed as follows:

$$\frac{\text{Operating Expenses}}{\text{Operating Revenues}} \times 100 \text{ percent} = \text{Operating Ratio}$$

For control purposes, the ICC permits carriers in a specific region an operating ratio of .93. This means, of course, that for every dollar of revenue, the carrier makes $.93 for expenses and $.07 in profits, income taxes, and interest. However, many carriers turn their capital over 20 times a year and hence earn $1.40 per invested dollar. While the operating ratio standard has been attacked as being no standard at all, it is useful for controlling overall earnings levels of firms that are not highly capital intensive and for which a majority of costs are variable.[14]

SOURCES OF FUNDS

Capital, like any other resource, seeks uses that pay the highest return. The capital market and other sources of funds are imperfect markets, and carrier managers should be aware of their existence and function when new equipment or routes are to be planned. Managerial acumen regarding fund sources and costs will enable a carrier to carefully compare and select financial resources that best enable the firm to achieve its objectives. In a comprehensive sense, there are five principal sources of funds for transportation carriers: stock markets, financial institutions, manufacturers, the government, and retained earnings.

Stock Markets

Many transportation carriers seek funds through the sale of securities and use an investment banker to initially handle the issue. In the event that the amount of funds sought is beyond the scope of an individual investment banker, a temporary syndicate may be found to underwrite and issue the securities. Frequently, stock issued by Delta Air Lines and the Southern Railway System have been placed in this fashion.[15] Recently, a trend has developed regarding private placement of securities directly from some carriers to financial institutions, such as pension funds.[16]

Fundamentally, there are two types of secondary markets for carrier securities: the organized exchanges, such as the New York Stock Exchange, the American Stock Exchange, and Regional Exchanges, and the over-the-counter market. While most rail and air stocks are traded on the organized exchanges, public motor carrier stock, for the most part, is handled in the over-the-counter market. Dealer costs vary considerably between the two secondary markets.[17]

Financial Institutions

Various sources of funds available to carrier firms for expansion include banks, pension funds, insurance companies, and financial organizations such as the Household Finance Corporation. Many carriers maintain lines of credit for day-to-day operations as well as acquisitions and expansion. Credit arrangements from financial institutions can be syndicated among institutions if debt is sufficiently large.

Manufacturers

Many manufacturers, such as International Harvester and Mack Truck, finance equipment acquisition. By engaging in the commercial paper business, manufacturers are able to develop reliable customers and frequently provide liberal trade-in allowances in order to encourage up-to-date equipment. This particular arrangement is primarily used in the motor carrier industry.

Government

Under the provisions of the National Transportation Act of 1958 and the Small Business Act, government guaranteed loans are available to railroads and motor carriers that are unable to secure funds from private sources at reasonable credit cost.[18] These programs are administered by the DOT and the Small Business Administration. Under the Merchant Marine Act of 1970, guaranteed loans are available for construction of new ocean vessels, as well as operating subsidies.

Retained Earnings

Although management philosophy regarding debt, leverage, and capital costs varies considerably from company to company, many companies prefer to finance new equipment and facilities through retained earnings. During the early growth period of the motor carrier industry, retained earnings represented the principal source of funds for expansion, due to the lack of available credit.[19]

LEASE-OR-BUY DECISIONS

The managerial question regarding leasing or buying a capital asset is one of the oldest controversies in the field of financial management.[20] The manner of resolving this question varies from company to company and from firm to firm. Whether a transportation carrier will buy or lease depends on many circumstances. Most airlines, for instance, lease aircraft from the Greyhound Corporation, banks, and other financial intermediaries. Lease expenses are deductible from ordinary income for tax purposes, and in some situations improve the pertinent debt-equity ratios, which are employed by analysts evaluating the firm. Leased equipment, on the other hand, is deducted from net worth and hence can distort a carrier balance sheet.

There are basically three types of lease agreements: finance, net, and maintenance. All leases contain provisions concerning the method of rate settlement; termination, replacement, and addition of vehicles; settlement of lessor's obligations; and maintenance and operating costs. A finance lease usually involves the lessee's paying for all maintenance outlays and guaranteeing against any substantial resale equipment loss. A net lease, conversely, charges the lessee with the responsibility for maintenance outlays and, after a final adjustment, the lessor reclaims the vehicles at the lease period's termination. A maintenance lease is confined to maintaining equipment, but its terms vary considerably. Braniff, for example, contracts for maintenance work.

Carrier managers should ideally consider the following factors when searching for a leasing company: stability and financial strength, capitalization cost and types of equipment, capability to fulfill lease agreements, company policies regarding net and maintenance leases, payment policies, and auxiliary services provided.[21] Lower operating costs, fleet control, insured maintenance, and proper and sufficient insurance, however, represent advantages gained from ownership.

Although capital cost constitutes an important variable to be evaluated by carrier management in lease-or-buy decisions, detailed analysis should be concentrated on the effect of leasing on overall profits. Management should recognize, moreover, that most administrative expenses are shifted to the leasing company. In short, several factors must be evaluated in lease-or-buy decisions.

FEDERAL FINANCIAL REGULATIONS

Under most circumstances, carriers issuing stocks and bonds must file their prospectus with the Securities and Exchange Commission.[22] Railroads, motor carriers, water carriers, and bus companies must first secure permission from the ICC before they can issue securities and debt. Regarding railroad equity and debt issues the ICC regulation states:

> . . . It shall be unlawful for any carrier to issue any share of capital stock or any bond or other

> evidence of interest or indebtedness of the carrier . . . or to assume any obligation or liability as lessor, lessee, endorser, surety, or otherwise, in respect of the securities of any other person, natural or artificial, even though permitted by the authority creating the carrier corporation, unless and until, and then only to the extent that, upon application by the carrier, and after inspection by the Commission of the purposes and uses of the proposed issue and the proceeds thereof, or of the proposed assumption of obligation or liability in respect of the securities of any other person, natural or artificial, the Commission by order authorizes such issue or assumption.[23]

The commission will not permit a rail carrier to issue securities, debt, or assume securities, unless the proposed issue is necessary for the carrier to perform service.

Regarding motor carriers and buses, section 214 of the Interstate Commerce Act exempts security and debt issues when the value of the offering, together with the value of other securities outstanding, does not exceed $1 million. Also, any note possessing a maturity date of two years or less and of not more than $200,000 does not require commission approval. This $200,000 exception is applicable only when the $1 million valuation does not include any short-term notes.[24]

SUMMARY

Ongoing capital acquisition programs are essential if carrier managers are to adequately provide quality services. By employing realistic financial analytical techniques such as payback and PI, alternative investment projects can be ranked and priorities assigned. Rate levels and sources of funds are important subjects to carrier management because of profits, capital costs, and aggregate revenues. Lastly, carrier executives must be able to resolve the basic controversy regarding lease or buy, as well as being aware of federal securities and debt regulations.

NOTES

1. See Joel Dean, "Measuring the Productivity of Capital," <u>Harvard Business Review</u>, January-February 1954, pp. 120-29,

where a broader presentation of capital expenditure programs is developed. Much of this section is heavily influenced by Dean's work.

2. Milton H. Spencer, Managerial Economics, 3rd ed. (Homewood, Ill.: Richard D. Irwin, 1968), p. 386.

3. Salvage is ignored in this example.

4. Interestingly, available data indicate that few firms actually use present-value techniques or sophisticated investment techniques, for that matter, when making capital expenditure decisions. Consult W. Warren Haynes and Martin B. Solomon, Jr., "A Misplaced Emphasis in Capital Budgeting," Quarterly Review of Economics and Business, February 1962, pp. 39-43; James H. Miller, "A Glimpse at Practice in Calculating and Using Return on Investment," N.A.A. Bulletin, June 1960, pp. 65-76; D. F. Istvan, "The Capital Expenditure Decision-Making Process in Forty-Eight Large Corporations" (Ph.D. diss., Indiana University, School of Business, 1959); and Walter W. Heller, "Anatomy of Investment Decisions," Harvard Business Review, March 1951, pp. 95-103; for evidence that few firms use correct procedures when making capital expenditure decisions.

5. Spencer, op. cit., p. 408. Spencer writes that nomographs do not ". . . provide explicitly for increased working capital need or for special expenses which will result from the project. Such increases, therefore, should be anticipated at the outset and treated as part of the equipment cost or gross investment in order to obtain a more reliable estimate of percent return on investment."

6. For an interesting and in-depth evaluation of carrier earnings levels, consult Alfred E. Kahn, The Economics of Regulation, vol. 1 (New York: John Wiley and Sons, 1970), pp. 26-54.

7. "Money Men: Wings of Paper," Forbes, February 15, 1972, p. 54.

8. Grant M. Davis and Stephen W. Brown, Logistics Management (Lexington, Mass.: D. C. Heath and Co., 1974), Chapter 14.

9. Value, of course, is a nebulous concept, given various arguments regarding reproduction or original cost. See Martin T. Farris and Roy J. Sampson, Public Utilities: Regulation, Management and Ownership (Boston: Houghton Mifflin Co., 1973), Chapter 6, for an extended review of the many controversies associated with original and reproduction cost.

10. J. Bryant and H. Herrman, Elements of Utility Rate Determination (New York: McGraw-Hill, 1940), pp. 46-113.

11. There have been few orders to reduce rates because of inflationary excesses during the past two decades. One problem confronting government regulators is the weak and strong road problem that brings about uneven carrier earnings.

12. Actual rates of return have tended to stabilize at 2 percent. Consult William E. Fruhan, Jr., The Fight for Competitive Advantage:

A Study of the United States Domestic Trunk Air Carriers (Boston: Graduate School of Business Administration, Harvard University, 1972), p. 26, for a review of air carrier earnings.

13. The CAB permits a 5.4 percent return on equity capital and 4.7 percent on debt.

14. D. Philip Locklin, Economics of Transportation, 7th ed. (Homewood, Ill.: Richard D. Irwin, 1972), p. 710.

15. This situation was brought about by the financial magnitude of the issues and the underwriting guarantee.

16. The teamsters union is active in financial arrangements.

17. See John W. Bowyer, Investment Analysis and Management, 3rd ed. (Homewood, Ill.: Richard D. Irwin, 1966), Chapter 5, for an excellent discussion of brokerage cost in the securities market.

18. U.S., Congress, PL 85-726, 85th Cong., 2nd sess., 1958; 67 Stat. 230.

19. Charles A. Taff, Commercial Motor Transportation, 4th ed. (Homewood, Ill.: Richard D. Irwin, 1969), Chapter 8.

20. Spencer, op. cit., Chapter 16, contains an extended discussion of leasing techniques.

21. Clyde W. Phelps, The Role of Fleet Leasing in Motor Vehicle Fleet Plans of Business Firms (Baltimore: Commercial Credit Co., 1969), pp. 30-36.

22. Exceptions include state and municipal bonds, receiver certificates, U.S. government notes and bonds, securities issued by commercial banks and savings and loan associations, railroad securities, and select issues not exceeding $300,000 at the Securities and Exchange Commission's option.

23. 49 USC 20 (a) (2).

24. Ibid., 214. Also consult John Guandolo, Transportation Law, 2nd ed. (Dubuque, Iowa: Wm. C. Brown Co., 1973), Chapter 51, for an excellent presentation on the regulated dimension of carrier finance.

CHAPTER 13
HUMAN RELATIONS, PERSONNEL MANAGEMENT, AND TRAINING

In this chapter the human element of the transport industry will be discussed. This variable affects every corporate organization and is important to profitability. People—both management and labor—are the most important assets of any transport company. The manner in which a carrier utilizes this asset is based on its philosophy of human relations, personnel management, and training.

EVOLUTION OF HUMAN RELATIONS

Concern for the individual worker by his employer has evolved from a complete lack to a state of sophisticated analysis by industrial psychologists. Today, employers are cognizant of worker wants, needs, and desires, because productivity and profits depend, to a great extent, on the interest and enthusiasm of the individual worker toward his company. This is especially true in transport.[1]

Unionization has brought concern for the individual worker into focus. To some degree, unionization arose out of the companies' lack of concern for individual dignity. The early Industrial Revolution, with its sweatshops and child labor, is a continual reminder of this lack of human concern.

Transportation firms did not learn the lessons of cooperation and concern for individual dignity overnight. They too went through a maturation process that started with a total lack of concern for wages, fringe benefits, working conditions, and safety. Today the industry is faced with increasing demands by workers to place worker interests and wants on a level with company existence.

Historically, transport companies have provided avenues for some people to gain self-actualization and bring the full fruits of their abilities to bear on the advancement of personal goals and objectives, while at the same time achieving company goals and objectives. Today, with a greater concern for the individual, larger numbers of individuals have the opportunity to work in a pleasant environment, enjoy good fringe benefits, and share in the growing demand for transport services. Many of these people hope to play an important managerial role in transport's future.

In order to succeed in building their companies and industries, transport firms were forced to establish a corporate function to handle personnel and training matters. During the development period, railroads needed trained labor gangs to lay ties and tracks, as well as to supply food, transportation, and protection. Large numbers of people were involved in sales, operations, and administration, as well as construction. These people had to be recruited, hired, trained, paid and, in some cases, terminated. The same was true for waterways, airlines, trucking, and pipelines.

Since there were different levels of skilled jobs, different approaches to personnel and training methods were required. Engineers, pilots, and drivers required more attention than gandy dancers, stokers, baggage handlers, and dock workers. However, each of these functions is important and contributes to profitability. As a result, some training and orientation to job responsibilities is required.

Today, job skills in transportation, and in industry as a whole, have increased in importance. An airline pilot with 250 passengers and a multimillion-dollar aircraft must be well qualified. The public conscience demands that the air pilot, as well as the rail engineer, truck driver, and barge captain, be qualified in terms of job expertise and physical capabilities. Because of transport's commitment and involvement with the public welfare, standards of job performance have been established and must be met. This societal concern is easily seen in the movement of people, but, because of the pivotal nature of transportation to the economy, it also applies to freight transportation.

Because society has a very definite concern, transportation carriers have responded with better employment practices and training procedures. A good public image is important and should receive the attention of carrier management.[2] Thus, carrier management philosophies must include attention to society's demands and provide for improvements in employee relations and qualifications. Alert carrier managers know that the end result will be long-run growth and profitability.

FACTORS AFFECTING CHANGE IN HUMAN RELATIONS

As times change, so do management concerns, techniques, and social concerns. In addition to the concern of workers for increases in wages, fringe benefits, and improved working conditions, and the concern of society for more efficient services, carrier management must react to the changing trends in corporate management philosophies, mobility, youth, and women.

Management Philosophy

Every carrier has a management philosophy, whether it is written or not, and this philosophy is a reflection of ownership and management. One facet of this philosophy will outline the corporate goals and objectives in a dynamic society. Profit growth, dividend payout, debt-equity ratios, and acquisitions are but a few of the goals and objectives that will reflect the management philosophy of the company. The overall purpose of existence is the overriding factor in every corporate management philosophy.[3]

Another very important aspect of a carrier management philosophy is concern for "people development," since this is its prime corporate asset.[4] This philosophy will be reflected in personnel, training, and hiring practices as well as the general attitude toward company employees.

The degree of management delegation of authority also reflects its management philosophy.[5] Through the expansion of delegation of authority, some companies have attempted to provide an environment conducive to each manager's realizing his full potential as a manager.[6]

Finally, the corporate organization structure also reflects management philosophies in the areas of delegation of authority, communications, development of management talent, personnel matters, and societal concerns.

Mobility

Today our society is more mobile than ever before. Carriers are faced not only with the task of hiring and training capable managers, but keeping them with the firm. While carriers have their own specific areas of operations and skills, managers are also involved with many general functions that are transferable from one carrier to another, or from one industry to another, and from one transportation mode to another. Movement of managers from one mode to another has been minimized up until now due to intense competitive conditions and hostilities between modes. Mobility of transportation managers to nontransportation positions has always been present.

As a result of increased mobility, it is common for the top executive officers of the carrier to have gained experience at two or more firms before joining their present company. This top executive is also approximately 10 years younger than his counterpart of 10 years ago.[7]

Mobility is broadening the dimensions of human relations within the corporate community, and carriers must also be prepared for new and creative problems and opportunities as a result of such developments.

Youth in Transportation

Just as the top executive's average age has dropped, so has the average age in most employment categories. This becomes evident by considering population and employment statistics. Carriers find themselves forced to choose more and more middle managers from the younger age groups. Although these youths are often better educated, they lack experience and exposure to the work environment, and thus will affect future corporate strategies.[8]

Further, the management philosophies of youth will sometimes clash with those of their older colleagues, but, one hopes, in a less than dramatic fashion. These younger managers have been referred to as the "younger college generation," and often have definite ideas about the humanization efforts within the firm.[9]

The average age of nonmanagerial employees in transportation has also dropped. This will almost certainly have an impact on labor strategies. It is to be expected that some rebellion against older established patterns and guidelines will result. Carrier management should recognize these developments and counteract with a younger and more professional outlook in their labor departments.

Women in Transport

Women have been discriminated against for years in employment, but the new female activists are changing all this.[10] Women make up 35 to 40 percent of all workers today. Unfortunately, women often receive an income that is 50 percent that of their male counterparts in comparable jobs. Even in the clerical work force, which is approximately 75 percent female, women receive one-third less salary than their male counterparts.[11]

Carrier firms have succeeded in hiring women in most job categories. Clerical job categories are most prominent, although some have found positions in sales and operations. It is also becoming more common to find a female branch manager in the trucking industry. Even so, women play a very minor role in the top management of carriers. Transportation, while built primarily by men, must adjust to these new developments. The adjustment must be philosophical as well as practical and creative.

PERSONNEL MANAGEMENT

Employees are involved with the personnel management function from their date of employment to their date of departure from the firm. Therefore, personnel practices reflect the carrier's commitment to human relations. Programs and activities that are usually found in the area of personnel management include hiring procedures; personnel fringe benefit coverage (such as hospitalization, medical, and life insurance; profit sharing; and pensions); termination procedures; wage and salary administration; and the relationship with the bargaining unit. In some carriers the personnel function may be separate organizationally from labor relations. In others they are combined. Labor relations and bargaining will be discussed in Chapter 14.

Personnel is inevitably involved with all the above factors affecting change in human relations, such as company management philosophy, mobility, youth, and women entering the employment market. Further, due to increasing amounts of legal action alleging job discrimination, sex discrimination, and other unfair labor practices, the legal side of the corporation has become a concern in the personnel department.

Personnel is actually different in purpose and function from management training and development. Organizationally, the two functions may be in the same department or under the same executive in some carriers, or separate for operational purposes in others. The larger carriers seem more prepared to pay the expense necessary to provide separate and specialized services for their large numbers of employees. Therefore, it is common to find distinct management training and development departments in such firms. The training and management development function will be treated separately here.

The more important categories of concern to transport personnel managers include employee selection and retention, fringe benefits, and wage and salary administration.

Employee Selection and Retention

In many areas of transportation there is a shortage of skilled workers, and some jobs are less appealing than jobs in other industries. Some modes have a much better image than others as well. Further, there is a very wide range of salary levels in transportation. Finally, the degree of public concern for safety and performance is also of importance here. All of these factors affect selection and retention.

Selecting Employees

The process of filling vacancies involves publicizing available job openings and interviewing and screening candidates to determine qualifications. A capable interviewer, in many cases the personnel manager, is required. Job skills must be well outlined so that both the employer and the prospective employee are aware of performance standards.

In order to select employees for a position, a pool of ready applicants should exist. There are a number of sources for new employees that transport firms may look to when openings occur. These include present employees who qualify, local job application files, present employee recommendations, local newspaper advertising, institutions of higher learning or specialty schools, the local union, and customers or clients.

When selecting employees, the person with the best qualifications for immediate performance and/or future growth is generally sought. Endless lists of outstanding individual characteristics could be noted, but only a few deserve mention here. They include professional competence or skills, the ability to command respect from others, the willingness and ability to communicate effectively, adaptability, personal honesty and integrity, prior job experience, a belief in the importance of his job, and exhibited personal stability. Naturally, the individual is sought who can best meet the specifications as required by the job or position description.[12]

There are certain recognizable characteristics that are undesirable in applicants, specially for those seeking supervisory positions. These include poor personal appearance, lack of competence, inability to communicate, and lack of commitment to job, self, and others.

When selecting employees, a reference check is essential. This is especially true here, since most employees in transportation are in labor positions that require a low skill level. This is not to imply that labor has a monopoly on deceit, but simply that labor positions have a higher level of job openings and turnover than white-collar jobs.

A job description and job information is vital when hiring employees. For example, the job requirements for an air pilot, railroad engineer, or road driver are more specifically defined than those for a baggage handler, porter, or dock worker. Physical standards are also vital in assessing job qualifications.

When dealing with applicants, personnel should furnish a well-defined job outline; qualifications required; reporting responsibilities; starting salary and salary range; specifics about hours and days worked, holidays, and so on; and job training availability. In addition to job information, job applicants at carriers will be interested in company characteristics including the company management philosophy; industry standing with regard to profits, growth, and revenues; well-defined company goals; pay, hours, and fringe benefits; and working conditions. Such company information may be important in a job decision.

Retaining Employees

Naturally, transport firms attempt to retain their productive employees. However, there are a number of factors that pose difficulties here.

In a competitive job market, the capable employees will be able to move from one job or carrier to another, and mobility continues to plague most carriers. Some positions are more susceptible to turnover than others. For example, salesmen and rate or traffic clerks have exhibited the highest turnover statistics in the past. One way in which carriers have lessened labor mobility has been through better hiring practices and better employee salaries and fringe benefits.

Terminations, within the conditions of the union contract, are sometimes necessary to rid a company of nonproducers. Managerial positions also have nonproducers, and their effects on company profits are normally greater than those of blue-collar workers.

The conditions for termination are important from both a practical and a legal standpoint. Performance reviews should determine the producers and the nonproducers. Exit interviews should also be conducted to determine why employees were separated from the company, and also to enable a company to look for trends regarding such things as reasons for separation and problems at a specific location. As a practical guide to record keeping, companies may classify employee separations according to the following descriptions: lack of work, retirement, left of own accord, discharged, leave of absence, and death.

Lack of work is self-explanatory, but must we well justified, especially in the eyes of the union. Retirement may be classified as voluntary, disability, compulsory--union contract, or compulsory--company policy. Left of own accord would include voluntary, to accept other employment, marriage, pregnancy, other domestic responsibilities, injury or illness, and leaving geographic area.

Separations by discharge are very difficult to accurately describe. The following codes for discharged employees serve to reinforce this: unreported absence, frequent tardiness, improper conduct, refusal to report, insubordination, dishonesty (signed statement), garnishment, failure to obey orders, fighting on company property, leaving work without permission, drinking on duty, reporting under the influence of alcohol, violation of safety rules, defective or improper work, carelessness, destruction of company property, labor dispute, and others.

A leave of absence may be granted for sickness, education, military, and other reasons.

Separated employees will normally be applying for other jobs and the new employer normally checks references at the last place of employment. Great care must be utilized in accurately describing the reason for separation, as it may (if severe enough) prevent the employee from obtaining new employment. Due to the legal ramifications involved, a complete file and record of occurrences leading to the dismissal are extremely important.

Turnovers normally cost a company four times the employee's salary. These are costs that can be reduced through better personnel and management development activities. Even in the face of natural employee changes, good corporate human relations can affect the ability to hire and retain qualified employees at all levels in the carrier organization.

Fringe Benefits

Fringe benefits will naturally vary from one transport firm to another. They will also vary in coverage among various employment classifications, such as union, nonunion clerical, supervisory, and executive.[13] The type of ownership and size of the firm will likewise have an influence on the type and extent of fringe benefits among carriers.

Union fringe benefits are paid for by the employer but are completely managed by the appropriate union. In some cases, the union fringe benefits are more appealing than those of company supervisory employees.

Types of Benefits

The types of fringe benefits existing in transport firms are similar to those found in most industrial firms, but are often not as attractive financially. Again, the extent of fringe benefit coverage will vary with the size of the company, union, and transportation mode. No motor carrier can equal the flying privileges of airline employees. However, such a fringe benefit to the airline employees may be offset by lower salaries than those of some other transport employees.

In the discussion of benefits, it should be realized that some carriers pay all or a portion of some coverage, while other benefits require employee contributions.

Hospitalization and Major Medical. Hospitalization and major medical normally covers such items as hospital room allowance, surgical benefits, and other items associated with hospitalization. Major medical covers more expensive and prolonged illness involving both in-patient and out-patient coverage. Deductibles and limits of coverage may be specified.

Pension Plan. The number of years of employment, retirement dates, and size of the monthly pension payments are important factors under the pension plan. Pension plans may or may not be contributory and may or may not be vested after a specified number of years. Pension plans are generally paid over and above, or in conjunction with, social security retirement benefits.

Profit Sharing or Bonus. Profit sharing or bonus plans allow eligible employees to share in company profits. These are often on a percentage-of-salary basis and go up to a maximum of 15 percent of the employee's salary. Profit sharing usually refers to a program of reinvestment of annual company contributions to the plan.

Bonus plans normally refer to a cash pay-out on a quarterly or annual basis. Formulas covering the extent of participation are complicated, but all are predicated on the basis of the existence of company profits.

Life Insurance and Accidental Death and Dismemberment. Most carriers carry a minimum-term group life insurance policy on all nonunion employees. Union employees normally have similar coverage. These programs, which are both contributory and noncontributory, usually allow the employee to increase his life insurance coverage at a very low group rate. Life insurance policies for the employee's spouse and family are normally available on a contributory basis.

Accidental death and dismemberment policies are normally available to employees on a contributory basis, and these policies normally provide for family coverage.

Vacations. It is generally accepted that employees should have annual vacations and certain holidays off, with or without pay. Union contracts are quite specific about vacations, while carriers will vary on their policies of allowable vacations.

Company vacation policies will also vary regarding the length-of-employment requirements for specific numbers of vacation days. For example, some carriers may require 10 years of continuous service for three weeks of vacation, while others may require five or even 15 years. Most traditional holidays, with some substitutions, are extended to transport employees.

Sick Leave. Although the sick leave program was developed for clerical, and primarily female, employees, it has generally been extended to all employees. Most plans allow employees to build up a reserve of sick leave (months or days worked without absence) so that sick leave pay will be forthcoming when a prolonged illness occurs.

Educational Assistance. Many carriers have recognized the advantage of well-educated employees and have instituted educational assistance plans. These plans generally reimburse an employee for receiving an acceptable grade in a company approved course. In many firms, such benefits have also been extended to union employees.

Stock Purchase Plans. Many carriers that are public corporations, and some that have privately held ownership, have allowed employees to purchase their stock at a savings. In most cases, the employee can utilize payroll deductions and may save the price of the initial brokerage fee, or may be able to purchase the stock below market price. Companies may contribute a portion of the stock purchase price for their employees. It generally holds true that stock ownership positively affects attitudes toward the company.

Savings Programs and Loan Programs. Many carriers utilize the service of a credit union or financial institution to allow employees to save and repay loans on a payroll deduction basis. Some companies provide an incentive to employee savings by matching their contribution to a savings plan on a percentage basis.

Many carriers have some type of special executive coverage or fringe benefits that are limited to certain employee groups. These programs vary considerably, but are usually designed to attract and hold key managers. Cash bonuses and stock options are popular programs, along with additional life insurance and disability coverage. Salary and organizational level normally determine which executives are covered by these and other programs.

Wage and Salary Administration

In addition to hiring and administering fringe benefits programs, the chief function of the transport personnel manager is to administer the wage and salary program for the company. In the face of continuous union demands, inflation, the changing cost of living, governmental guideline programs, and salary competition for the well qualified, the personnel manager has a very difficult task. Efficient wage and salary administration is based on three factors: job description, performance appraisal and standards, and progressive promotion. Further, constraints are imposed by federal regulations, and must be considered.

Job Description

Job descriptions should cover the exact requirements for the job. If the job is for a specific task, then that task should be clearly defined. If the job calls for an employee to do a number of tasks, then the job description should reflect this. The lack of specific job descriptions or poor communications in outlining an individual job greatly affects employee turnover. There should not be variation between the job description and the actual work performed.

Job descriptions should be written and available for examination by the employee applicant. These descriptions should also be relevant and kept up-to-date with changing corporate job requirements. Depending on the individual company management philosophy, job descriptions may be rather narrowly defined or may be general and flexible.

Obviously, every specific, minute detail of a job cannot be defined. However, the generally acceptable descriptive functional categories would include the basic individual qualifications necessary for the job, the job tasks to be performed and equipment to be used, the reporting responsibility of the individual (chain of command), the specific authority and scope of responsibility that the individual performing the job has, the productivity standards and work load, the salary level, the probationary or training period, the working conditions, the promotional and career opportunities, and, in some cases, the length of employment. The shift to be worked, length of the shift, meal times, and coffee breaks, fall more into the administrative areas of the individual job, although they should occur in accordance with job descriptions and commitments.

Performance Appraisal and Standards

Performance appraisals and standards are used primarily for salary review and promotions. Such techniques allow a company to evaluate employees against standards, and thus reduce favoritism between supervisors and subordinates.

Employee job performance should improve when sound methods of appraising job performance are utilized. Coaching of employees on how best to meet standards provides an excellent opportunity for positive supervisory-subordinate communications.

Carriers can also plan for the future by developing a system that will rate each employee as to his present status and as to future performance capability. Employees who need additional training or additional experience, or who are incapable of performing in a higher level job, are identified. The programs also help companies evaluate their recruiting and management development efforts based on employee performance.

Various rating scales are utilized by carriers to measure employee performance. In most cases these rating scales or standards have been developed for that specific job on a company basis. Similar standards for the particular mode may be applicable, but in many cases they are difficult to use. For example, pounds per man-hour, if accurately recorded, may not be applicable from one carrier to another due to freight mixtures, types of packaging, and the presence of automated equipment. On the other hand, the passenger-occupancy ratio for particular aircraft should be standard from one airline to another, if the number of seats on equipment is the same.

Evaluation interviews may be used to further reinforce the importance of having job standards and the need for productivity improvement. The employee is able to evaluate his job progress and honestly knows where he stands with his company.

There are a number of difficulties in keeping employee evaluations and appraisals completely objective. Although managers may feel employee evaluations are necessary, they may be too diplomatic in their efforts and unrealistic. A manager who is unsure of how to grade his employees may be too busy to judge his subordinates, or he may feel that production is his main duty, and thus is unenthusiastic about performance appraisals.

Employees may be suspicious and hostile toward performance appraisals, especially if they are uninformed of their purpose.

Although people generally want to be told where they stand with a company, there is no guarantee that a change for the better will occur.

The key to a good performance appraisal system is a good supervisory-subordinate relationship. A history of personal honesty and fair dealings resulting in a proper understanding of functions and roles greatly assists the communications effort.

Progressive Promotion

Progressive promotions tend to prearrange movements within the corporate organizational structure. Instituted as an avenue for stability, the process does insure well-trained replacements. The shortcoming of progressive promotion is that it can curb creativity and cause inbreeding.

Progressive promotion systems are more commonly found in older, more established firms that have larger numbers of employees. For example, traffic departments in railroads tend to utilize progressive promotion more than smaller truck lines do.

Progressive promotions are not restricted to specific organizational levels. Within modes, this practice, or variations of it, can be found at the top management level as well as at the first-line supervisor. Branch managers can be predesignated and groomed for the position as well as presidents. From the individual carrier manager's viewpoint, the individual would at least know his place in the organizational structure, and his prospects for future growth.

The disadvantages of progressive promotion are numerous, and include the development of the "crown prince" concept; an emphasis on status quo; a high turnover of management personnel due to lack of advancement or slowness of advancement; a lack of creativity due to an absence of new thinking; a deterrent to recruitment of personnel; a high average age for employees if advancement is slow; and a possible deterioration of company morale and esprit de corps.

Carrier personnel policies are affected by the operations to be performed, and such progressive promotions may or may not be desirable for a particular firm. A continued record of growth and profitability tends to reaffirm the existing structure. However, history has taught us that conditions do change and past growth trends do not necessarily continue into the future.

Administrative Constraints by the Federal Government

The personnel departments of carrier firms are affected in many ways by federal government regulations. For example, union contracts are legally enforceable; discrimination suits by organizations, individuals, and the government are becoming quite common;

and federal policies with regard to wages are applied to the transport employee.

Transport firms adhere to union contracts, which cover a variety of fringe benefits and working situations. Union contracts are sometimes violated by employee and employer with resulting legal action. The Justice Department and the National Labor Relations Board play an important role in these areas and cause growing concern among transport firms. Legal actions alleging discrimination on the basis of race, sex, religion, and other factors have proved expensive for carriers as well as all industrial concerns.

Of recent vintage are the federal wage-price guidelines. These guidelines outline the nature of rate increases available to carriers, and the extent of wage and salary increases to employees. Union contracts that were negotiated prior to the enactment of the wage-price program were exempt from the plan in most cases.

TRAINING AND MANAGEMENT DEVELOPMENT

Supplying and developing well-trained supervisors is a major concern for carriers due to the changing complexities of the business environment and the need for capable management assets. Unlike the personnel function, which is concerned with many aspects of hiring procedures and avenues for satisfying human needs, the management development function is concerned with changing worker behavior, if necessary, to produce desired profitable operating results.

The Need for Management Training

Carriers have grown rapidly in recent years, in terms of operating equipment, operating facilities, and number of employees. Too often, carriers have not grown in terms of effective managers. A growing firm that has the ability to attract, hire, train, and place capable management talent to supplement the already present management is headed for a sound future. Also, a part of management development is the training and educating of those already employed.

Supervisory Training

Supervisory training normally refers to the training of supervisors and various levels of management, as opposed to the training of employees who are a part of the bargaining unit. While the total concept of training at all levels is important, more attention tends to focus on training of the first-line supervisory levels.[14]

Front-Line Supervisor

The front-line supervisor is the management level closest to the bargaining and operating level of transportation. He supervises the employees' work and is in a position to affect costs and profits on a day-to-day basis. Therefore, he is of primary importance to carriers of all sizes and modes.

Although the first-line supervisor may not have as much education and experience as those at other managerial levels, he does require a number of diverse management skills in order to be effective. The need for training is evident. On a daily basis, he must practice good communications; good supervisory techniques, such as giving recognition, reprimanding, and record keeping; and must know the bargaining contract from the employer's point of view. He must also be sufficiently aware of general company operations if he is to perform his function effectively.

The subject of first-line supervisory training gains increased importance when one considers that this level of management is also greatly affected by turnover. There are many reasons for this; among them are working conditions, tough unions, shift work, straight salary with no overtime, lower salary than unionized employees, management pressure for productivity, and irregular work weeks. It sometimes appears that carriers are spending many dollars to train first-line supervisors, but will not spend a few additional dollars in the right places to insure a low turnover rate. Adequate training and preparation plus company fringe benefits can often reduce first-line management turnover.

Other Levels of Management

Managers above the first line are also in need of training and development. They need to be kept abreast of the changing facts about their company, changes in carrier services, communications, and other management and supervisory techniques. Although there is a definite difference in job function and level of responsibility, these middle and top managers must remain dynamic and not static. They need training and mental stimulation too. Their contribution to profits may not be gauged on a daily basis, but is important to reaching overall company objectives.[15]

Specific programs may be developed for both sales and operations employees. Normally the objectives of training are the same, but the content and materials may vary significantly. Training for middle and upper management is normally more sophisticated and may involve additional classroom work, seminars, and special consultation with an in-house professional trainer. This training usually includes more emphasis on overall company policy and theory, as opposed to the day-to-day techniques of how to improve production.

Nonsupervisory Training

Members of the bargaining or operational unit should receive training for their jobs, since they directly affect carrier profitability and because they are important members of the firm. Carriers have diverse job requirements depending on the specific mode, but all employees are in need of future job development. The skilled jobs are vital to the functioning of transport firms. Airplanes, railroads, pipelines, trucks, and barges are complicated pieces of machinery. The employees who operate them and the employees who load and unload them are dealing with the concerns of the public commodities. Should these pieces of equipment and commodities not be handled properly, society will suffer.

Carriers should not forget their nonunion employees and should give equal attention to directly or indirectly training them for specific job requirements. Some employees may learn while they perform their specific jobs, while others may spend considerable time training before their first day on the job. The degree of job difficulty is a vital factor in this regard.

Training Techniques

Training techniques are as different, and as similar, in carriers as they are in most industrial firms. Individual carriers prefer some techniques over others.

On-the-Job Training

The most widely used training technique in the transportation industry as a whole is on-the-job training. In this manner, a new employee learns from someone who is already employed how to do the job. This technique has a number of advantages and disadvantages.

For some positions, on-the-job training is not enough. Pilots, for example, must receive extensive training before they can qualify to fly passengers. The same holds true for railroad engineers, truck drivers, and those in similar employment categories. Although they do receive on-the-job training as part of their orientation, their practical classroom and job experiences are vitally important.

On-the-job training is valuable since the employee learns to perform certain functions in a practical manner in a real job situation, and can raise questions and learn while he is performing the job. The individual can also obtain the localized terminology, knowledge of past job practices, and proper methods not covered in the book for satisfactory performance.

The primary disadvantages of on-the-job training rest with the trainer, or the person training a new man on the job. More than likely the individual is not a good trainer. He performs the job in his own way, sometimes utilizing short cuts to accomplish results. He may have also developed a number of bad job habits that can provide incomplete training for the new man. His own personality, feelings, and biases will be projected to the new man, which can also pose a number of problems for a new employee.

Since many carriers lack company employed professional trainers, on-the-job training becomes very important and is often the only training available. In order to improve training in this area, some of the larger carriers have decided to spend the money for salaries and expenses to provide good in-house training for both supervisory and nonsupervisory employees, in the hope that they, in turn, can train operational employees. Smaller firms have chosen to utilize transport seminars on specific subjects, such as sales, operations, claims, and general management, for some of their supervisory employees. The first-line supervisors receive on-the-job training primarily.

Training Facilities

Training, other than on-the-job training, can be accomplished in various types of meeting rooms or classrooms. Motel meeting rooms are popular as training facilities, since carriers and other firms usually find them readily available and inexpensive. These types of facilities are preferable to in-house training facilities, since the participants get away from the work location and are not confronted with daily crises.

A few transport firms do utilize specially built facilities, but in most cases the capital has not been expended for a separate training facility.

Types of Training Instruction

Seminars and discussion groups provide the most appropriate means of imparting knowledge in transport training. Audiovisual instruction is also widely used due to the increasing availability of management films relating to transport.

Role playing is a technique often used in training sessions dealing with management techniques, supervisory skills, and labor. This forces participants to adopt style, temperament, and knowledge of another person in his job situation. Realizing why a person reacts as he does greatly assists supervisors in the coordination of their tasks.

Attitudes and Other Factors Affecting Training

There are many factors that affect training in carriers. One of the most overriding is the commitment of top management to upgrade supervisory and worker knowledge. Assuming this commitment is honest and firm, which is not always the case, the primary concern then becomes the individual participant in the training efforts.

Training involves an effort toward changing behavior, and many participants feel this is impossible. Thus, the attitude of the participant is most important. He must feel that the training efforts are for his benefit as well as for the betterment of company operations.

Labor Proximity and Attitude

The worker's attitude toward his job and his training can be affected by the location of his training and the location of his home in relationship to his job.[16] Training efforts should be conducted at locations as convenient to the employees as possible. Secluded training locations are sometimes appropriate, but most often consideration should be given to the accessibility of these locations to the employees. Workers have moved farther away from their work place due to a shorter work week, some creativity in shift assignments, the development of better roadways, and changing worker attitudes toward the job. Thus, employees have more time to think about themselves, their jobs, and their training, as they commute to and from work.

Worker proximity will differ with each mode of transport. Many air pilots live in one city but are based, for flying purposes, in a city 200 to 500 miles away. Along with an awareness of changing worker proximity, carriers must be more aware of creative techniques to keep the worker enthusiastic about his productive efforts on the job. The same holds true for company training efforts.

Worker Wants and Attitudes

Carrier management needs to decide if employees are really interested in improving their job knowledge and status. What do transport workers really want out of their jobs? Salary? Fringe benefits? Promotion and growth? If workers want promotion and growth, for example, they will become discouraged when promotions and company growth are not an alternative.

Higher salary is not the desire of all employees. In a recent study conducted in the motor carrier industry, it was found that "good wages" actually ranked three out of ten in order of importance.[17] Of even greater significance was the fact that supervisory employees were not accurate in their perception of what the employee wanted from his job. These results would be similar in most, if not all, carriers. This clearly outlines the problem for management: it is essential to know the job wants of employees and subordinates. Past studies have shown that differences do exist in employee attitude, supervisory work attitudes, and supervisory perceptions of employee work attitude.[18]

For more effective job wants to emerge (effective in terms of continued job success and positive employee attitudes), a participative management approach, gained by respect, effective communications, and understanding is necessary. In order to accomplish such tasks, it may be necessary for firms to implement a training program designed to help supervisors gain a better understanding of their total job environment and especially of their own wants. Once these wants are known and understood, it may be possible for companies to have better production as a result of better supervisory-subordinate relationships.[19]

Change and Job Complexity

Changing work requirements necessitate some form of training for most firms today. As the economy becomes more complex and dynamic, jobs become more complex. Training is one way of easing the frustrations of the complexity of changing work conditions. Some transport workers may feel that their jobs are the only ones that are changing. Communication of the total effects of change may be helpful to those workers affected by change.

College Recruiting and Management Training

College recruiting is an avenue used by many carriers to attract young men and women to the industry. In no way does a college degree assure success in transportation or any other business. But a degree does mean that the individual has had a certain amount of theoretical instruction in the institutions of higher learning and has a genuine interest in transportation as a career.

One of the biggest challenges facing growing carriers is the need to hire, train, and develop additional capable management to assure a smooth management transition during growth. It is not an easy task to find qualified individuals. Some can be found with other transport firms, in diverse professions, or on the college campus.

A carrier planning for long-range growth and profitability may find it more advantageous to hire someone off the college campus and teach him all aspects of the business, rather than hire someone who may have developed many bad habits with another firm or carrier.

Young ideas are fresh and take time to develop to their fullest. Thus, individuals must have a chance to synthesize the operation of a going concern with their more formal educational exposure. A training program is essential. The end result is, one hopes, an individual who is aware of his total surroundings in the firm and who has a strong feeling of self-confidence as a result of his combined academic and practical techniques.

Longer training programs, in excess of six months, are oriented more toward making an individual a specialist in operations, sales, or other traffic functions. The training programs of six months or less are primarily designed to give the trainee an overview of the functions performed in a carrier organization and make him aware of supervisory techniques. Typically, it is not until after the training period is over that the individual will be on his own and will make his first real carrier management decisions.

A typical management training program proceeds through four steps. First, the college graduate is recruited and led through a series of selection procedures, including a terminal and general office visit, and then hired into a carrier firm. Second, the recruit is placed in a training program designed to expose him to the overall aspects of the business (sales, operations, clerical functions, and general management). Third, the recruit spends a substantial amount of time at one central terminal or general office location, or he may spend some time at a number of facilities. The goal here is a more in-depth training. Finally, upon the completion of the formal training program, he is placed in a position as a full-time supervisory employee, and discards the trainee designation.

A total program of recruiting, training, and placement is most desirable. This means, among other things, that the more personal attention the person gets, the better he or she will make the adjustment from the campus to the firm. Further, the trainee should be made very much aware of his potential in the firm, but only after learning the business through experience. Giving an individual attention and assistance in no way implies that he or she does not have to perform satisfactorily. If anything, it means that the trainee should perform over and above the normal newly hired supervisory employee. Finally, a firm's management training program, and its entire philosophy of bringing new management into the firm, is a result of the total management of the corporation. The company's personality will obviously reflect this philosophy.

In most cases, college recruiting will produce approximately 25 percent or less of the new hires in a given year. Thus, well-qualified and experienced supervisory employees will also be needed in addition to those recruited on campus. The biggest advantage an experienced employee has to offer is the ability to produce in a relatively short period of time, whereas it takes college-recruited trainees longer to reach this stage.

SUMMARY

In this chapter the components of human relations, personnel management, and training have been discussed as they relate to carriers. Although the operations and sales aspects of carriers may appear to be the major factor in carrier success, it is really the human aspect of the firm that counts most. The greatest asset any firm has is its human talent at all levels. Profits are made and lost by individual efforts in the firm, and thus the need for the development of people and people-related aspects of the transport firm continues to increase and be of pivotal importance.

NOTES

1. Jack J. Holder, Jr., "Labor Proximity to a Modern Metropolitan Terminal Location," _Terminal Operator_, October 1971, p. 71.
2. Bernie Smart, "Youth Views Trucking," _Fleet Owner_, June 1970, pp. 61-66, 93.
3. Jack J. Holder, Jr., "Management Development Today . . . Solving Tomorrow's Transport Problems," _Alphian_, November 1972, pp. 17-20.
4. Warren J. Wittreich and John B. Miner, "People: The Most Mismanaged Asset," _Business Horizons_, April 1971, pp. 69-77.
5. Jack J. Holder, Jr., "Achieving Goals and Objectives in the Motor Carrier Industry," _Transportation Journal_, Spring 1971, pp. 51-59.
6. Jack J. Holder, Jr., "Goals and Objectives--Insights in Depth," _Alphian_, June 1972, pp. 5-8.
7. Eugene E. Jennings, "Two Worlds of the Executive," _TWA Ambassador_, March 1971.
8. "The Job Gap for College Graduates in the 1970's," _Business Week_, September 23, 1972, pp. 48-54.
9. Smart, op. cit.
10. David Gilbert, "The Changing Female Role," _Nation's Business_, December 1972, p. 39.
11. Michael R. Notaro, Jr., "Women's Lib . . . Next Business Disruption?" (Speech given to the Advertising and Sales Executive Club, Kansas City, Missouri, 1971).

12. Jack J. Holder, Jr., "Hiring an Assistant Supervisor," Supervisory Management Magazine, April 1972, pp. 25-30.

13. Niels H. Nielsen, "Being Businesslike About Benefits--The Allis-Chalmers Way," Corporate Financing, January/February 1971, pp. 35-39, 46, 66-67.

14. Jack J. Holder, Jr., "Evaluation of an In-Company Management Training Program," Training and Development Journal, April 1972, pp. 24-27.

15. Herbert H. Hand, "The Mystery of Executive Education," Business Horizons, June 1971, pp. 35-38.

16. Holder, op. cit., "Labor Proximity to a Modern Metropolitan Terminal Location," p. 7.

17. Jack J. Holder, Jr., "Motor Trucking Supervisory Perceptions and Employee Job Wants," Terminal Operator, September 1970, pp. 6-12.

18. Paul Hersey and Kenneth H. Blanchard, Management of Organizational Behavior (Englewood Cliffs, N.J.: Prentice-Hall, 1969).

19. Robert H. Schaffer, "The Psychological Barriers to Management Effectiveness," Business Horizons, April 1971.

CHAPTER

14 LABOR RELATIONS AND COLLECTIVE BARGAINING

Labor relations in transportation are unique. There is probably no other area in which the public has greater concern. Since the transportation of goods and people is mandatory for business to exist in the U.S. economy, any stoppage due to a strike or a lockout calls forth public reaction and concern. The economy simply cannot exist without transportation, as has been demonstrated again and again. Therefore, it is essential that labor relations and bargaining be successful in transportation. To attempt to insure this success and to avoid work stoppages, substantial federal control which does not exist in other industries exists in the area of labor relations in transportation.

From the carrier viewpoint, labor costs approximate 60 percent of total costs in rail, motor, and air transportation.[1] As a substantial cost item, the wage bargain (and the fringe benefits that accompany it) has a large and direct effect on carrier costs and profitability.

Finally, from a historical viewpoint, workers have been organized for many years in transportation. Indeed, much of the early labor movement started in transportation, and railroad strikes played an important role in the history of the labor movement in America. Just as important historically has been society's attempts to insure continuous service in transportation by specifying various legal devices and regulations under which labor relations and bargaining must take place. For carrier management, it is important to understand the development of these federal acts and regulations in order to appreciate the reasons why the modern wage bargain and labor relations are carried on in the manner in which they are today. Labor relations in transportation are different, and a great deal of that difference is due to the legal and institutional environment that surrounds them.

LEGAL ENVIRONMENT OF TRANSPORTATION LABOR RELATIONS

Using a historical approach helps the reader to appreciate how the present-day laws and regulations developed. Since they were so important, railroad labor relations were regulated first, and it was in that mode that the legal environment of transportation labor developed.

The Labor Environment Prior to 1926

Railroad unionism began around the time of the Civil War with the organization of engineers, conductors, firemen, and switchmen. Their unions, known as the "big five," were the Brotherhood of Locomotive Engineers (1863), Order of Railway Conductors (1868), Brotherhood of Locomotive Firemen and Engineers (1873), Brotherhood of Railroad Trainmen (1883), and Switchmen's Union of North America (1894).[2] Unions in the nonservice crafts were organized toward the end of the nineteenth century, but contained a minority of the workers until World War I. The government encouraged unionization during that conflict and these nonservice unions have generally been part of the American Federation of Labor (AFL), unlike the operating brotherhoods, which have been independent.[3]

Congress acted to solve labor problems in the railroads before the turn of the century. The Arbitration Act of 1888 provided for voluntary arbitration of disputes between carriers and their employees, but no procedures were enacted to implement or enforce the provisions. The Erdman Act of 1898 was concerned with the settlement of disputes involving employees who operated trains. Even though the Erdman Act did establish procedures for mediation and arbitration, it too was ineffective. The Newlands Act of 1913 attempted to solve arbitration machinery weaknesses by providing for a Commissioner of Mediation and Conciliation. This was a workable solution until 1916, when the brotherhoods struck for an 8-hour day.[4]

The Adamson Act of 1916 provided for the 8-hour day and was bitterly opposed by the railroads. The act was appealed to the Supreme Court in the face of a national strike, and upheld on the basis that Congress had the power to meet national emergencies. The 8-hour day became standard under governmental operation of the railroads during World War I (1917-20). During the war years labor made many advances in wages, the standardization of policies and practices, the organization of the union, and the entire process of collective bargaining.

The Transportation Act of 1920 was enacted as a result of the problems caused by the return of the railroads from government to private control. This act created two ways of dealing with the railway labor problems. Local, regional, or national boards of labor adjustment could be established by agreement between employees and the railroads to solve disputes concerning grievances, rules, and working conditions. The second provision created the Railroad Labor Board to solve these disputes if the adjustment boards could not. Unfortunately, neither the adjustment boards nor the Railroad Labor Board was effective in resolving labor disputes, and the act as a whole did not really achieve its objective.[5]

The Railway Labor Act of 1926[6]

The Railway Labor Act of 1926 was a major piece of legislation that attempted to incorporate all of the measures used for the preceding 40 years. Its coverage was extended to all railroad workers, and the provisions of this act, in terms of machinery for settling disputes, is still in use today.

There were a number of major provisions in the act, but essentially it outlined a series of procedural steps that had to take place before a work stoppage could occur. These procedures are illustrated in Figure 13.1, basically, two special boards and two areas of labor relations are involved--contract interpretation and contract negotiations.

In disputes concerning contract interpretation and grievances over rates of pay, rules, or working conditions, the first step is holding carrier-union conferences. It is anticipated that conferences will settle the majority of the disputes in this area. Should this not be the case, appeal can be made to the National Railroad Adjustment Board. Originally the act called for a bipartisan appeals board, but in 1934, Congress created the National Railroad Adjustment Board, which is composed of 36 members, 18 from each side. The board is divided into four divisions, each having jurisdiction over a separate class of labor. If a deadlock occurs, a neutral third party is selected to serve. Should there be no agreement on a neutral third party, the National Board of Mediation, which was also created in the 1934 amendments, appoints the neutral party. The interpretation on appeal is binding.

The traditional collective bargaining procedures are relied on as the first step in contract negotiations. Later in this chapter we will be concerned with the length and scope of these contracts. It is assumed that collective bargaining will be successful in reaching an agreement in most cases of contract negotiations. However, should this not be the case, either party can call on the services of the National Mediation Board (or the board may act on its own motion).

FIGURE 13.1

Settlement Procedure Under the Railway Labor Act

Grievance and Contract Interpretation

Carrier-Employee Conferences

↓

Appeal to

↓

National Board of Railroad Adjustment
18 employee and 18 employer members
Neutral third party

Decision final

(appoints if deadlocked → Neutral third party)

Contract Negotiations

Collective Bargaining

↓

Mediation

↓

National Mediation Board
3 members serve 3 years
appointed by President

↓

Voluntary Arbitration Option

↓

Temporary Arbitration Board
One-third carrier representatives
One-third union representatives
One-third chosen by above two-thirds

(appoints if disagreement → One-third chosen by above two-thirds)

If arbitration started, award is final

Emergency Board Option
(if arbitration refused)

↓

National Emergency Board
If National Mediation Board certifies dispute threatens to interrupt interstate commerce, President appoints board of outstanding citizens.
30 days to investigate and report plus 30 days cooling-off period

Award not binding - Public opinion only force used

↓

Presidential or Congressional Action

This board is composed of three members, serving three years each, and appointed by the president with the consent of the Senate.

Essentially, the National Mediation Board attempts to mediate or find common ground in the dispute. The board does not take sides or make awards. Unlike the adjustment board, it is made up of impartial public officials not connected with either management or labor. As noted above, the mediation board may be called on to appoint a neutral third party if a deadlock occurs on the National Railroad Adjustment Board.

If the second step of mediation fails and no common ground is found or settlement reached, the act orders the National Mediation Board to work for the option of arbitration. Arbitration is voluntary, and both sides must agree to this process. Under arbitration, a temporary board of arbitrators is chosen to hear the dispute, investigate, and make the award. One-third of the arbitrators are chosen by management, one-third by the unions, and the final third by the carrier-unions arbitrators collectively. Should there be disagreement in the choice of the neutral one-third, the National Mediation Board chooses them. Once agreed to, arbitration is binding.

Should arbitration be refused, the National Mediation Board may evoke a fourth step, the emergency-board option. Upon certification to the president that the dispute threatens to interrupt interstate commerce, the president may, within his discretion, appoint a National Emergency Board made up of outstanding citizens. This emergency board is given 30 days to investigate the dispute and to make a report. During this time of investigation plus 30 additional days, no change may take place (this is called the 60-day "cooling-off" period). While the National Emergency Board has no power to enforce its report and recommendations, it is hoped that public opinion will induce acceptance of the findings of the board.

The final step is not specified in the Railway Labor Act of 1926, but has come about through practice. Should public opinion fail to force a settlement along the lines of the emergency board's finding, either the president or Congress will generally intercede to prevent work stoppage. On some occasions, work stoppages have actually begun, and congressional action has taken place in the wee hours of the morning to keep the commerce of the nation from grinding to a halt. In other cases, the president has actually called the negotiators to the White House and forced a settlement by persuasive powers (a procedure used by President Johnson). In recent years, Congress has been forced to act literally at the last moment to settle disputes in railway labor.

Presidential Railroad Commission of 1960

By 1960, it appeared that the procedures of the Railway Labor Act were no longer viable. Accordingly, President Eisenhower established the Presidential Railroad Commission to investigate. The commission was made up of equal representation from the public, labor, and management, but failed to satisfy all parties in its final report, which dealt with wages, rules, working conditions, and social security. The commission reported basically that the entire structure of labor-management relations in the railroad industry should be drastically overhauled. The report failed to solve the problems, and chaotic conditions have followed, with additional disputes and strikes.[7]

Air Transportation and Labor

In 1936, the Railway Labor Act was extended to employees of airlines engaged in interstate commerce. Although the act called for a National Air Transport Adjustment Board to deal with labor disputes, it has never been established. Other provisions of the act apply to airlines but have not been utilized, due to agreed-upon settlements between carriers and unions.

In the initial stages of the airline industry, the primary unions included the International Association of Machinists, the Transport Workers' Union, and the Airline Pilots Association. Ground service employees and stewardesses have since become a significant factor in union-management negotiations, and the introduction of jet aircraft and the following sense of job insecurity has caused a number of labor disputes in air transportation.

The airlines have successfully used a mutual aid pact since 1958 in their efforts to withstand strikes against individual airlines. This pact calls for air carriers to pay a carrier that is on strike an amount equal to their increase in revenues attributable to the strike, less direct expenses.[8] This agreement has been used on a number of occasions, the most recent being the strike against Trans World Airlines in the late fall and early winter of 1973.

Labor difficulties in the airline industry have not been associated with the violence that has marked union-management controversies in the railroad and motor industries.

The Motor Carrier Industry and Labor

The Railway Labor Act does not apply to motor transportation. The International Brotherhood of Teamsters, Warehousemen and

Chauffeurs is the largest union affecting the motor carrier industry. The International Brotherhood of Teamsters is not a member of the AFL-CIO, but is completely independent.[9]

It is quite common to find a truck line terminal manager dealing with many aspects of the teamsters' union in labor negotiations at the terminal level. For example, road drivers, dockmen, city drivers, office workers, and maintenance employees may all be members of the teamsters' union but belong to a different local in a city. Each local will have a union steward and business agent working with the terminal manager to resolve disputes affecting their local.

Grievances that cannot be resolved locally will be taken to a Joint Area Committee for further deliberation. Grievance committees at the local and Joint Area Committee levels are composed of three teamsters and three employers, who must decide on the grievance. The chairman of the committee is usually one of the teamsters on the committee.

Under James Hoffa, the teamsters' union moved from a multiemployee, area-wide agreement to a national master contract affecting all motor carriers. To combat the teamsters at the national level the motor carriers formed Trucking Employers, Inc. (TEI), which is a national bargaining group made up of representatives of motor carriers. In addition to a national master freight agreement and contract, area supplemental contracts are negotiated that reflect certain management-labor practices in different geographic areas.

The first national master freight agreement signed between TEI and the International Brotherhood of Teamsters was in 1967. A short lockout by TEI was one of the activities particular to the 1967 contract. In 1970, certain teamsters locals chose not to go along with the national agreement and struck all of the motor carriers in certain cities for a few weeks. Cities such as Los Angeles, Oakland, St. Louis, Kansas City, Chicago, Akron, and Cleveland were involved. The strike in Chicago lasted the longest, running almost 80 days. The contract in 1970 called for a 39-month contract, while the 1967 contract ran only 36 months. The 1973 agreement once again called for a 36-month contract, and in 1973, TEI and the teamsters reached the national agreement on schedule and avoided the violence that characterized the 1970 strikes.

Since the departure of Hoffa from the helm of the teamsters, internal struggle for leadership has occurred. Some observers feel that these struggles were primarily responsible for the strikes in 1970. The teamster leadership since Hoffa has courted national politicians on a very close and successful basis.

A national strike in the trucking industry for any length of time would drastically affect our country's economy. Thus, a national interruption of service seems quite unlikely. In recent years, "no-strike" legislation has been proposed in the transportation industry to prevent a national transport crisis.

Other Variables Affecting Transportation Labor Relations

Legislation and union-management confrontations are not the only variables affecting labor in the transport industry. Legislation and the grievance hearings are only the result of conflicts that cannot be reasonably settled. Other important factors that directly enter into the union-management relationship must be considered.

National Labor Relations Board

When employees feel they have been unfairly treated they may utilize the National Labor Relations Board (NLRB) to bring suit against a transport carrier. These suits are increasing and require management to conduct a legal battle or make a settlement in each case. Carriers have been concerned about the increasing number of suits and how they can work within their company, and within management ranks, to prevent them.

Department of Transportation

The DOT has established a number of requirements on the operation and reporting activities of carriers. Many of their requirements are concerned with hours of service and other factors affecting the employees of transport firms.

Department of Labor

In 1970, Congress enacted the Occupational Safety and Health Act, to be administered by the Department of Labor. This act directly concerns working conditions and job safety in all companies--including transport firms. Upon complaint by an employee, the Department of Labor will investigate. This act has caused transport firms to become concerned about the safety of their facilities and equipment. Employees of transport firms can, and do, file complaints, and thus more conflict arises between management and the bargaining units.

Interstate Commerce Commission

The ICC, which is the primary regulatory body for transport firms, has affected labor relations since its inception. ICC decisions obviously affect carriers and may result in a requirement for more or fewer employees at one location or another. The union will certainly be involved in resolving such disputes with appropriate groups of management. A good example of their influence is the investigation of railroad and motor carrier mergers in the last five years, and the corresponding actions required by employers and management to resolve conflicts and changes in their respective labor pools.

Fair Labor Standards Act of 1938

The Fair Labor Standards Act of 1938 had a number of provisions that have shaped the standards of working conditions, wages, and hours worked. The primary purpose of the act was to eliminate the working conditions that served to burden commerce among nations and states without curtailing employment or earning power. The two main provisions concerned the minimum wage an employee could earn and the maximum number of hours an employee could work. Both provisions have obviously had a direct effect on transport firms and all industry.

The minimum-wage provision is continuously under scrutiny by the labor unions, politicians, and the Department of Labor. Over the years since the enactment of the act, the minimum wage has been substantially raised by various amendments. The maximum-hours provision of the act refers to the wage per hour in excess of 40 hours a week, including provisions for time and a half, double time, and holiday pay. Many of these provisions have become part of union contracts and union-management agreements. One can readily see how these provisions would be of great concern to transport management.

Equal Employment Opportunity Commission

Born out of the Civil Rights Act of 1964, the Equal Employment Opportunity Commission has as its direct concern the equal employment opportunities of all minority groups. These provisions are directly applicable to the transport industry, and its subsequent changes in employment activity have not always been easily accepted or implemented. As a result, the Justice Department has filed a number of individual and class-action suits against both employers and unions to legally enforce the provisions of the commission. It should be stressed that both employers and unions are liable under this act.

TECHNOLOGICAL CHANGES

Technological changes have directly affected the labor movement in transportation. Whether it be the reduction of train crews or the reduction of dock employees due to automated freight-handling equipment, labor is affected and initially reduced. Such technological changes have caused many labor-management disputes throughout the transportation industry.

In order for carriers to continue to be profitable in future years, more automation in equipment will be necessary. Retraining and reclassification of employees is a permanent part of labor-management responsibility. Increased productivity is a key ingredient to profitable operations in carriers and investment in laborsaving devices will undoubtedly continue.

SOCIETAL FACTORS

In addition to technology, our society is changing drastically, and these changes are affecting people, most of whom are employees. Carriers have not been noted for quick and effective employment of psychological and human relations techniques, but future management must be aware of the broad factors affecting their employees in contemporary society or they will witness a further deterioration in their union-management relations.

Labor Proximity

The proximity of employees to their place of employment is changing. A recent study of labor proximity to a metropolitan motor carrier terminal indicated that 35 percent of employees lived 10 or more miles from the terminal.[10] Employees are moving farther from their work place in an attempt to escape to the suburbs. Companies have been known to follow the supply of employees and to also move their headquarters to suburban locations.

Better highways and human transport facilities have aided the worker who wants to move out of the city and commute to his place of employment. Better working hours and a reduction in the number of hours worked have aided this move.

Other Important Factors

Carrier management should be concerned about the reduction in average age of employees as a result of changing age levels of the population. Mobility in management ranks has increased considerably, within the firm, between carriers, and between modes. The employment and advancement into management ranks of women and minorities has caused most transport firms to re-evaluate and change their hiring practices, fringe benefits, and, in general, their attitude and philosophy. As noted in Chapter 13, all of these factors have great effect on personnel and human relations.

Additionally, the nature of work and the work place have changed over time. Railway yards, barge docks, and truck terminals are still found in the depths of the inner city. Airlines have moved past the suburbs into the country, but are faced with many problems as they are surrounded again by the populace.

Pollution controls of all types have caused concern for carriers, both in terms of needed capital for improvements and in the effects of air and noise pollution on employees.

THE CARRIER LABOR DEPARTMENT

Each transport carrier has one or more departments to deal with contract negotiations, grievances, and general labor-management relations. In most cases, a vice president is the top organization level for labor relations in a carrier, even though the president of the company may be deeply involved in labor matters.

In addition to a vice president for labor, there is usually a staff at a central location or dispersed throughout the company on a regional basis that handles labor matters in its particular territory. The territories are usually established along the lines drawn by the labor agreement; for example, Western Conference, Southern Conference, Eastern Central, and so on, in trucking. While the vice president for labor may be actively handling grievances and labor problems in one part of the country, his normal duties would include the administration of the total labor program for the company. The extent of the problem depends on the size of the carrier, of course.

It is common to find a number of attorneys involved in labor matters for national or regional companies. Labor contracts are legal documents and in most cases are difficult to interpret. Many of the federal and state agencies with which the carrier labor department must deal employ attorneys to handle their regulatory affairs, and thus a need exists for legal balancing. Unions often employ attorneys to conduct their matters with carriers, too.

In many carriers, and especially in the trucking industry, the labor departments are composed of former union employees who know both sides of the contract. They also have the advantage of knowing firsthand the past practices that have resulted in a written contract. It is very difficult for a person who is new to an industry to readily grasp and effectively solve labor difficulties without such background information. Personal relationships and past associations are vital to an effective carrier labor representative.

As an extension of the carrier labor department, the local branch or area manager may be involved in grievance and local labor-management conflicts. This is especially true in a carrier that has branches on a profit-center basis. The local branch manager may extensively utilize the carrier labor department for assistance in presenting his case at the grievance hearing. Because of the changing nature of labor, a carrier operating on this basis must make a concerted effort to keep its branch managers aware of recent developments. It must also train and inform branch managers in labor strategy on a continuous basis.

SUMMARY

Special procedures affecting labor relations in transportation have been historically developed to deal with railroad labor disputes. Airlines are also covered by these railway labor acts. Motor carriers have not had to contend with specific federal legislation to solve their union-management difficulties.

Labor-management peace is of vital interest to the economy, since the impact of industry-wide and area work stoppages is tremendous. Labor-management peace in transport companies is not limited to legislative concerns, but is dependent also on our changing society and its effects on employees.

In view of the considerable impact of the transportation wage bargain on carrier profits, it behooves carrier management to be well informed on the history and development of society's attempts to protect itself from transportation stoppages.

NOTES

1. Dudley F. Pegrum, Transportation Economics and Public Policy, 3rd ed. (Homewood, Ill.: Richard D. Irwin, 1973), p. 474.
2. Roy J. Sampson and Martin T. Farris, Domestic Transportation: Practice, Theory and Policy, 3rd ed. (Boston: Houghton Mifflin Co., 1975), p. 426.
3. Pegrum, op. cit.
4. Hugh S. Norton, Modern Transportation Economics, 2nd ed. (Columbus, Ohio: Charles E. Merrill, 1971), pp. 209-10.
5. Pegrum, op. cit., pp. 478-79.

6. This section borrows heavily from Sampson and Farris, op. cit., pp. 430-32.

7. Pegrum, op. cit., pp. 482-83.

8. Sampson and Farris, op. cit., p. 433.

9. Norton, op. cit., p. 206.

10. Jack J. Holder, Jr., "Labor Proximity to a Modern Metropolitan Terminal Location," Terminal Operator, October 1971, p. 7.

CHAPTER

15

THE LOCATION OF TRANSPORTATION OPERATIONS

Chapter 1 presented a physical inventory of existing transportation assets in terms of miles of highways, airways, waterways, pipeline, and rail trackage. For the most part these facilities are fixed, and thereby inject a certain degree of rigidity into the domestic transportation network. Carrier managers, however, should refrain from considering the network as static because the U.S. population is highly mobile, and manufacturing centers have shifted from the East and the North to the South and the Southwest. In short, markets for freight and passengers are in a constant state of flux and should be carefully analyzed from a managerial perspective before a carrier's resources, in terms of new or replacement terminals and facilities, are committed, or before acquisition and merger plans are laid.

The primary purpose of this chapter is to provide carrier managers with exposure to the following areas of location analysis: significance of fixed facilities in transportation, shifting markets, techniques for locating operations, other factors to be considered in new route and terminal decisions, and the legal dimension of new transportation operations.

FIXED TRANSPORTATION FACILITIES

Transportation resources devoted to the public consist of variable equipment, such as trucks, buses, tankers, locomotives, and boxcars, and fixed facilities, such as terminals and docks.[1] The location of variable facilities is flexible and can be optimized by careful and efficient scheduling. Fixed facilities, on the other hand, create managerial problems because of factors such as shifting markets, fuel, changing customer needs, and social and ecological changes.

Detailed marketing research must be undertaken before investing in fixed facilities. Essentially, the following factors should be considered:[2]

1. location of the carrier's primary customers
2. availability of adequate interchange facilities
3. labor supply and cost
4. tax structure
5. insurance costs
6. education facilities
7. recreation potential
8. projected customer growth
9. population trends

Other variables, such as political structure, may be examined if they can, in any way, influence the location of the carrier's operations.

SHIFTING MARKETS

Transportation demand is a derived demand, as we have prevously noted, and hence is influenced by technology, population, and other demographic factors. In this regard, carrier managers must be attuned to continuing alterations in market structure and location in order to plan for route expansion and modified levels of service. Indeed, one principal responsibility of management is to seek clues that will indicate changes in the location of business activity.

Population trends have changed dramatically in the United States during the past five decades. Major regional population changes in this country during the period from 1960 to 1972[3] are depicted in Table 15.1. Although the Northeast has experienced an absolute increase in population from 44.8 million in 1960 to 49.8 million in 1972, the area has experienced a relative decline from 24.9 percent of the domestic population in 1960 to 23.7 percent in 1973. The north central region declined from 28.7 percent to 27.4 percent in population during this period. The population shifts to the South and the West are particularly evident both in absolute numbers and in relative share (percent). Needless to say, these population distributions and related changes harbor significant marketing location implications for transportation companies.

The basic location of manufacturing industries, moreover, has changed considerably during the past 20 years. Benjamin Chinitz and Raymond Vernon contended that improved transportation service

TABLE 15.1

Regional Population Trends in the United States, 1960, 1965, 1970, 1973
(millions)

	1960		1965		1970		1973	
	Number	Percent	Number	Percent	Number	Percent	Number	Percent
United States	180.0	100.0	193.5	100.0	203.8	100.0	209.9	100.0
Northeast	44.8	24.9	47.5	24.5	49.2	24.1	49.7	23.7
North Central	51.7	28.7	54.2	28.0	56.7	27.8	57.6	27.4
South	55.2	30.7	59.6	30.8	63.0	30.9	66.0	31.4
West	28.3	15.7	32.2	16.6	34.9	17.1	36.6	17.4

Source: U.S. Bureau of the Census, Statistical Abstract of the United States: 1974, 95th ed. (Washington, D.C.: Government Printing Office, 1974), p. xiii.

is one of the prime reasons for manufacturing concerns' shifting from the Northeast and the Midwest to the South and the West.[4] That is to say, with the growth and refinement of trucking and containers, an element of flexibility is injected into a firm's marketing and distribution strategies, which tends to draw it closer to markets.[5]

Because of increased flexibility, carrier management should ideally closely analyze changing consumption patterns and movement of manufacturing concerns to markets. Long-range analysis of future market structure and demand will enable carrier executives to petition for modified operating authority and other new services or acquisitions.

SOME LOCATION TECHNIQUES

Location analysts have consistently attempted to clarify and quantify the two factors--economic and environmental--that influence industrial location.[6] There are economic factors that directly affect a manufacturing plant's operations. These factors, moreover, have a direct and immediate impact on a firm's revenues and manufacturing process. Examples of direct economic factors include wages, freight rates, material costs, taxes, and insurance. On the other hand, environmental forces influence the sociopolitical aspects of a geographic area or region. The impact of such factors as labor skills, recreation facilities, and education systems is indirect and the effect on plant cost and earnings is difficult, if not impossible, to accurately measure.[7] Also, attention is now being directed to studying how regions, states, and communities influence the location of industry. Tax reform, labor training, and outright subsidies are examples of subjects being examined.[8]

In Chapter 9, a number of growth indicators were discussed, some of which are important to location. When contemplating entering a particular territory, carrier management should examine several sources for data concerning these areas. Traditional sources include the following:

1. Local chambers of commerce are excellent sources for company listings, employment trends, profits, education systems, transportation facilities, and business community forecasts.
2. Trade associations are good sources for specialized carriers intent on developing traffic in a limited number of commodties.[9] These associations can provide extensive information concering factors such as traffic management and industry trends.
3. State industrial development commissions provide information concerning the number of carriers authorized to serve a state

or city. Population, transportation facilities, and growth projections are also provided.

4. State and federal government agencies publish statistical information, such as the censuses of population, transportation, and business, that can be used to evaluate a potential city area.

Before investing in a new fixed facility, a two-part analytical procedure should be employed.[10] First, the carrier planning committee should use a skimming technique in order to discard any marginal sites or regions. Second, once marginal areas have been rejected, more in-depth analytical techniques should be employed. Air and motor carriers, because of the passengers and freight transported, usually seek to enter markets where a high level of retail sales occur.

By using BPI, QI, and ISA, carrier managers can rapidly eliminate marginal or undesirable locations. BPI is a relative measure of consumer purchasing power. The formula for computing the index is as follows:

$$BPI = \frac{5D + 3S + 2P}{10}$$

BPI = percentage of potential U.S. buying power

D = net effective buying income (disposable personal income), expressed as a percentage of national disposable personal income

S = retail sales, expressed as a percentage of national retail sales

P = population, expressed as a percentage of total national population

BPI is a measure of the relative ability of an area to purchase consumer goods. If areas A and B are being evaluated, and area A has a BPI of .10 and area B has a BPI of .05, A's market potential is twice that of B. In the United States, California has the highest BPI and Alaska the smallest. When using this particular index, caution must be exercised, because it must be used in conjunction with other factors such as population. Sales Management Magazine computes and publishes BPIs for states and SMSAs.[11]

Two additional measures, QI and ISA, can be used when identifying quality goods markets, areas responsive to promotion, and locations possessing inordinate amounts of discretionary income. QI is a relative measure of the per capita purchasing power of a geographical market and is computed thusly:

$$QI = \frac{BPI}{P} (100)$$

P = population, expressed as a percentage of the total national population

Since the QI for the nation as a whole equals 100, a QI of 120 would indicate a quality market, while a QI of 80 would indicate a low-grade or inferior market. A quality index has to be used in conjunction with some indicator of market size, such as population or retail sales. For instance, a QI of 150 for a city in Alaska that has a population of 25 is virtually meaningless.

ISA is a relative measure of retail sales activity that is relevant to products sold through retail stores. Its basic use by carrier management is to identify areas of active retail sales. Conceivably, areas having high ISAs could require high levels of customer service. The index is computed thusly:

$$ISA = \frac{S}{P} (100)$$

S = retail sales, expressed as a percentage of total national retail sales.

P = population, expressed as a percentage of total national population

Because the ISA's national average is 100, an ISA of less than 100 is generally poor, while an ISA of greater than 100 is normally good. Like other skimming indices, ISA must be used in conjunction with other measures of market size.

When attempting to decide where to commit funds for expansion, many factors are important. After using BPI, QI, and ISA as skimming devices, carrier managers are now prepared to probe deeper into the search for a specific location.

Carrier managers should strive to pinpoint active and potential trading centers, because these frequently represent excellent locations for traffic growth. By locating a series of interrelated trading centers, networks of terminals can be established. One possible technique that can be employed to determine the drawing power of a natural trading center was developed by William J. Reilly.[12] His law of retail gravitation can be adapted to ascertain the potential market served by a given terminal.

Reilly's fundamental hypothesis is that the ability of a shopping center to attract customers is directly proportional to the square of the distance between the shopping center and the prospective buyers. Shopping centers, of course, can be easily changed to freight terminals with no modification in Reilly's formula required. The formula is as follows:

$$\frac{T_1}{T_2} = \frac{P_1}{P_2} \left(\frac{D_2}{D_1} \right)^2$$

$\frac{T_1}{T_2}$ = ratio of shippers from an intermediate location who will patronize terminal 1 (T_1) to those shippers who will patronize terminal 2 (T_2)

P_1 = population of terminal 1

P_2 = population of terminal 2

D_1 = distance between terminal 1 and X, an intermediate location

D_2 = distance between terminal 2 and X

To demonstrate the application of Reilly's Law, assume that REA Express is debating the relative merits of locating a terminal in either of two places. The population of proposed terminal 1 is 400,000, while the population of proposed terminal 2 is 100,000. REA's management is interested in an intermediate location that is situated 40 and 10 miles, respectively, from terminals 1 and 2. Reilly's Law enables REA's management to calculate how many people and businesses it can service from X to the two terminals. Figure 15.1 depicts the data and basic problem confronting the company. With respect to this data, contained in Figure 15.1, Reilly's formula can be applied as follows:

$$\frac{T_1}{T_2} = \frac{P_1}{P_2} \left(\frac{T_2}{T_1} \right)^2$$

$$= \frac{400,000}{100,000} \quad \frac{10}{40} \quad 2$$

$$= 4\ (1/4)^2$$

$$= 1/4$$

In other words, for every customer from the intermediate location X served by terminal 1, four potential customers can be served from terminal 2. REA should locate the terminal at the second location, all other things being equal, because four times as many customers will be attracted from X than would be if the firm were to locate at the first one. Also, REA should strongly entertain the possibility of establishing the proposed terminal in the intermediate location X.

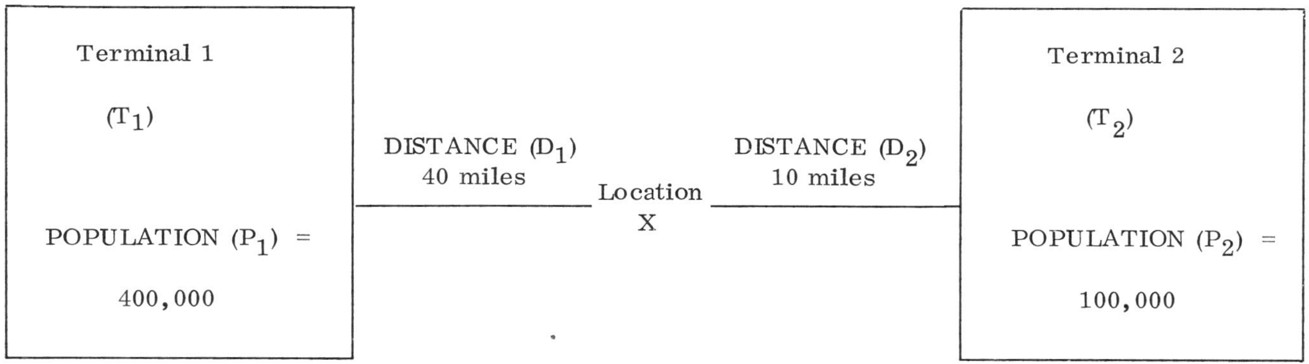

FIGURE 15.1

An Example of Reilly's Law in Location Analysis

When establishing terminals, carrier managers are interested in clearly identifying the mileage boundaries between proposed locations. Once established, management wants a terminal to service as large an area as possible, given certain legal constraints. Although designed primarily for shopping centers, the following formula, developed by P. D. Converse, can be used to show the boundary between two terminals:[13]

$$DB_2 = \frac{Dj}{1 + \sqrt{\frac{(P_1)}{(P_2)}}}$$

DB_2 = distance of the boundary from terminal 2

Dj = total distance between the two terminals

P_1 = population of terminal 1

P_2 = population of terminal 2

Employing the same data as above, the physical boundary between the two proposed REA terminals is computed as follows:

$$DB_2 = \frac{Dj}{1 + \sqrt{\frac{(P_1)}{(P_2)}}}$$

$$= \frac{50}{1 + \sqrt{\frac{400{,}000}{100{,}000}}}$$

$$= \frac{50}{1} + \sqrt{4}$$

$$= \frac{50}{1 + 2}$$

$$= \frac{50}{3}$$

$$= 16.6 \text{ miles}$$

A customer located up to 16.6 miles away can be served by either of the two terminals. However, X is located only 10 miles from terminal 2; therefore, the physical boundary is 6.6 miles to the left of X. This particular form of analysis is useful when determining physical boundaries between trading areas and cities. Also, this analytical technique is important in establishing terminals in large areas. Yellow Freight, for example, serves Los Angeles from four terminals.

A further locational problem involves terminal spacing. Carriers faced with high customer service requirements will often establish a series of break bulk points and terminals. When locating these facilities, the carrier manager should attempt to place each facility, insofar as possible, where no territorial overlap occurs. That is, a terminal should be located so that it serves a distinct area. The maximum area that a terminal can serve can be determined by solving the following equation:[14]

$$D = S \cdot T$$

D = maximum distance from terminal to terminal

S = average speed for delivery

T = maximum time allowed in transit

Assume that the hypothetical State Truck Line must guarantee a one-day delivery service to customers in order to meet rigorous competition. The firm, moreover, only works an eight-hour shift, and its customers take two hours to pick up a shipment and load it onto a truck and two hours to unload the line-haul truck and deliver a shipment. Assuming no overtime is incurred, the maximum transit time is four hours. If average speed is 30 mph the spacing of the terminals is computed as follows:

$$\begin{aligned} D &= S \cdot T \\ &= 30 \cdot 4 \\ &= 120 \end{aligned}$$

Thus, the terminals should be spaced 120 miles apart. When using this formula, care must be exercised, because terminal intervals will change with any variation in factors such as speed, congestion, or pickup and delivery time. Additional network analysis can be used in terminal spacing. Nevertheless, this equation is useful when screening possible mileage intervals for future terminal locations.

OTHER FACTORS IN LOCATION OF TRANSPORTATION OPERATIONS

In addition to the above considerations, other factors can be important in location decisions for motor carriers, railroads, freight forwarders, water carriers, and express companies. Due to projected growth and noise, airports are now being located at considerable distances from central business districts. Other carriers, however, attempt to locate in or adjacent to business districts, and railroads attempt to develop industrial parks. In short, location is an important carrier management strategy responsibility.

Cost control constitutes an important factor in terminal location. The location of a motor carrier terminal, for instance, is based on five important cost elements: level of customer service offered, highway access, energy, socioeconomic factors, and construction factors.

The level of customer service that a carrier is willing to provide will indicate the number of terminals that will be located. In cities such as Los Angeles and Chicago, some carriers have elected to build several small terminals in lieu of one central facility. The advantages of smaller terminals include lower terminal costs, reduced stem time, reduced fuel expenditures due to proximity to customers, easier pickup and delivery scheduling, reduced congestion, and overall better customer service.

The critical variable in locating terminals in the motor carrier industry is access to highways, which is crucial because of access to routes and stem time. Highway access is also important because of interline agreements and the actual mileage to the next relay point with line-haul equipment.

Energy problems also affect the location of terminals. Fuel costs are increasing, but by locating close to customers, overall fuel expenditures can be reduced. Local ordinances regarding fuel storage should be carefully evaluated if fuel is to be stockpiled as a hedge against rising energy prices.

There are essentially seven socioeconomic factors affiliated with terminal location: size of terminal payroll, other funds expended by terminals for local operations, proximity to employees' residences, easy access to and from freeways, personnel problems arising from terminal location, and highway congestion. The facility proper is a seventh socioeconomic factor. What atmosphere does it develop? How is it structurally established? How are the terminal employees affected by the facility?

Construction and site selection should ideally be predicated on need. That is to say, past profits and revenues should be examined and, if renting or leasing, present and future rent should be compared. When selecting acreage, management should carefully estimate future growth and buy additional acreage if needed for expansion. Highway access, contracts, zoning, weight limitations, and ICC regulations concerning debt must also be considered, in addition to clear titles and lead time for completing the terminal.

Once the land is cleared and free, actual construction can commence. The terminal size, of course, will be determined by the amount of traffic anticipated. Some modifications may be needed because of docks, offices, fuel, and scales. OSHA regulations, moreover, can affect the actual construction of a building.

LEGAL CONSIDERATIONS

As we have noted repeatedly, regulation provides a constraint on carrier decision making. In location decision, the regulatory constraint on mergers, which we analyzed in Chapter 4, is of some importance, and should be reviewed once more as it affects location.

Regulated carriers must receive route authority from the various regulatory agencies before they can acquire new operating authority or merge with an existing carrier to enter a new market. Motor carriers have traditionally expanded their geographical operations through acquisition.[15] There are two types of mergers in the regulated segment of the motor carrier industry: Section 212 mergers and Section 5 mergers. A Section 212 merger involves two carriers whose combined revenues are less than $300,000 annually.[16] The legal requirement for a merger of this nature consists of the ICC's finding the unification consistent with the public interest.

A Section 5 merger, on the other hand, applies to all railroad mergers and mergers where motor carriers whose combined revenues are more than $300,000, and to individuals controlling carriers. This classification of merger is rigorous and the commission approves such mergers when it finds that the public interest demands the unification. The ICC not only closely examines the fixed cost and capital structure resulting from the merger, but also examines the impact on competition and employee deplacement.[17]

Even though most carriers expand into new markets by acquisition, each carrier has the right to petition for new operating authority on the basis of public convenience and necessity. The CAB's principal consideration in such cases is competition and maintaining competitive balances among carriers that it regulates, as noted before. Similarly, the ICC focuses on shipper needs, existing service, competition, and traffic interline arrangements.[18]

SUMMARY

An examination of the domestic transportation system reveals a substantial investment in terminals, docks, and yards. Transport demand is of a derived variety, and fixed facilities should be located only after careful and detailed geographical analysis, because of shifting markets. In this chapter, six areas of location analysis were examined. These included the monetary significance of fixed facilities in transportation decisions, market modification, site location techniques, decision variables, and the legal dimension involved in new operations.

NOTES

1. Chapter 1 contains considerable information on miles of way, number of vehicles, average haul, and so on. For more detailed statistics, consult Transportation Facts and Trends, 10th ed. (Washington, D.C.: Transportation Association of America, 1973).

2. This is only a partial listing, and factors to be considered will vary from carrier to carrier. For other areas requiring analysis, see W. I. Little, "Location Selection Through Integrated Systems Management," Land Economics, February 1969, pp. 97-103; and Edmund S. Whitman and W. James Schmidt, Plant Relocation: A Case History of a Move (New York: American Management Association, 1966), p. 42.

3. See U.S. Bureau of the Census, Statistical Abstract of the United States: 1970, 93rd ed. (Washington, D.C.: Government Printing Office, 1973), p. xiii.

4. Benjamin Chintz and Raymond Vernon, "Changing Forces in Industrial Locations," Harvard Business Review, January-February 1960, pp. 126-36; and "Zero Growth, We Couldn't Stand It," Forbes, July 1, 1972, pp. 17-18.

5. Grant M. Davis and Stephen W. Brown, "Physical Distribution Strategies," Transportation and Logistics Review, Summer 1972, pp. 88-89; L. W. Weiss, "Geographical Size of Markets in Manufacturing," Review of Economics and Statistics, August 1972, pp. 245-57; and L. J. Struyk, "Evidenceon the Locational Activity of Manufacturing Industries in Metropolitan Areas," Land Economics, November 1972, pp. 377-82.

6. Through their rate-making process, carriers can actually determine the location of industrial selling and buying markets. For a good discussion of this power (which is omitted in this section), see D. Philip Locklin, Economics of Transportation, 7th ed. (Homewood, Ill.: Richard D. Irwin, 1972), Chapter 3.

7. V. M. Rittan and L. T. Wallace, "Developments in Plant Location Theory," Industrial Development, June 1961, pp. 57-58.

8. Many states, for example, will construct physical facilities for a new firm and will also train its labor force.

9. Common carrier operating certificates specify what commodities can be transported.

10. This section borrows heavily from Grant M. Davis and Stephen W. Brown, *Logistics Management* (Lexington, Mass.: D. C. Heath & Co., 1974), Chapter 4; and Grant M. Davis and Phillip H. Taylor, "A Three Dimensional Approach for Locating Distribution Centers" (Paper presented before the Southern Regional Science Association, Rosslyn, Virginia, April 5, 1974).

11. For a map of BPIs of the United States, by state, see John F. Magee, *Physical-Distribution Systems* (New York: McGraw-Hill, 1967), p. 33.

12. William J. Reilly, *The Law of Retail Gravitation* (New York: William J. Reilly, 1931), Chapters 1 and 2.

13. P. D. Converse, "New Laws of Retail Gravitation," *Journal of Marketing,*" vol. 14, no. 3 (October 1949), pp. 379-84.

14. Walter B. Wentz and Gerald I. Eyrich, *Marketing: Theory and Application* (New York: Harcourt, Brace and World, 1970), Chapter 18.

15. For support of this observation, see Duncan W. Edwards, "Economic Concentration of Regulated Class I Motor Carriers" (M.S. thesis, Auburn University, 1972); and James C. Nelson, *The Effects of Entry Control in Surface Transport* (New York: National Bureau of Economic Research, 1965), pp. 381-442.

16. 49 USC 212 (b).

17. Erie R. Co. Merger, 312 ICC 185, 247; Oklahoma Ry Co. Abandonment, 257 ICC 177.

18. North American Van Lines, Inc. purchase of Fort Smith Furniture Transportation Co., 15 Federal Carrier Cases, 35, 504.

PART

III

THE OUTLOOK FOR CARRIER MANAGEMENT

Now that the five constraints on carrier management have been analyzed in Part I, and the specific managerial responses and techniques detailed in Part II, our concluding task is to look ahead and make an educated guess on the future of carrier management.

CHAPTER

16

CARRIER MANAGEMENT AND THE FUTURE

We have argued here that carrier management is different from management in general. The major difference is that transportation is a regulated industry and management must therefore operate in a regulatory environment that takes the form of five managerial constraints: the regulatory system itself, regulated transportation competition, a regulated route structure, regulated ownership patterns, and regulated pricing and rate making. In each of these instances, management discretion and freedom of action is constrained. While in most industries management usually can set prices at will, this option is restricted in transportation. While management can typically change operational patterns as it sees fit, in transportation such factors as route structure, competition, and ownership, are controlled.

In spite of these controls and constraints, considerable latitude exists for carrier management to exercise its talents. In Part II we detailed ways in which operational management responds to constraints, marketing methods in a regulated environment, the role of public relations and advertising, equipment selection options, finance and credit alternatives, human relations-personnel-training opportunities, labor relations and bargaining responses, and locational options. This second part was actually predicated on the idea that constraints can be opportunities.

Now we will consider the future of carrier management, and offer a few suggestions that might be appropriate to present and future carrier managers. In a sense, these remarks reflect the biases of the authors, but they also reaffirm our firm conviction that the future of carrier management is indeed bright.

First, we foresee a continuation of the present type of economic system. We believe that the majority of future economic activities will take place in an environment relatively free of restrictive controls. It is our conviction that the total economy operates best when the free market mechanism is allowed to operate with a minimum of restrictions.

Second, although we reaffirm our belief in free enterprise, we do not foresee any major change in the regulatory constraints confronting carrier management. Our transportation regulatory system can be subjected to considerable criticism. Indeed, we have individually and collectively questioned various parts of regulation in writing, in public addresses, and in the classroom. The regulatory system can certainly be amended, updated, and changed. Yet we believe that regulation will remain and will continue to be a force in future transportation events.

Third, since we believe regulation will survive, we also believe that government ownership will not be the pattern of the transportation of the future. While current developments such as Amtrak and the Regional Rail Reorganization in the Northeast seem to be moving the United States toward governmental ownership of transportation, we take heart in the fact that Congress continues to strive to preserve private ownership, the common carrier concept, and use of the profit motive, wherever possible.

Fourth, we believe that there is a future for carrier management. This follows from our first three beliefs--our present economic system, our system of regulation, and avoidance of government ownership. If these three premises were not true, our fourth premise would not be as strong.

A rationale for our belief in the existence of a future for carrier management is the fact that transportation seems to grow as fast as or faster than the economy. We foresee continued economic growth and therefore continued growth in transportation. While the number of carriers may not increase as the economy grows, transportation business does grow with the economy. With more transportation businesses, more carrier managers will be needed. To our way of thinking, there is a bright future for managers in transportation, and we predict a great deal of future opportunity and challenge for those entering the field.

This is not to say that the carrier management of the future will be the same as the carrier management of today. This is one of the premises on which this book was written: the carrier management of tomorrow will differ greatly from the carrier management of today.

The carrier manager of the future will have to be more sophisticated and better trained. Life becomes more complicated daily, and transportation--already a complicated area--will become similarly more complicated.

Future carrier managers will have to be knowledgeable about such things as electronic data processing and computers, capital budgeting and investment techniques, human relations--indeed, everything we have discussed here, and more.

The only logical approach to the future of carrier management is to have better educated managers. While it is difficult to define precisely what this "education for the future" should be, any good education should train people to think, to analyze, and to develop their intelligence. It will be the manager who has these qualities who will succeed in the future.

Transportation education takes many forms. Membership in and attendance at meetings of Traffic Clubs, Delta Nu Alpha chapters, and National Defense Transportation Association meetings are all types of education available to all transportation managers and potential managers.

Attendance at seminars and short courses sponsored by transportation groups, associations, or institutions of higher learning can also be helpful. Very often these will be sponsored by carrier organizations and will be held in conjunction with academic institutions. We urge attendance by carrier managers and potential managers, irrespective of the level of their formal training.

We strongly suggest that programs designed to "professionalize" transportation are extremely worthwhile educational ventures. The American Society of Traffic and Transportation (AST & T) holds competitive nationwide examinations every six months for those desiring certification as professionals in transportation. Study groups in preparation for these examinations are sponsored by Delta Nu Alpha and others. We feel strongly that this program is an excellent way to become educated in transportation. Parenthetically, we admit a bias in favor of the AST & T programs, since all three of us have been deeply involved in them as examiners, associate examiners, or members of the board of directors.

We recommend to those interested in education in regulatory matters the twice-yearly examinations for admission to the bar of the ICC. One does not have to be a law school graduate to plead cases before most regulatory bodies (including the ICC), but one must demonstrate competence and understanding of the complicated area of transportation law.

Formal education in transportation is becoming more and more important for carrier managers. Fortunately, such formal education takes many forms and is available at several levels. Downtown "traffic colleges" still exist in some cities and have highly specialized traffic courses, which are usually given in the evenings. Another type of formal education is the popular community, junior, or technical college, which generally has a two-year curriculum. Many of these have transportation courses. We recommend these schools to carrier managers and potential managers.

Finally, a number of universities and four-year colleges have courses in transportation. A larger number of them have courses in business administration, which can be helpful in developing carrier managers and potential managers. If a curriculum in transportation education exists at a nearby university, it should be supported and assisted by carriers acting in their own self-interest. Scholarships, prizes, offers of tours of facilities, help with class projects, financial aid for research and faculty travel, hiring of graduates, and other devices of support are appreciated and useful to such programs. These programs can and do "turn on" the young men and women who will be the carrier managers of tomorrow. With help and support, the educational product can be better, and there will be more people who have been exposed to transportation education from which carriers can choose. We strongly recommend these programs to all carrier managers and suggest that transportation education is only as strong as the carriers make it.

In closing, we must admit our bias toward formal transportation education. All three authors have taught in institutions of higher learning and have earned doctorate degrees. We remain firmly committed to transportation education.

It is our conviction that carrier management has a considerable future and that this future depends on education. Working together with enlightened carrier management, and with its support, we foresee nothing but a bright tomorrow for transportation education and hence for transportation.

NAME INDEX

SUBJECT INDEX

ABOUT THE AUTHORS

GRANT M. DAVIS is Orren Harris Professor of Transportation at the University of Arkansas. He has been admitted to practice before the Interstate Commerce Commission and is an Educational Member of the American Society of Traffic and Transportation. He has served on the National Education Committee of Delta Nu Alpha and is an Associate Examiner for the American Society of Traffic and Transportation.

Professor Davis is the author of The Department of Transportation (1970), coauthor of Logistics Management (1974) and Rate Bureaus and Antitrust Conflicts in Transportation (Praeger Publishers, 1974), and author of numerous articles in leading business journals.

Dr. Davis has had industrial experience with Mason and Dixon Lines and the Ford Motor Company. He earned his B.B.A. at Georgia State University, and his M.A. and Ph.D. at the University of Alabama, and has taught at the University of Alabama, Arizona State University, Auburn University, and the University of Arkansas. In 1971, he was selected National Transportation Man of the Year by Delta Nu Alpha.

MARTIN T. FARRIS is Professor of Economics and Transportation at Arizona State University. He has been admitted to practice before the Interstate Commerce Commission and is a Certificated Member of the American Society of Traffic and Transportation. He has served on the National Education Committee of Delta Nu Alpha and was Examiner for Transportation Economics for the American Society of Traffic and Transportation from 1962 to 1974.

Professor Farris is coauthor of Domestic Transportation: Practice, Theory and Policy (1966, 1973, 1975), Modern Transportation: Selected Readings (1967, 1973), and Public Utilities: Regulation, Management and Ownership (1973), and author of numerous articles in leading economics and business journals.

Dr. Farris earned his B.A. and M.A. at the University of Montana, and his Ph.D. at Ohio State University. He has taught at the University of Montana, Ohio State University, the University of Hawaii, and Arizona State University. In 1973, he was selected National Transportation Man of the Year by Delta Nu Alpha.

JACK J. HOLDER, JR. is Vice President of Yellow Freight Systems, Inc. He is a Sustaining Member of the American Society of Traffic and Transportation and serves on the Board of Directors of the Society. Dr. Holder is a publicly elected Trustee of Johnson County Community College in Overland Park, Kansas, and a member of the Executive Council of the Indiana University Alumni Association.

Dr. Holder is author of _Corporate Support Programs to Institutions of Higher Learning_ (1967), coeditor of _Transportation and Logistics Challenges 1974-1980_ (1974), and author of numerous articles in leading journals of transportation.

Dr. Holder earned his B.S., M.B.A., and Ed.D. degrees at Indiana University and taught at Ohio University before joining Yellow Freight Systems, Inc. in 1968. He is well known nationally as a speaker before traffic and industrial groups.

RELATED TITLES

Published by
Praeger Special Studies

RATE BUREAUS AND ANTI-TRUST CONFLICTS IN TRANSPORTATION
Grant M. Davis and
Charles S. Sherwood

MANAGING MULTINATIONAL CORPORATIONS
Arvind S. Phatak

HOTEL SECURITY MANAGEMENT
Harvey Burstein

INDUSTRIAL LOCATION DECISIONS IN METROPOLITAN AREAS: A General Model Tested for Boston
Donald N. Stone
Foreword by Benjamin Chinitz

TRAINING JAPANESE MANAGERS
Allen Dickerman